Sacred Marriages

MW01602246

This book represents a new direction in the study of religion and marriage by using a postmodern theoretical framework focusing on gendered discourse and culture, to examine the meaning of sacred marriage within social contexts. Drawing upon data from in-depth interviews of couples in long-term, sacred marriages living in the American Midwest, together with an analysis of Christian marriage advice manuals, *Sacred Marriages* explores how couples use religious and nonreligious discourses and cultures to give their marriages meaning, and how those sacred meanings are used in their daily lives and the spaces that they embody. The study shows how religious and secular beliefs are combined to formulate cultural strategies for approaching the sacralization of marriage, and how religious and nonreligious discourses and cultures are ordered, depending on circumstances and social contexts. This often results in other relationships being subordinated in favor of the sacred bond believed to exist between husband and wife. The book argues that sacred marriage is a malleable concept, as people bend religious culture to form new and altered sacred marriages during emotional extremes. A thoughtful examination of long-term Christian marriages, this volume will appeal to scholars of religion and sociology with interests in marriage and the family.

David F. Mullins is Professor and Director of the Sociology Program at the University of Saint Francis, USA.

Routledge Studies in the Sociology of Religion

A platform for the latest scholarly research in the sociology of religion, this series welcomes both theoretical and empirical studies that pay close attention to religion in social context. It publishes work that explores the ways in which religions adapt or react to social change and how spirituality lends meaning to people's lives and shapes individual, collective, and national identities.

Sacred Marriages
A Discourse Analysis
David F. Mullins

For more information about this series, please visit: www.routledge.com

Sacred Marriages
A Discourse Analysis

David F. Mullins

Routledge
Taylor & Francis Group

LONDON AND NEW YORK

First published 2019 by Routledge

2 Park Square, Milton Park, Abingdon, Oxfordshire OX14 4RN
52 Vanderbilt Avenue, New York, NY 10017

Routledge is an imprint of the Taylor & Francis Group, an informa business

First issued in paperback 2019

British Library Cataloguing-in-Publication Data
A catalogue record for this book is available from the British Library

Library of Congress Cataloging-in-Publication Data
A catalog record for this book has been requested

ISBN: 978-1-138-09809-1 (hbk)
ISBN: 978-0-367-89719-2 (pbk)

Typeset in Times New Roman
by Apex CoVantage, LLC

To Tammy and Gabi, with love beyond words

Contents

Acknowledgements

I would like to thank Dr. John P. Bartkowski for his guidance over the past 15 years. He is the essence of a scholar teacher, and I am fortunate to know him and grateful for his sage advice. I also appreciate the opportunity afforded me by Neil Jordan at Routledge to write this book. I would further like to extend my thanks to all of the anonymous reviewers and colleagues who have critiqued my work. Additionally, I cannot express enough my appreciation to the administration and board of the University of Saint Francis who provided funding and a sabbatical in support of my research. Finally, I am indebted to the couples I interviewed for this study. They invited me into their homes, and shared the most private moments of their lives with me. I cannot thank them enough.

1 Introducing discourse and religious culture

This book is about religion and sacred marriages. It represents a continuation of a body of scholarship that extends over a century. According to Burr et al (2012), the first generation of this scholarship began in the late 1800s and lasted through the end of the 20th century. It was marked by a focus on global markers of religious involvement (e.g., participation and affiliation) and their influences on marital satisfaction and stability. In the late 1980s, a second generation of scholarship emerged offering a more nuanced appreciation for the complexities of religion, encompassing specific beliefs and practices and their impacts on different dimensions of marriage and family processes. The most recent scholarship examines proximal measures of religiosity by focusing on the influence of the sanctification of marriage and family processes based on measures of the degree to which people perceive various aspects of life as having divine character and significance (Pargament and Mahoney 2005 and 2009). Much of this work originates in the field of psychology, and accordingly, researchers have attempted to quantify and measure the degree to which people perceive aspects of life to be sacred using indexes like the Manifestation of God and the Index of Sacred Qualities. Sanctification has largely been viewed as a "psychological process with a spiritual reference point," influencing how people feel and act, stemming from their beliefs or experiences of the divine and sacred qualities (Hernandez et al 2011: 775).

Sacred marriages are social

In this book, I suggest an extension and redirection of the scholarship examining sacred marriages with a stronger focus on the social. The present paradigm in the study of religion relies on asking standard questions about how often people go to church, if they believe in God, how they perceive God acting in their lives, and what it means to be a Christian (Ammerman 2014). This includes strict standards of what it means to believe, to be religious, and to belong to a denomination or congregation. But, at times, these expectations of religion do not capture how people live. Words like faith, belief, salvation, spiritual, and sacred are polysemous – holding multiple, at times contrasting meanings for people. The salient aspects of religion and the sacred in people's lives should be *how* they live and what they *do* because of their belief in the sacred. To more fully understand the potential effects of religion and the sacralization[1] of marriages, this study draws from religious and nonreligious spheres in the discourses and cultural scripts within written texts and the stories of people living in sacred marriages.

Data and methods

I conducted in-depth interviews with couples who were married more than 40 years and who said they believe marriage is sacred for religious reasons (see Appendix for a discussion of the sample and methodology). Following Swidler (2001), rather than compare multiple groups representing different cultural backgrounds, or present an exotic culture unfamiliar to the reader, this study examines what some might consider the most common and typically American cultural experiences of a dominant, homogenous group of mostly working-class, white, educated, U.S. Midwesterners. Indeed, many couples I interviewed claimed they were, "no different from anyone else." Yet, when asked about loving, long-term marriages, they offered unique sociocultural experiences, and passionate, conflicted narratives that shaped their understandings of how religion influenced their marriages and families. I also analyzed 58 Christian marriage advice manuals to identify dominant religious discourse pertaining to marriage (see the Appendix for a discussion of the sample of Christian marriage advice manuals and the methodology I used to analyze them). The manuals were specifically recommended by participants, located in the lending libraries of participants' churches, or acquired from publishers recommended by the participants based on their religious denominations.

Need for the study

Given the plethora of studies of religion and marriage, and the perceived global deinstitutionalization of both religion and marriage, one might ask why offer yet another perspective on the influences of religion on marriage? Despite changes in marriage, it continues to be the most frequent form of family structure in the U.S. Americans are also overwhelmingly religious (Pew Research Center 2010 and 2012). The U.S. continues to be a highly religious nation containing millions of married couples.

Despite more than a century of scientific research, religion's influences on marriage and family are poorly understood. The conceptual reification of religion as an external reality that acts *on* people's lives has not adequately captured people's lived experiences of religion and the sacred *in* their lives. For example, studies that include measures of relationship quality by assessing individual spouse's levels of happiness and satisfaction with their marriage assume that happily married couples are likely to remain married. While this may be the case, many couples who have enduring marriages are unhappy (Hawkins and Booth 2005; Heaton and Albrecht 1991). And in contrast to this logic, some Christians[2] believe that secular culture promotes divorce by overemphasizing happiness and personal satisfaction in marriage; suggesting instead, that unhappiness, conflict, and discord in marriages are opportunities sent from God to be more holy (Thomas 2000). Additionally, despite the salience of gender in both religion and marriage, it has been largely overlooked in the study of sacred marriages.

There is a need for a different paradigm in the study of religion's influences on marriage and family because previous attempts to explain the effects of religion on marriage have produced largely weak, mixed, and often conflicting results. This is in part due to the significant historical changes marriage has undergone according to Coontz (2005), who suggests that contemporary marriage and family life is an overdetermined phenomenon – meaning it has so many causes that eliminating multiple elements of the change would not reverse it. Consistent with Kaslow and Hammerschmidt (1992) and Kaslow and Robison (1996), Bachand and Caron (2001: 117) have concluded that, "There appears to be no one factor or group of factors that have overwhelmingly contributed to the longevity of marriages." And Shiota and Levenson (2007: 673) have argued that there is a "need for researchers to think of long-term marriage as a process, embedded in shifting roles in and demands by the outside world, not as a static and isolated unit." This book represents a new, needed way of conceptualizing religion and marriage.

Religion as discourse and culture

The first interview I conducted demonstrates the need for reconceptualizing sacred marriages. Larry and Helen[3] are self-described "cradle to grave" Catholics. Both try to attend mass several times a week, and they are leaders in their church. They have a large, Catholic family, and their religion is a prominent part of their identity as individuals and as a couple. But while Helen professes a devout belief in God as a supernatural being, her husband Larry does not. For him, being Catholic is not about shared belief in a divine being or his degree of perception of that divine being's influences in his life. Like most of the people in this study, religion is a way he talks about and gives meaning to his marriage and family. From the way they mark the passage of time with religious references to first communions, christenings, weddings, and baptisms, to their personal sacrifices to allow their children to attend parochial schools, people like Helen and Larry use religion to love, to raise children, to seek out communities of believers with similar values and shared cultures, and to construe a future together that is founded on the negotiation of elite religious discourse and the actions they take to cope with challenges and crises.

Larry is a devout Catholic. He is ardent in his belief that marriage is sacred for religious reasons; but, he does not believe in God as an entity. His faith lies in religion and the community of believers. "We're all God. It's all of us that make up God," according to Larry.[4]

Following Ammerman (2014), I seek not to categorize religion or define words like sacred through a scientific power discourse but rather to include the voices of participants like Helen and Larry in their everyday lived experiences of religion and their understanding of sacred marriages in the way they live. Moving away from the quantification of participants' degree of religiosity or degree of perception of the sacred in their lives, this study relies on the power of culture and discourse to examine how people think, feel, act, and talk about religion and the sacred in their marriages. The locus of religion's power to shape sacred meanings is social and driven by interactions premised on culture and gendered power regimes in discourse.

Theoretical framework

Ann Swidler (1986) likens culture to a tool kit in which people use cultural tools to negotiate their social worlds and form meaningful identities and significant relationships. Symbols are meaningful objects in people's social environment and may include ideologies (Christianity), inanimate material objects of significant meaning (a Bible or rosary), or representations of people (husband or wife). Culture is produced through social practices, that can be used strategically to form subjectivities and navigate social worlds through strategies of action. Culture matters and acts in people's lives not by defining ends of action, but instead by providing the cultural resources they use to construct strategies of action. Cultural strategies of action are not "consciously devised plans to attain goals," but rather "persistent ways of ordering action through time." Strategies of action are "a general way of ordering action . . . that might allow one to meet several life goals." People do not form strategies of action from scratch, but rather from chains of links using existing cultural resources.

Several studies offer rich applications of Swidler's (1986 and 2001) metaphor of cultural toolkits and cultural repertoires in their studies of religion (Baggett 2009; Bartkowski 2001 and 2004; Gallagher 2003; Jenkins 2005; Konieczny 2013). Collectively, these studies note the varied presentation of symbolic forms and strategies of action within religious communities by which new cultural meanings are set in motion. They suggest, religious culture[5] is not static, but rather strategies and symbols are malleable and plastic, bending and giving to reinterpretation, producing new cultural repertoires and religious meanings at the margins of nonreligious and religious social worlds.

While early research suggests that being socially engaged in institutionalized and private expressions of religious culture benefits marriage (Call and Heaton 1997; Curtis and Ellison 2002; Heaton 1984; Heaton et al 1985; Heaton and Pratt 1990; Lehrer and Chiswick 1993), research also suggests that the likelihood of divorce increases when husbands attend services more frequently than wives, and when wives hold more conservative beliefs than their husbands (Vaaler et al 2009). Thus, while sacred marriages are produced through cultural strategies and cultural symbols, the effects of religious culture are not guaranteed to be positive, and the effects of religion in sacred marriages differ by gender.

From a sociological perspective, the sacred meanings of religious texts like scripture, or the words of a powerful sermon, or the vows stated during a wedding ceremony, do not reside statically in the texts or words themselves. Rather, the texts and words become sacralized through strategies of action premised on ritual practices and everyday habits. And, as Bartkowski (1996, 1997, and 2001) points out, these strategies vary by social context. While religious elites are formally trained to interpret religious discourse within the formal framework of institutionalized faith practices, laypeople are more likely to interpret elite religious discourse in light of their everyday problems rather than through abstruse theological concepts. This study gives credence to the power of discourse in how people produce and negotiate religious culture in their lived experiences of sacred marriages, especially in situations where they search for solutions to their problems of action.

The links between discourse and culture cannot be overemphasized because culture frames discourse and discourse shapes culture. John Dewey ([1910] 1997: 171) argued that only through symbolic representations found in culture are humans able to create understanding and actions. Hence, semiotic culture and discourse depend on interactions. Dewey argues that the use of discourse allows the training of thought to convey meaning and order actions.

> If a man moves toward another to throw him out of the room, his movement is not a sign. If, however, the man points to the door with his hand, or utters the sound "go," his movement is reduced to a vehicle of meaning: it is a sign or symbol. In the case of signs we care nothing for what they are in themselves, but everything for what they signify and represent. *Canis, hund, chien*, dog – it makes no difference what the outward thing is, so long as the meaning is presented.

It is through discursive representation of culture that humans are capable of sharing thoughts, ideas, theories, or any other mental construct. The sacred is no different. Since cognitive representations are intangible, there is no mechanism afforded humans to physically share the ontological sacred. Dewey recognized that ideas are dependent upon shared meanings because it is only through shared meanings that abstract concepts like religion, sacred, marriage, and family can exist.

There is power in texts and words (Chodorow 1999; Fairclough 2003; Hook 2001). Texts, language, and symbolic and material objects shape our understanding of the world and our actions. They are part of our psyche, our psychological unconscious mind, and they are part of culture. We talk to ourselves as both subject and object in countless ways to make sense of our world. A large portion of that self-talk is a negotiation of culture and the circumstances and social contexts in which we find ourselves. Those broader discourses, social contexts, and self-talk are reflexively shaped by, and framed within, culture. Both religion and marriage are discursively and socially constructed (Berger 1966) within specific social contexts and lived experiences (Hall 1997).

Culture and discourse inform our subjectivities. According to Lupton and Barclay (1997: 8), "Subjectivity . . . may be defined as the varying forms of selfhoods by which people experience and define themselves." Poststructuralists largely reject a positivist perspective of "the self" as a fixed identity in favor of a more dynamic and heterogeneous negotiation of selfhood predicated on disunity and conflict. This multifaceted dimension of the individual's internalized identity is reflexive in nature being strongly influenced by experience, sociocultural history, and reflexively anchored in discourse. The production and maintenance of subjectivity is dependent upon discourses that people draw upon from the wider culture. People construct sacred marriages that are multidimensional and responsive to their social environments by weaving together discourses to adapt to changing social forces in the production of new sacred meanings.

In the past decade, there has been a significant increase in the use of discourse theory in social science research and Foucault's work related to discourse is inevitably attached (Hook 2001). According to Foucault, power should not be viewed as an external influence located in social institutions like religion. Instead, power is a system that produces knowledge and simulated realities. The importance of power in the present study is in the intertwining of culture and discourse. Power shapes discourses which reflexively influence culture. As Lupton and Barclay (1997: 11) note, "We are always the subjects of power." Thus, we are not merely malleable entities upon which culture is written any more than discourse is a straightjacket upon us that removes our agency and freedom to act. But rather, power relations are resistant and discourses are conflicting, resulting in culture that draws upon these competing power systems and discourses through a negotiation of oppositions, rejections, and transformations of interaction within social contexts.

Given this theoretical framework, neither religion nor marriage are wholly social structures that impose rules, norms, and values upon actors. Instead, each person is constantly negotiating power systems, competing discourses, and social forces in the construction of culture (Shotter and Gergen 1989; Weedon 1992). Religion, the sacred, marriage, family, and gender reflexively encompass nexuses of strands of culture through discourses and power systems. These strands of culture can be used to construe future realities and discoursally constituted ways of being. Fairclough (2003: 207) has termed these future realities "social imaginaries." Culture can be discursively projected onto future networks of social practices giving meaning, including sacred meanings, to social relationships. Social imaginaries allow people to manipulate culture, to try out their cultural toolkits, and to compare potential outcomes of various strategies of action before they act or are acted upon. Culture is connected to discourse in the social construction of strategies of action, symbolic meanings, and reflexive social practices in which social actors influence others in the present and the perceived future.

Agency

It is important to note, that I contend that there is no reason to assume that everyone is equally capable or adept at using or producing culture to solve problems of action in their lives. While there may be more than enough culture available to use, as Swidler (1986) suggests, there is no evidence that people have the same ability to develop or use their cultural toolkits, or to pursue strategies of action that will lead to solutions to their problems. Actors have different cultural repertoires and different cultural tools available to them. I assert that some people may be more or less able to effectively employ those cultural tools and repertoires in different social contexts. Likewise, it is not likely that everyone is influenced by or uses discourse with the same efficacy to solve their problems of action. It is completely plausible that some people may have a higher ordered understanding and ability of manipulating cultural strategies to their benefit to solve problems of action, while others may have a far less developed understanding of culture and discourses concerning marriage and family. Ultimately, even the best use of culture and discourse would prove ineffective in solving problems of action if those cultures and discourses are not shared within the community in which a person is acting.

Emotions

And, while sacred marriages are constitutive of religious discourse and religious culture through social interaction, people do have biological urges and sensate experiences. People fall in love. Emotions are particularly important in the study of sacred marriages, because they influence how people talk, think, feel, and act in their sacred marriages. But more than that, religion evokes emotions within sacred marriages. Emotions are personal and social, biological and cultural, and are located at the intersection of social agents and social structures. Emotions are imbued with religious discourse and religious culture, framed within encounters with the living, the dead, the imagined, and the transcendent. "Religious emotional regimes" (Riis and Woodhead 2010) include super-social relations and experiences of the sacred (e.g., sacred sites, sacred landscapes, sacred artifacts, and sacred beings). By attending to self and society, culture and self, and culture and society, religious emotional regimes speak to married couples' collective sensate emotions, personal resistances, selections of cultural scripts, and the emotional dimensions of their agency.

The sacred is not a panacea (Mullins 2016). Deep investment in the sacred may have deleterious effects in people's lives (Krumrei et al 2009; Mahoney et al 2003; Pargament et al 2005). Burr and his colleagues (2012: 22) offer four specific ways that the sacralization of marriage could be harmful to families. First, perceiving marriage as sacred raises the stakes. When people view divorce, loss, violation, or desecration as divine punishment, these negative life events become more distressing (see Jenkins 2014 and Riessman 1990 concerning sacred divorce). When goals are realized, sacralization magnifies the success, but in failure the pain is more acute. Second, when family members misunderstand religious teachings or take them to the extreme, their behavior can be harmful. Sanctifying strict, punishing, or controlling behavior can lead to rejecting and disowning children. Third, when expectations of sacred marriages do not meet the realities of people's lived experiences, it may trigger feelings of spiritual failure, exacerbating maladjustment. Fourth, throughout history religion has been used to justify inequality through racial and gender discrimination.

Study overview

While at times I describe the influence of religion in sacred marriages in terms of embodied habitus, structural schemas, and performative practices, this study's primarily focuses on the social, cultural, and symbolic dimensions of sacred marriages. Rather than thinking of religion as a social and cultural force that acts externally on marriages, I assume that sacred marriages exist through religion's social, cultural, and discursive processes. In this study, I seek out the power of discourse in constructing and constituting the realities and semiotics of sacred marriages. Discourse and culture constrain and enable people through the ways they talk, think, feel, and act in response to their problems. Ultimately, religion and the sacred are culturally structured ways of speaking that give meaning to experiences, emotions, and actions. Semiotic discourse and culture associated with sacred marriages exist within sociocultural contexts. A study such as this must question whose interests are served by the use and availability of specific religious discourse as well as how power relationships are sustained and justified by culture. Any discussion of power relationships in marriage must acknowledge the inevitable interrelationships between wives and husbands and the ways in which gender influences resistances and alternative discourses in response to dominant religious discourse.

More than representing human relations, religious culture and religious discourse includes semiotic emotions shaped by encounters with the super-social. The scheme I propose recognizes not only social agency of each spouse, but their perception of supra-human social agency in their lived experiences of marriage and family. There is an extra-human semiotic discourse throughout the texts and narratives I analyzed in this study which is found in the interactions between selves, culture, discourse, and community in sacred marriages. This extra-human discourse generates, focuses, and communicates religious meaning in sacred marriages. At times, however, this discourse loses power to competing discourses and strategies of action when it fails to evoke intended emotions, sentiments, or social imaginaries of a shared future together. It is important to consider how and when couples use religion to construct supra-human social agency through their individual agency and their collective social agency as a couple.

Given these considerations, there are three overarching themes that inform this study.

1   Marriage is painted as sacred, yet fragile. The discourse of privatization and divorce is gendered and pushes wives and husbands to engage in ongoing gendered questioning of self-talk, talking with their spouse, and elite and dominate religious discourse to work towards the ideal of sacred marriages by ongoing self-reflection.

2   Sacred marriages are reproduced through religious culture and discourse at a human level of action. There is also an extra-human level of meaning and action in love, sex, and childbearing. These aspects of marriage and family exhibit gendered emotional sensations originating from individual's earliest experiences of marriage during their childhoods. It is during this time period

that people develop their understandings of religious semiotics and expectations of marital satisfaction and marital quality.

3   Dominant religious discourse about marriage is gendered and suggests that marriage is a logical, natural expectation; a fragile process requiring work and commitment; an opening and structuring of emotions and sexual drives; a demanding but supernaturally rewarding endeavor filled with stresses and strains; and, an opportunity for a deep, fulfilling love, and exclusive intimacy.

Chapter by chapter

Love has been largely overlooked in the scholarship of sacred marriages. Chapter 2 examines the sacralization of love as used to evoke, manage, legitimize, and moralize emotions and strategies of action in sacred marriages. The sacralization of love focuses not on compatibility, relationship quality, marital satisfaction, or conflict, but instead on religious ways of feeling, talking, thinking, and acting with love in their sacred marriages.

Chapter 3 examines gendered religious discourse in the sacralization of sex and childbearing in sacred marriages. The manuals sacralize sex and childbearing by framing husbands and wives as co-creators with God, requiring men to control their sexual aggressions and women to embody the qualities of virginity and motherhood. The couples negotiate the limits of physical, social, and emotional resources alongside religious scripts concerning sex and childbearing. Participants drew on fragments of religious and secular discourses and cultures to solve their problems of action related to sex and childbearing. And, while few fully accepted or followed all Church teachings concerning sex and childbearing, equally few indicated Church teachings should change.

Chapter 4 examines the blending of religious and secular discourses and cultures to promote resilience in sacred marriages. Participants in sacred marriages ordered religious and nonreligious discourses and cultures in the selection of strategies of action to solve their problems. Through the blending of religious and nonreligious spheres, participants constructed a sacred consciousness within their cultural repertoires. While specific religious discourse and religious culture varies across participants based on individual sociocultural histories, the people in this study share in a sacred consciousness in marriage that is social in origin.

Religious rituals structure and order religious and nonreligious discourses and cultures through gendered embodiment in the sacralization of marriage using everyday spaces in which sacred marriages are lived. Chapter 5 examines these spaces and how people use the discourses and cultures in rituals to orient themselves to and reproduce meanings in their sacred marriages as they face problems of action that threaten their marriages. At the same time, rituals can be a source of stress in sacred marriages. Some couples deal with this stress by privatizing sacred meanings and reconstructing new or altered meanings to rituals based on their lived experiences.

Couples often disagree about the use of religious discourse and religious culture to solve their problems of action. Chapter 6 examines the resulting religious dissonance, and the compromises it promotes in response to changes in sacred marriages, which play a salient role in marriage self-regulation. In the process of seeking compromise, they make choices together through collective agency that may subjugate the individual agency of either or both spouses promoting a perception of supernatural intervention in their lives. Supernatural intervention, at least in part, is the force of collective social agency couples create through discursive relational dialectics to solve problems of action.

Drawing from religious and nonreligious spheres, participants in this study used religious culture to moralize their experiences of their marriages. Ultimately, their sacred marriages are not dependent on relationships with the supernatural or specific sacred experiences. Chapter 7 describes religious traditions and how they invoke religious narratives and experiences, regardless of internalization or understanding in sacred marriages. Rather than promulgating specific religious truths about marriage, most of the people in this study shared stories about the way people ought – and ought not – talk, think, feel, and act in sacred marriages as part of the larger relationships – both human and divine – to which they belong.

In a reflexive reconstruction of sacred marriages, the people in this study not only used religion to talk, think, feel, and act in religious ways in their lived experiences, their lived experiences reflexively shaped the ways they acted, felt, thought, and talked about religion and their sacred marriages. In Chapter 8, I describe how participants used religion to frame their lived experiences of marriage when religion solved their problems of action. When religious discourse and religious culture were not sufficient to solve their problems of action in their lives, their stories bended religious culture in meaningful ways that ordered their experiences and solved their problems of action in their sacred marriages. By invoking religious associations in the sacred consciousness of their marriages in their stories, while subordinating specific religious schema, they reproduced altered sacred marriages that maintained a niche position within the community of sacred marriages despite their broader marginalization.

In the Conclusion, I describe sacred marriages as existing within the nexus of private and public, and religious and nonreligious spheres. The Conclusion addresses the discursive construction and positioning of sacred marriages within contrasts and broader narratives of sacred marriages in communities. I explain how sacred marriages are produced through gendered embodiment and lived within broader religious and nonreligious cultures, religious and nonreligious spaces, and situated within specific times and places. People's ability to bend religion to construct new sacred marriages through dialectical relations associated with compromises they make in response to change are also addressed. Finally, I describe why people generally eschew changes in religion because it provides familiar cultural tools they use in their sacred marriages that they generally know how to manipulate to solve their problems.

Appendix: methodology

The appendix describes the methodology used for conducting and analyzing participant interviews. Participants were drawn through snowball sampling from the

U.S. Midwest and consisted of 43 heterosexual couples married over 40 years who were self-proclaimed Christians who hold religious beliefs that marriage is sacred. The interview questionnaire used in the study is included in the Appendix. Methodology for selecting and analyzing 58 Christian marriage advice manuals is also described. Implications of the choice of methodology on the study are discussed.

Notes

1 Given the power of language, and sacred language in particular, I intentionally use the word sacralization instead of the preferred term in most studies of sacred marriages, which is sanctification. Following Williams (2008), through a process of desacralization my intention is to position sacred marriages in the public, academic domain as opposed to the theological domain of a particular faith community. In contrast, sanctifying implies consecrating something as holy and pure to be set apart from other marriages. By referring to the sacralizing of marriage this study takes seriously both the religious and nonreligious spheres in which sacred marriages exist and operate. This study deconstructs the sacred following Pinto's (2003) conceptualization of the transcendent divine as a positivity based on experiences and knowledge of gendered reality. Although the manuals and most participants equated the sacred to God as a divine being, some participants did not. Many participants referred to supernatural interventions in their sacred marriages with words like "providence," "luck," and "destiny." This study views the sacred not as descriptor of a reality, but rather as an etic for academic analysis.
2 Although the term Christian is sociologically inaccurate, it has a common understanding and meaning among the participants in this study. It is how most of them self-identify. I have also chosen it because although this study investigates the influence of religion on their sacred marriages, the study sample is exclusively drawn from Catholics and Protestants who self-identify as Christians. Thus, the findings of this study may not be generalizable to non-Christians or non-sacred marriages, and I make no such generalization to any dissimilar marriages outside this study.
3 All names of people, places, and churches in this book are pseudonyms.
4 While over half of the couples in this study self-identify as Catholic, there are innumerable practices and styles of American Catholicism (Arbuckle 2013; Burns 1992; D'Antonio et al 2001; D'Antonio et al 2007; Davidson 2005; Dillon 1999; Lawler 2002; Salzman et al 2004).
5 I have chosen the phrase "religious culture" with intention. Religion may refer to a social institution. I have opted not to use the phrase "culture of religion" because my focus is on that which refers to religion – hence, religious – and not the institution itself. I have also chosen the singular "religious culture" over the plural "religious cultures" not because I do not recognize that there are many religious cultures, but because my focus is on the power of culture itself and not any specific cultures. Thus, I use "religious culture" to refer to the power in culture that relates to religion, and not the power of religion itself.

2   Love

Research over the past 50 years has consistently demonstrated that the vast majority of Americans marry for love and say they would not marry someone with whom they were not in love, even if that person possessed all the other qualities they desire in a spouse (Kephart 1967; Caughlin and Huston 2006). Love plays a salient role in the decision to marry in countries other than the U.S. as well (Abdhalla 2009; Levine et al 1995; Xu and Whyte 1990). Some have argued that love is more important in marriages today than at any other time in history due to the privatization of marriage which has left it a more fragile institution dependent on individual emotion and choice for its endurance (Amato and Irving 2006; Cherlin 2009; Coontz 2005). A growing body of evidence also suggests that love is a core component of individual emotional quality, which has been shown to be an important predictor of relationship endurance (Nock 2001; Wilcox and Nock 2006; Sayer and Bianchi 2000).

Many have argued that the body of literature that does exist concerning love is largely confusing (Caughlin and Huston 2006) and overly focused on romantic love (Amato 2007). Previous studies have primarily been premised on incomplete assumptions about love, failing to recognize that positive affect and negative affect are relatively independent and not polar opposites (Berscheid 2010). Married couples can exhibit high levels of apathy, conflict, and love simultaneously. Even scales of liking someone and loving someone are only moderately correlated, suggesting people sometimes love others they do not necessarily like (Rubin 1970).

Some of the most recent work in sacred marriages (Brown et al 2011; DeMaris et al 2010; Dollahite et al 2012; Mahoney 2010; Mahoney et al 2003; Pargament and Mahoney 2005) gives little primacy to love. Despite evidence suggesting improved marital outcomes associated with sacred meanings in religion (Black and Lobo 2008; Dollahite and Marks 2009), little is known about the influence the sacralization of love in these marriages. Some have concluded love's relative absence in the literature stems from a paradigm in which marital satisfaction is believed to be the cornerstone of marital stability, despite scholarship demonstrating that decreased levels of love are more likely to lead to divorce than high levels of conflict (Berscheid 2010; Roberts 1992). The relative dearth of sociological studies of love in sacred marriages is particularly striking given the dyadic nature and experiences of love – people love one another – and the evidence from the social psychology of emotion which demonstrates that the locus of the emotions and behaviors associated with love lies not only in the individual actors but within the interactions between them (Rietti 2009) as organized through discursively constructed social forces like culture, gender, and social class (Peräkylä and Sorjonen 2012).

Giddens (1992), in his description of confluent love, has concluded that love wanes, lasting only as long as it is mutually satisfying. Love itself is at the mercy of individual choice because no social force requires people to love one another, and the legal bonds of marriage have become increasingly privatized and permeable in an age when people marry, divorce, and remarry almost at will. Love relationships teeter on the brink of dissolution based ultimately on personal choice. Beck and Beck-Gernsheim (1995) in, *The Normal Chaos of Love*, suggest that love in relationships has taken center stage since the Industrial Revolution because religion's influence over relationships, and marriage in particular, has declined. In response to the decline of religion's influence, love has become a secular religion of its own.

In contrast to those who suggest that love is finite, or that love is its own religion, I suggest, following Swidler (2001), that it is because relationships and love are fragile that people do cultural work using different cultures of love to sustain their marriages and love relationships, and that religious discourse and religious culture organize and structure competing cultural schema of love in sacred marriages. While Swidler's (2001) study of love represents ground-breaking work in the understanding of love and relationships, her work is not exclusive to marriage or sacred marriages. And, while she does include religion in her study, it is not the primary focus of her analysis.

The present study fills a gap in the current literature of sacred marriages through the use of a combination of cultural theory based on Swidler (1986 and 2001), the study of religion and family based on Bartkowski (2001 and 2004), Wilcox and Wolfinger (2016), and the study of emotion based on Chodorow (1999) and Hochschild (2012). This study also incorporates religion's influences on emotions – like love – following Riis and Woodhead (2010). Collectively, this scholarship recognizes that cultures of love are produced through people's actions. Practicing cultural repertoires allows people to selectively pick up and put aside cultural themes to implement various strategies of action. Religion, therefore, is not a straightjacket that causes and affirmatively directs love in sacred marriages, but rather people develop religious repertoires they use to form strategies of actions in their lived experiences of their sacred marriages. The sacralization of love blends the private and the public, the cultural and the discursive, to evoke, manage, legitimize, and moralize emotions and strategies of action in sacred marriages.

In the remainder of this chapter, I attempt to describe the process of sacralizing love based on my analysis of the data. My separation of different forms of love is consistent with the literature, but it is also artificial because love coexist in people's lives as a fluidity that is both responsive to circumstance and dependent on social contexts. The following typologies of love cannot be disaggregated from people's lived experiences of love within social, sensate, and religious emotional contexts which influence subjectivities and interactions (Denzin 1983). My purpose is not to reify these typologies, but rather to contrast the study participants' perceptions of a secular culture of love with sacralized love, constructed through religious discourse and religious culture. The juxtaposition of religious and secular cultures is a fundamental aspect of the process by which marriages are sacralized. The sacralization of love in sacred marriages is produced through a discursive positioning of the perceived divine qualities of sacred love in marriage with a characterization of secular culture in general, and secular love in particular, as detrimental to sacred marriages by framing secular love as unnatural, base, misguided, and animalistic.

Sensate emotions

According to the manuals and the couples I interviewed, love is constitutive of many, sometimes conflicting, feelings. Despite the importance of feelings in religion and love, the sensate aspects of emotions have often been largely avoided in the literature. Burr and others' (2012) recent work examining the role of the sacred in families dedicates considerable attention to the performance of love as measured in people's actions by constructing love "as a verb and not a noun." However, this conceptualization of love elides the sensate emotionality of love in people's bodies. Focusing on actions associated with love provides little consideration of how people think, talk, or feel about how they acted in their sacred marriages. The sensate dimensions of love and other emotions are important, and the sensate is important in the study of religious culture in particular (Bartkowski 2004; Brasher 1998; Griffith 1997). Additionally, sensate experiences play a vital role in the religious emotional regimes described by Riis and Woodhead (2010).

The manuals and the couples I interviewed were trepidatious at times in their approach to the sensual nature of love. Some characterized the sensate emotionality of love as potentially, if not outright, harmful to sacred marriages because they attributed feelings of love to a secular culture of unregulated lust and sexual perversions, satisfying personal desires. In contrast, they framed sacralized love as premised on the values of giving of oneself for the benefit of the other through selfless commitment and dedication. The result of these giving and selfless actions, especially when the recipient of love was not deserving, was framed as the source of "the positive feelings" of love. Making the "daily choice to love your spouse no matter what" an essential expectation in sacred marriages. This decision was believed to be rewarded through positive sensate experiences of love personally, as described by one husband's comment, "You feel how you act, and if you give love, you feel love."

Companionate love

Companionate love was an important part of several of the manuals and participants' experiences of love in their sacred marriages. Companionate love encompasses strong affection for family members, pets, close friends, or others with whom people's lives are closely intertwined. Companionate love is based on a deep sense of friendship, companionship, and liking another person (Hatfield and Rapson 1993). While a few couples in this study described their courtship and eventual marriage as stemming from a companionate love relationship, almost all of the couples incorporated aspects of companionate love in their narratives. They shared stories of interactions with their pets, siblings, close friends, children, grandchildren, and sometimes great-grandchildren filled with emotions that guided their behaviors. They felt these relationships mostly strengthened their relationships with their spouses.

Companionate love was not always supportive of other forms of love between spouses in sacred marriages. Couples reported that levels of romantic love were often negatively impacted in the presence of increasing levels of companionate love for people who were not their spouses. Many couples described times in their lives when their experiences of romantic love suffered due to increased levels of companionate love for their children and grandchildren. Placing the needs of children and grandchildren above the level of romantic love they perceived their spouses' needed was common. In some cases, high levels of companionate love for people other than spouses was associated with infidelity by spouses, feelings of disenfranchisement from parenting processes by spouses, and decreased levels of sex and feelings of intimacy between spouses.

When I asked Corrine if she felt she had given up anything of herself to be a wife and mother, she replied, "I never gave up anything. I always wanted to be a wife and a mother. Everything I ever did was because I love my kids." Later, while telling me about her husband's infidelity, she paused and said, "I guess I did give up something for my kids. I gave up time with my husband that he needed. When the kids were all out of the house, I didn't know who I was anymore." Couples' feelings and expectations associated with companionate love often decreased feelings and behaviors associated with romantic love.

The importance of companionate love to husbands was particularly striking. On numerous occasions, when I asked husbands how they knew their wives loved them, they began to cry. This reaction was surprising given the frequency with which men cried after being asked this particular question. Their explanations of their tears and sentimentality centered around sensate experiences of companionate love.

Bill said, "I don't know what I'll do when she's gone."

Earnest described crying himself to sleep every year when his wife takes her annual trip for one week with her high school friends for their "girls week." These husbands described an emotional attachment with their wives based on companionship and a sense of consistency that was literally tear-jerking.

Wives' levels of happiness associated with companionate love were an important aspect of husbands' experiences of companionate love. Several husbands told me the "secret" to marriage was making sure their wives stayed happy. Twenty-five out of 43 husbands I interviewed – over half – said some variation of the following: "If your wife isn't happy, no one is happy." Their desire to make their wives happy was rooted in companionate love. Husbands described times when they changed not only what they said to their wives, but how they said it to make their wives happy. They described "honey-do" lists that included various house-hold chores they completed to make their wives happy. They also described ways of talking about their wives with respect as part of companionate love. Several retired husbands described changes in their feelings and behaviors when they retired because their increased presence with their wives was disruptive to their wives' routines and caused stress in their marriages.

Jack explained, "You don't ever go out talking bad about your wife. She's your wife and the mother of your children. You talk about her with respect, even when she's acting crazy. [Laughter]."

While these husbands' attempts to increase the level of companionate love in their relationship are filled with a power discourse of gender (i.e., implying hus-bands can control wives' happiness and satisfaction through husbands' actions, pejoratively describing household chores as "honey-do's," and simultaneously describing their wives as objects of respect and irrationality), they are clearly concerned about companionate love in their relationship, consistent with the find-ings of others (Cancian 1986; Thaagard 1997). Both husbands and wives rec-ognized that being together for family events, doing things together as a family, and tackling "life's ups and downs together" was an essential part of their mar-riages. They were also attempting to exhibit more feminine characteristics of love (Clack 1996), and potentially assume a more masculine role as religious leaders and providers in their homes by investing in a masculinized form of emotion work (Wilcox 2004).

Attempts to enhance levels of companionate love in sacred marriages were an important aspect of couples' narratives and the manuals. Given that a core component of love is personal choice, attempts to manage companionate love are an essential aspect of marriage endurance. Knowing that marriage is fragile, and that love is equally fragile and can end based on another's will, couples often employed specific plans to strengthen companionate love relationships with family and friends. This was particularly true for women who frequently shared stories of strong feelings of companionate love for their husbands when they were "just there" for them. Although this could partially be attributed to a generational culture in which men financially supported women, almost all the couples I interviewed included wives with equal educational attainment to their husbands and who worked outside the home for pay at various times in their lives. These wives did not need their husbands to care for them. Instead, many wives felt increased marital satisfaction, relationship satisfaction, and increased levels of companionate love for their husbands when their husbands met their expectations as fathers, as "men of God," and during periods of involvement with extended family, friends, and religious congregations, even when they faced career instability and financial troubles as a couple. Their feelings of love were not about physically or emotionally supporting each other as caregivers. They experienced sensations of love by the mere presence – and the persistence of the presence – of their spouses.

The importance of emotional investment in forming loving relationships with others through companionate love is a salient aspect of relationship quality in many of the sacred marriages in this study. Most wives especially wanted their husbands and their children to form strong companionate love relationships with extended family and friends. One couple I interviewed, for example, went to lunch once a month with a group of friends they have had for over 60 years. As the group of friends shrinks in size due to death and illness, the companionate love they expressed for their remaining friends played an increasingly salient role in their love for one another. Husbands focused more on a disciplined commitment to relationships in their descriptions of their companionate love for others. Wives described the value they placed on companionate love relationships, especially with their husbands, in terms of a sense of familiarity with known expectations of their husbands' emotional investment in their relationship and their relationships as couples with others.

Investment in emotion work is an important aspect of relationships (Hochschild 1979, 1983, 1989, and 2013). Husbands and wives differ in the ways they do emotion work, the degree to which they participate in emotion work, and the ways they perceive and experience the effects of emotion work in their marriages. While both husbands and wives need to invest in emotion work, research suggests that husbands' emotional investment does not have to be the same as wives for wives to report significantly higher levels of marital quality just by husbands exhibiting some level of interest and involvement in emotion work (Wilcox 2004). This is partially the effect of wives' lowered expectations of husbands' emotional involvement. However, gender is at work here as well through cultural scripts of masculinity that devalue emotionality in men and the feminization of love (Cancian 1986), despite men's ability to be sentimental and expressive in their love. This was certainly the case for over half the men in this study who cried openly when asked about their wives' love for them, as I mentioned previously.

Romantic love

Both the manuals and the couples in this study suggested romantic love held significant sway in their marriages, especially early in their relationships. Expectations of the couples about levels of romantic love, as well as the value of romantic love in their marriages, changed through time. However, the sensate aspects of passionate and erotic feelings and experiences associated with romantic love played an important role in the marriages of the couples I interviewed throughout their lives.

Amato (2007: 306), suggests that there are many definitions of romantic love but fundamentally it "is a strong emotional bond with another person that involves sexual desire, a longing to be with the person, a preference to put the other person's interests ahead of one's own, and a willingness to forgive the other person's transgressions. Seen in this light, one might conceptualize commitment, sacrifice, and forgiveness as components of love." However, romantic love can include "both intense positive and negative emotions" (Sprecher and Fehr 2011: 559).

Although sexual desire for another person is not a prerequisite to marriage, the texts and interviews I analyzed for this study are ripe with references to romantic love in sacred marriages.

When I asked, "Why did you marry your wife?"

Dan replied, "Why do you think I married her? You know. Why does anyone get married? To be together. You know – physically. [Laughter]."

Although some couples had sex before they married, it is important to draw a distinction between religious objections to premarital sex and a generational culture that discouraged premarital sex. When asked if he and his wife did not have sex before marriage due to his religious objections, Dan quickly replied, "No, I never had a chance to think about it like that. Back then you just didn't do that." Other husbands shared that they tried to attend roller skating parties, dances, or school-sponsored sporting events in other communities, so they could meet and have sex with women unknown to their parents and extended family to reduce the risk of "getting caught." While some of the men described attempts to engage in premarital sex, they did not describe these encounters as being associated with romantic love for their sex partners. Brian, a devout Catholic, summed up romantic love by explaining that there is a difference in "lust" and "love" and while he had sexual desires for his wife before they married, to them, their sex life was an expression of their love and passion for one another that reflected "God's blessings" in their marriage. In Brian's words, "Not everyone is blessed with children or physical love for one another. It's just not in God's plan . . . We've always tried to do what's right, and God's blessed us for the decisions we've made in his name."

As Brian's comments suggest, husbands in this study described romantic love and sexual intercourse as being different but related. Although they are clearly linked, the sensate experiences of romantic love occur in the absence of sex, but sex fuels erotic and passionate feelings included in romantic love. Equally, the degree of romantic love in their relationship, especially husband's perceptions of their wives' degree of romantic love in their relationships, influenced their sex lives, which I discuss in more detail in Chapter 3: Sex and childbearing.

In comparison to husbands, most of the wives described romantic love in non-sexual terms. While many wives shared that they had physical passion and sexual desire for their husbands, they were far more likely to describe romantic love in terms of feelings they attributed to their husbands being good fathers, loving men, or romantic as exhibited by writing them love letters, poetry, or love notes. Wives described "date nights" and feelings of closeness as part of romantic love. Often they described romantic love in opposition to what they believed their husbands perceived romantic love to be. For example, Betty shared that when she and Frank were first married she wanted to hug him or hold his hand because she felt "romantic and in love." "But I had to tell him, listen, every time I touch you, don't think it's going to lead to the bedroom!"

The data in this study suggests that romantic love is expected in sacred marriages, and that although the physical act of sex becomes less frequent with age, the importance of sensory and emotional experiences of intimacy as well as romantic behaviors remains important. Additionally, romantic love is evoked through inter-actions between couples. Couples often sought out shared experiences to promote and maintain romantic love in their relationships (e.g., "date nights").

Importantly, romantic love is regulated for nonreligious reasons. One wife described intense emotions and "acting crazy" when she learned she was unable to bear children out of concern that her husband would no longer feel or exhibit romantic love for her or find her sexually desirable. Some wives described fears that their husbands would engage in extramarital sex as they aged due to changes in the wives' bodies. Some wives, and some husbands, reported changing their behaviors and their appearances in attempts to manage their spouses' degrees of physical attraction and romantic love for them. Couples also felt that their degree of romantic love was impinged upon by external forces to their marriages (e.g., outside employment and parenting responsibilities). Negative emotions or behav-iors were often couched within a framework of romantic love which attributed spouses' shortcomings and failures to external causes and beyond the spouse's control.

The regulation of romantic love also occurred in relation to commitment. For the two couples I interviewed who were pregnant at the time of their marriage, family forces in addition to religion played significant roles in the ways these couples felt, talked, and thought about their relationships and their love for one another. Both husbands described their parents' insistence on them marrying their wives. The couples spoke of their decisions to marry as pragmatic rather than reli-gious. They did not describe romantic love in terms of sex but rather in terms of an obligation to a lifelong commitment to one another, to marriage itself, and to their unborn children. Committing to one another also entailed a component of com-mitting to "being an adult" and gendered expectations of men to be married, resi-dential fathers (Lupton and Barclay 1997). One husband explained his experience in strongly gendered terms, "I wasn't a boy anymore. It was time to be a man." The other husband, Tom, shared that his best man repeatedly asked why they were getting married so quickly. Tom said, "I just told him I loved her." Both Tom and his wife Jessica laughed at Tom's comment, and Jessica added with laughter, "We didn't know what love was back then." Then Jessica patted Tom's thigh and gave him a quick kiss. They held hands through the remainder of the interview.

The ways couples feel, talk, and think about romantic love in sacred marriages need not be fully internalized or understood for them to experience romantic feel-ings, talk about romantic love, and give private meanings to romantic gestures and behaviors outside of religious meanings. The decisions couples make in their marriages influence their feelings of romantic love towards each other, as well as their perceptions of being romantically loved by their spouse.

Compassionate love

Compassionate love refers to a love for all of humanity focused on the well-being of others without regard to motivation and without a requirement for reciproc-ity, although eventual reciprocity may be a latent expectation (Sprecher and Fehr

2011). Underwood's (2005) study of compassionate love among Trappist monks is based on two fundamental definitions of love focused on others: "giving of self for the good of the other" and "other-centered love." Compassionate love forgives others while attending to their needs through understanding, caring, and concern, particularly when others are suffering or in need.

While compassionate love would appear to be universally beneficial to all relationships, it can be problematic, especially when it crosses boundaries within marriage (Collins et al 2014). For compassionate love to be beneficial in a relationship, the care must be noncontingent and both partners must be willing to receive care and trust in the caregiver's altruistic motivations (Iida et al 2008). Additionally, the beneficial effects of compassionate care can be affected by the character of the provider, the partner's request for support, and the support history within the relationship. The temporal aspect of compassionate love confounds its effects in relationships given that short-term selfless caregiving differs significantly from permanent selfless actions associated with long-term caregiver roles.

While couples in this study rarely described their love for one another as being based on their spouses love for humanity, some did:

"Edna is such a good person. She loves everyone and would do anything for anyone – even a stranger!" Howard, a retired dairy farmer, said of his wife. "How could I not love her more each day? Who wouldn't love a person like that?"

More often, compassionate love played a role in caregiving for spouses and family members. Many of the couples had experienced significant health deterioration and an increasing dependence on others for physical and emotional support associated with the aging process. Additionally, after so many years together, many of the people I interviewed viewed their lives as depending on their spouse for simple matters like wives cooking meals, husbands managing the couples' financial affairs, and each spouse maintaining personal interests while intertwining them with the interests of the other spouse. They depended on each other to maintain their lives together as a couple, not because of romantic love or companionate love, but because they each played their own caregiving role in the relationship. They frequently referred to a need for self-sacrifice to support their children and their children's families. However, their understanding of their obligation to help others and to have a love for humanity differs significantly from their compassionate love for one another as a couple. For these couples, compassionate love for each other and their families largely resulted from a blending of romantic and companionate love.

Compassionate love also includes a desire for the spiritual growth and well-being of the other (Underwood 2005), and the couples and texts in this study are rich in descriptors of this aspect of compassionate love. However, it is important to note that compassionate love need not be based on religion (Post et al 2000). Participants often referred to increases in the degree of romantic love and companionate love when their levels of dyadic religiosity with their spouse increased. Attending religious services together, praying together, and attending religious rituals like christenings, baptisms, and first communions were significant events that evoked various emotions affecting levels of compassionate love for one another. Frieda explained that she "loved Ted for going to mass every morning" because she knew he prayed for her and their children. Chuck, a devout nondenominational Christian, said, "I just don't feel close to God," when he and his wife did not read the Bible and pray together each day because he believed it was his responsibility as a husband to help his wife "lead a closer walk with God." Clearly there are links between compassionate love and religion, but there need not be. Having and exhibiting a love for humanity can be based on nonreligious foundations.

The sacralization of love

Couples in sacred marriages clearly have many nonreligious cultural tools at their disposal to construct cultural repertoires of love in their marriages. Love has been strongly shaped through social structural changes associated with the division of labor in families, commercialization, changes in gendered behaviors and gendered expectations in marriage, economic factors, the sexual revolution, globalization, modernity, and a culture of privatization (Beck and Beck-Gernsheim 2014; Bellah et al 1985; Hochschild 1979, 1983, 1989, and 2013; Hopkins et al 2009). These changes in love not only influence the cultural repertoires people use to form love in their relationships, these changes influence people's feelings of love. As Illouz (2012: 6) describes in her book, *Why Love Hurts*, love is not purely private but is also institutional. Feelings of happiness, joy, exuberance, and ebullience that accompany the sensate experiences of love may also be fraught with self-doubt, anxiety, unease, restlessness, and dissatisfaction "because love contains, mirrors, and amplifies the 'entrapment' of the self in the institutions of modernity." Culturally shaped dynamistic imbalances in power within love relationships can shape love relationships.

While I have noted the external influences that shape the felt experiences of love consistent with the larger body of research, I have given little consideration to the notion that the sensate experiences of love shape structures like marriage, gender, and power discourses. As Flam (2009) suggests, much of the sociological study of emotions has focused on the ordering and structuring of emotions through external forces, but little attention has been given to a potential reversal of causality in which emotions order and generate new elements of culture, social structures, and interactions. Emotions like love can play a generative-causal role in relationships. With these provisions in mind, in the remainder of this chapter I describe the sacralization of love in sacred marriages with a focus on the power of love to alter religious culture and transform relationships in sacred marriages.

People's religious emotional lives are shaped by super-social relations encompassing interactions with the living, the dead, the imaginary, the transcendent, the inanimate, and all that is termed sacred (Riis and Woodhead 2010: 7). Religious emotion is predicated on interactions between self and society, self and symbol, and symbol and society. Therefore, religious emotion includes both individual emotion and collective emotion. Sacred objects and religious practices reflexively shape individual emotions that reflexively reinforce collective emotion and inform cultural strategies. As with discourse and sociobiological emotion, people negotiate conflicting and undermining processes resulting in disconnections while striving for broader connections in the future. These conflicts are negotiated through what Riis and Woodhead (2010: 10) have termed "religious emotional regimes." These regimes are premised on a sacred, ideal world against which individuals and collectives confront the secular world and interpret one in relation to the other. Religious emotional regimes can be part of cultural repertoires based on a far-reaching perspective of life beyond the finite lifespan. They guide how people feel about themselves and others. Religious practice emotes love by framing it within broader family emotions that are connected not just to kin but to ancestral families, the broader family of believers, and heavenly families. Religious culture can exhort love and define its meaning while guiding it towards proper objects, regulating its expression, ruling out inappropriate love, and sanctioning incompatible emotions.

The process of sacralizing love in sacred marriages has no specific starting point because the process is not ordinal or additive in nature. One aspect of that process however, is downplaying of emotionality and sensate experiences of love in favor of a focus on actions. The manuals and many of the couples I interviewed placed high value on a decision to love one's spouse regardless of emotional state, marital satisfaction, or marital quality.

> Wedding vows are not a declaration of present love but a mutually binding promise of future love. A wedding should not be primarily a celebration of how loving you feel now – that can safely be assumed. Rather, in a wedding you stand up before God, your family, and all the main institutions of society, and you promise to be loving, faithful, and true to the other person in the future, regardless of undulating internal feelings or external circumstances.
>
> (Keller and Keller 2011: 91)

The sacralization of love demands a focus not on compatibility, relationship quality, marital satisfaction, or the existence of conflict, but instead on religious ways of feeling, talking, and thinking about love in sacred marriages. Love is sacralized in sacred marriages in a variety of ways in the texts I analyzed as "divine love," "enduring love," "Christ-like love," "God's love," and "the ultimate decision to love." The authors of these manuals argue that regardless of the level of marital quality, love was not optional but rather commanded in sacred marriages. Couples' narratives were peppered with terms and phrases like "supernatural," "divined," "God's will," and "preordained," in describing their love for one another. They insisted that their love was "deep," "not gushy," "beyond the physical," and "rooted in our beliefs." Many of the people I interviewed reported that their religious beliefs and practices emoted a sense of a sacred love within their marriages, that they believed was unique and different from love in secular marriages. The sacralization of love as something extraordinary and divined provided stability as it produced feelings and behaviors attributable to supernatural love beyond the control of the participants, originating not within the individual but rather from "God putting a love for my husband in my heart," to use one wife's words.

Here I offer four quotes from marriage advice manuals as evidence of the process by which love is sacralized. I follow these quotes from the manuals with excerpts from participants' narratives in which they use language to describe love in their sacred marriages that parallels the manuals. Often the couples' stories mirror elite religious discourse while contrasting and incorporating their sensate experiences of their marriages. The authors of the manuals seek authority to their claims that love in sacred marriages differs from other forms of love by using elite religious discourse. In all other forms of love, according to the manuals, there is a principle of investment in the well-being of one's spouse for the benefit of that spouse. In contrast, sacred love for one's spouse, especially when one's spouse is difficult to love, is discursively framed as a means to be nearer to God and to promote oneself along the path to holiness. The sacralization of love comingles love for one's spouse with a religiously, self-serving construction of love that produces sacred sensate experiences of love, especially in the perception of an absence of reciprocation of love from one's spouse, fundamentally restructuring love culture.

In a popular pre-marriage counseling manual for Catholic couples, Anthony Garascia (2007: 11) writes the following:

> Just as you do, the Church has great expectations for your married life. We expect that the love you have for one another not only will express your lived commitment but will point towards a deeper mystery of God's love for the world . . . . Remember that in the end it is the grace of God that sustains our commitments and creates possibilities out of seemingly impossible obstacles.

Morse and Kerekes (2013: xi) describe the sacred nature of love in Christian marriage as follows:

> Almighty God wants me to love my spouse for the rest of my life. I am making a commitment to love this person, even if he or she becomes difficult. Even if my spouse becomes nearly impossible to live with, I will continue to act in an attitude of love toward him or her. Loving my spouse is part of my personal path to holiness.

The vocation of marriage gives meaning to commitment to one's spouse, to prayer, to attendance and participation in rituals, to communication, and even to sex (Lasnoski 2014). Popcak (2008: 19–20) explain the meaning of the sacrament of marriage as a vocation to one's spouse.

> There is only *one reason for marrying* that guarantees the lifelong happiness and relevance of a marriage, only one reason that even comes close to addressing the true meaning of a Christian marriage. More than love and

companionship, the real function of a Christian marriage is *for a husband and wife to help each other become the people God created them to be.* . . . God gives each one of us a sacred trust; to prepare our mate to spend eternity in heaven with *Him.* . . . When you marry in the Church, you are acknowledging that from now until the day you die, *God has made you responsible* . . . to see that your husband or wife becomes the person God created him or her to be.

[Emphasis in original]

Bosio's (2012: 14) sacralizes love within a broader societal context.

When you believe that marriage gives you a role in society, that your commitment to each other is a response to God's invitation, that you are a gift to your spouse . . . your motivation to stay together no longer comes from how you feel today, or from what is convenient for you, or from what is fashionable among your friends. Your motivation comes from the irrevocable commitment you made to each other, to God, and to society. It comes from your knowledge that others need you and count on you to be a good husband or a good wife.

Almost all the couples I interviewed shared stories of love in their marriages by comparing their love for one another with God's love for the world in some fashion. Randy, a farmer who converted from a Methodist to his future wife's nondenominational Christian church, said, "Love is like religion. Faith without works is no good, and works without faith is no good. Isn't God's love for us awesome, the way he laid out marriage?" Both he and his wife Vicky repeatedly stated their believe that God had "given them to each other as an example of his love for the world."

Several couples shared stories of loving each other when the other person was difficult to love. These stories ranged from one man's father who refused to leave his wife who suffered from severe, undiagnosed mental illness, to a woman who made a "decision every day" to love her husband despite his ongoing infidelity. In such cases of selfless love for an "unlovable" spouse or family member, respondents used words like "crowns in Glory," "showers of blessings," or other language indicative of God's blessing on their decision to love and to endure in their marriages.

In most cases, these gifts or blessings were believed to be bestowed on them in the afterlife, but sometimes participants believed their "righteous rewards would occur on Earth." One of the most direct corollaries between elite religious discourse in marriage advice manuals and interview narratives was in couples' descriptions of their marriages and love for one another as "vocations," "paths to holiness," and "Godly marriages." Echoing this elite religious discourse, participants portrayed their attempts to love their spouses with "Christ-like love," "eternal love," and "everlasting love."

While the realities of couples' lived experiences of religion, love, and marriage were often at odds with elite religious discourse, their conflicting narratives and the way they presented the influence of religion in their marriages and families were not. Perhaps the most striking example of the negotiation of love and the realities of marriage was in the joint interview of the dairy farmers, Joe and Monica.

Joe held Monica's hand as he said, "God gave this woman right here to me. Not many women can live this life. I couldn't do it without her. I'm blessed."

Monica was serious at first and said, "I love Joe because he's a true man of God. He's a good husband and a good father." Laughing, she added, "I just wish he loved me like he loves those cows!"

Although other interviews were not as poignant, they too were filled with stories that blended the realities of everyday life, like the work that accompanies dairy farming, and a presentation of the couples' love in religious ways.

Although couples used similar religious discourse to couch their love for one another within a socially accepted presentation of religion and marriage (e.g., "we are blessed"), when pressed to articulate religion's specific positive influence on their choice of spouse, love for their spouse, or marriage longevity they were largely unable to express direct impacts of religion in their lives. For example, when asked, "Has religion ever hurt your marriage or your relationship with your spouse?" only a handful of participants shared a specifically negative event (e.g., one wife shared that she believed her husband had spent too much time volunteering at church so he could avoid parenting responsibilities). Couples described an oft-confusing, quasi-hierarchical sacred love they suggested should subordinate their sensate emotions and expression of nonreligious forms of love based on romance and support for one another's physical and emotional needs.

Chuck and Christine's narratives exemplify this contradictory and conflicting negotiation of individual feelings of love and the demands of relationship maintenance in marriage with their beliefs about love in sacred marriages. During their interview together, they blended gendered expectations of parenting and marriage with their beliefs anecdotally by describing difficulties they were experiencing with their new pastor.

Chuck explained:

> I got in an argument with our pastor a while back. He's a young pastor and causes a lot of problems in our church. He would miss an elders meeting because he was going to a soccer meeting. I asked him, what part of this don't you understand? I showed him in the Bible. I couldn't find it now because I don't know where it was, but it says put Jesus Christ first. Not second, not third, first! Ahead of your wife your family, first. So he was putting his family first. He said I think you ought to put your family first. So I asked him again what part of this don't you understand? So anyway, in my life I always try to put my wife first. Not ahead of God, but first. In any decisions I tried to think of her first. It didn't matter what it was. Whether it was going someplace or

sex, I always tried to put her first. At least that's what I always figured was put her first. I think if you put your wife first, and I always try to put her first, then that shows a lot of love.

Christine added:

We wouldn't make it through all these years and a lot of these young kids have this problem because they don't know who Jesus is and they won't go to church. . . . My beliefs in the church is tied to me attending. I feel so much better when I go. It's the going in and setting and singing those pretty songs and praying when you have prayers and that just means a lot to me. It really does. It's a feeling I get when we're doing those things. [. . .] Chuck is just like his dad. And I have accepted that. I show him I love him. I go up and give him a hug and a kiss, but he doesn't do that to me. That's just the way he is. And I know. I know that. [. . .] But I raised his kids and put their needs first because he didn't need me then like he does now. I take care of him. I fix a good supper every day. And, I pray and I go to church, and I put him first too. Not before God, like he said, but first after the kids back then.

Chuck and Christine's narratives of love twist and turn in a somewhat convoluted manner. But, taken as a whole, they illustrate religion's influence in the sacralization of love in their marriage. Their shared belief that religion positively impacts their marriage plays a paramount role in their description of their love for one another. Chuck describes his love for Christine by rejecting what he perceives to be the new pastor's over-involvement as a husband and father, which is consistent with his own more limited involvement as a father and husband based on Christine's narrative. At the same time, Chuck positions his love for Christine at the highest possible level, a sacred level, by stating that he places her first in his life, other than when he places God above her needs. Christine echoes those love sentiments for her children, which she explains in terms of caring for their children's needs above the needs of her husband. She also notes Chuck's lack of affection and focuses her narrative on her acceptance of this shortcoming as an attribute of her sacred love for Chuck because she cares for him, prays, and goes to church. Both of their narratives are devoid of personal gratification seeking. Instead, they talk and think about the sacred love they have for one another as being premised on caring, compassion, and companionship because of their mutual believe in a sacred obligation to love one another.

One reason that people like Chuck and Christine may not have been able to articulate a specific definition of love is that love, like many abstract concepts, may not have a formal definition. Instead, love may be a concept that is defined reflexively by comparing it to a model relationship. In the case of sacred marriages, the model is that of the love of Christ for the Church. According to Hegi and Bergner (2010), there are two distinct aspects to people's perceptions of love in their lived experiences. The first aspect is definitional and pertains to that which people believe to be essential to love itself. The second concept is a prototypical understanding of love premised on the attributes of good, love-based relationships. Relationships based on love contain the definitional aspects of love itself but also contain other characteristics of love-based relationships. People's understanding of love contains both aspects of the definition of love and elements of good, loving relationships as a subset of the definition of love. That which makes sacred love unique and different from other forms of love is that it is based on a divined model of ultimate love expressed in terms of people's experiences of religion and the sacred.

If love can be construed as a prototypical concept that people give meaning to by including characteristics of cultural religious models of love, it follows that people would also exclude characteristics of relationships they do not believe to be sacred love relationships. The sacralization of love is patterned after elite religious discourse concerning marriage and the blending, intertwining, and potentially the rejection of more secular meanings and definitions of love. (See Northrup et al 2012 for an example of a secular model of love in contemporary culture).

Sacred love in marriage is a "social emotion" (Wilkins 2008) that is created, sustained, and made meaningful through community participation. People are coached in love. People are taught how to talk about and label experiences as sacred love in marriage. People are taught to think of their controlled emotions and actions as sacred love. People craft appropriate ways and places to talk, think, and feel about sacred love. People are taught to monitor and think about their emotions in marriage as stemming from the most sacred, supernatural origins. Love in sacred marriages is framed as innate and divined, insinuating that it is real, pure, unassailable, and the epitome of the sacred. Sacred love is a powerful emotion that couples use to define good and moral love in their marriages – and the marriages of others – as opposed to a perceived culture of love that is quotidian, unctuous, and a malignancy in relationships that lives in personal choice, unregulated emotionality, and lust that represents the essence of immorality and corruption of God's plan for humanity (Archdiocese of Philadelphia and the Pontifical Council for the Family 2014; Broyles 1993; Eggerichs 2005; Hahn 2001; Shimoff 2010; von Hildebrand 1991). Violations of the sacred nature of love in marriage are grounds for anger, distrust, and contempt, although the manuals suggest that Christians are commanded to love one's spouse unconditionally.

Couples were largely unable to recognize social effects on their love for one another, which I attribute at least in part to the privatization of love in marriage. The processes by which this cultural and social emotion has been internalized are largely hidden to participants who believe their love for one another is spontaneous, unmediated, and in some cases divined, granting this social emotion religious and sacred authenticity by regulating their own genuine emotions. Consistent with the Christian marriage advice manuals, many of the couples in this study indicated that feelings of marital dissatisfaction signaled immorality, and even those whom outsiders might judge to be in loveless marriages would not admit to low levels of marital satisfaction, marital quality, or low levels of love in their marriages because they believe that marriage is sacred and they deemed marriages that are not happy and filled with love "immoral," "the result of personal sin," or due to "selfishness and outright disobedience to God."

Love is not a panacea in marriage. There are pitfalls. Like any emotion, the management of love in marriage is susceptible to the same negative effects associated with managing any emotions. As Rietti (2009) points out, attempts at managing, modifying, regulating, and suppressing one's own emotions and the emotions of others reinforces social inequalities in which people's legitimate feelings and behaviors are labeled wrong, sinful, and immoral. Love in sacred marriages can at times constrain individual agency. The representational content of sacralized love based on a model of divine love can be incongruent with phenomenological aspects of emotional experiences in which peoples' private experiences of marriage and family life are inconsistent with the social dimensions of models of sacralized love in sacred marriage. This can place a high value on sacralized love in marriage that is incongruent with idealized expectations of romantic love. The sacralization of love was most detrimental when it implied an inferiority-superiority relationship between spouses, between a spouse and the religious community, or when comparing the spouse's extended family members in religious ways.

I cannot overemphasize the importance of love in the sacralization of marriage. A consistent theme in the manuals is that love in marriage – which is argued to be a sacred gift from God – stands in opposition and superior to the "secular perversion of love as an individual choice." The manuals proclaim that love in sacred marriages is authentic based on commitment. The manuals craft a sense of a sacred consciousness in which pure, rich love is structured and sheltered from the "impure, immoral corrupt world." As von Hildebrand (1991: xi) puts it, "We must bind ourselves through sacred vows so that the bond will grant our love the strength necessary to face the tempest-tossed sea of our human condition." Love in sacred marriages is protected by God from the temptations inherent in human existence, but this protection comes exclusively within the sacrament of marriage.

As the secular world corrupts and impinges on authentic love in sacred marriages, the manuals call upon Christians to defend marriage through their commitment to each other. There is a responsibility and duty to remain married to save "God's sacred gift of love." While proclaiming the doctrinal insolubility of marriage, the authors of the manuals recognize that marriages do end. There is not only a recognition of the fragility of marriage, but there is also a call to action to remain married in the face of the declining power of the Church in marriage. According to the couples I interviewed and the manuals, protecting "God's gift of love in marriage" is dependent on "fighting against oneself" for the sake of one's spouse. The decision to end a marriage is easy according to the manuals. Deciding to remain married is a "sacred act" because it requires a "victory over one's self" and the "culture of divorce." Sacred marriages are painted as a "battle against the outside world" that can "save God's design for authentic love" through the sacralization of love.

While the manuals refer to sacred texts, theology, and religious leaders to sacralize love in sacred marriages, their descriptions and explanations of love are surprisingly devoid of formal religious theology. While they often make reference to Bible verses that command Christians to love one another, the focus of the manuals' descriptions and explanations of sacred love in marriage overwhelmingly refer to the realm of the sacred beyond religious participation, religious doctrine, or theology of marriage. On the whole, they offer little religiously prescriptive descriptions of love. Unlike the 10 commandments, for example, that clearly state thou-shalt-nots, the manuals rarely refer to love in sacred marriages in terms of dos and don'ts based on religious doctrine. Rather, they discursively construct a sensate perception of love that is bounded not by religious teachings, but by its sacred place and sacred symbolism of God's design within sacred marriages. Perhaps most importantly, love in sacred marriage is sacred by framing it as "everything that human love is not." The manuals sacralize love between spouses in sacred marriages as "protected from outside intrusions," as "not vulnerable to everyday challenges," as "eternal," and as "beyond the comprehension of man's limited understanding."

Even in theologically based advice manuals for Christian marriages there is a preference for sacred imagery rather than religious teachings to describe love. While *Love is Our Mission* (Archdiocese of Philadelphia and the Pontifical Council for the Family 2014) is not a Christian marriage advice manual *per se*, it was referred to me by several Catholic couples I interviewed because its publication coincided with the 2015 World Meeting of Families in Philadelphia that took place during the time of my research. As a self-described catechesis for the meeting, I expected it to describe love in terms of doctrine and theology. And while it clearly has a doctrinal and theological basis, its focus is on sacralizing marriage. Throughout its pages, love is described in terms of God's love for others, the image of God, God's love for ourselves, "God's covenant with us," communion with God, "God's way of loving" as "superior to human love," the love of "God as a father," the love of "God as a mother comforting her children," God's love as a "friend who lays down his life for others," and God's love as a "teacher who leads us to love one another." Adherents are expected to be humble, "conform their hearts to God," and to see the world through "God's eyes" with recognition that "God's way is better, but not easier." Love is sacralized in sacred marriages by framing it as "deep like God's love" and an expression of "God's ultimate sacrifice for salvation." Marriage is presented as a metaphor for God's relationship with humanity. The sentimentality of love in marriage is deemphasized in favor of an image of God loving humankind "despite man's sinful nature." Likewise, sacred love in marriage should withstand because "God will not abandon" humankind. Love is described as a choice and includes the erotic and affective, but is not "deterred by them."

Much of the description of sacred love in marriage in the manuals lies in juxtaposition to a construction of a secular culture riddled with problems caused by divorce. Premarital sex, singlehood, infidelity, multiple marriages, cohabitation, and same-sex marriage are described as destructive elements of a social climate that supposedly promotes divorce and eschews reconciliation due to the advancement of agendas of selfishness and individualism. There is great value in considering the discursive construction of divorce in this exploration of love in the manuals.

According to the manuals, divorce is common and actively promoted in secular society. "You wouldn't believe how many people encouraged us to get a divorce when we were hurting," writes one Christian marriage counselor when describing commonalities in his clients who are struggling to remain married (Foley 1992: 26). Friends, family, and coworkers are described as divisive, trying to offer support to one spouse by denigrating the other spouse. Divorce is described as liberating and attractive. Secular support groups and secular marriage counselors are portrayed as supportive of divorce and encouraging of placing blame solely on the spouse. Divorce is often described in terms of superlatives, overwhelmingly without supporting evidence. Family problems and the breakup of marriages rank as the highest cost to employers and the most expensive social problem of our day, according to Foley (1992), although he cites no scientific study to support this claim. Love in secular marriages is described as part of the larger "throwaway society" with little meaning and only "ephemeral satisfaction." The secular world's "lack of moral direction" promotes an "unwillingness to reconcile" pushing couples to "run off to the divorce courts" without "deciding to love."

The manuals and many of the couples I interviewed sacralized love in marriage by diminishing the salience of sensate experiences of love and reframing love as a decision and a commitment. They suggest that people who divorce have "chosen not to love" because "they do not feel love's presence." Divorce is framed a "decision not to act in a loving way" towards one's spouse. Divorce also represents a failure to think of the needs of one's spouse above one's own need for love. "Just as God's love is eternal and without bounds," sacred love in marriage is described as being reflective of self-sacrifice, commitment, and "denying one's own feelings" for the good of one's spouse, all of which promotes a portrayal of a person who divorces as a "self-serving, irresponsible, quitter who is emotionally immature." Ultimately, the lack of sacred love in marriage resulting in divorce requires reconciliation with the Church (Shelly 2011).

Although each manual takes a different approach to reach this point, the manuals sacralize love in sacred marriages by comparing it to Christ's love for humanity and the Church. According to the manuals, authentic love cannot exist outside the bonds of marriage because it "pales in comparison to the eternal love Christ has" for each spouse and for humankind. The image of the infinite depths and superiority of God's love over the temporal nature of all other love sacralizes love within sacred marriages. A bedrock of the sacralization of love in the manuals is that love in sacred marriages is a supernatural gift from God that is only authentic within marriage, is eternal and mirrored after God's love for humankind, and must be defended from attack by the secular world. Aspects of the sacralization of love pervade the stories people shared with me about their lived experiences of their marriages, and I return to the sacralization of love in sacred marriages throughout this book.

3   Sex and childbearing

If love is a forgotten variable in the study of religion and marriage, then the sacralization of sex and childrearing are practically nonexistent (Hernandez et al 2011). While there is interest in the study of religion's influences on sex and childbearing (Wilcox and Wolfinger 2016), there is almost no research concerning religion's effects in sex and childbearing in sacred marriages. This chapter first examines the processes by which sex and childbearing are sacralized in the Christian marriage advice manuals through gendered religious discourse, and then examines how the sacralization of sex and childbearing influences how couples think, feel, talk, and act in their everyday lived experiences in their sacred marriages.

Sensate links

In the previous chapter, I examined the sacralization of love in sacred marriages. While I argued that sacred love is a social emotion framed within religious culture, there is also a felt, sensate experience of sacralized love in sacred marriages. Sacralized love in sacred marriages has a sensate component that is linked to sexual intercourse and childbearing. Research indicates that emotions like love are linked to physical sex outside of religion as well (Dunbar 2012; Turner and Stets 2005). In fact, according to Wilcox and Kline (2013), non-conceptive sex, childbearing, and parenting can all be associated with biochemical and physical changes in the bodies of both men and women that influence their emotions. Although sex and childbearing are biological in nature, they are subject to cultural definitions and constraints on how they are to be experienced and expressed physiologically, psychologically, and socially. Religious culture has influenced the ways people act, think, talk, feel about sex and childbearing throughout recorded history (Lawrence 2011).

Much of the social experience and expression of love and physical sex occurs through discourse in which people talk to themselves and to others using linguistic labels to express internal sensations (Peräkylä and Sorjonen 2012). Discourse shapes the expression and experience of sex and love through facial, voice, and paralinguistic movements that influence interactions. People can think about physical sensations of sex and love as both subject and object in which they love others and are loved by others. According to Damasio (1994), people re-experience similar, although potentially not as intense, physiological reactions when they think about themselves as subject and object of love. Even the words love or sex could serve as a stimulus, bringing forth a wide range of emotions depending on the quality of the relationships to which reference is being made. Love and sex can evoke deep meaning as part of people's sociocultural histories and their social imaginaries of the future. Both biological sex and childbearing are sacralized as part of the sacralization of marriage through gendered discourse in religious culture.

I am intentionally emphasizing the links between love, sex, and childbearing not because sex cannot take place outside of love relationships resulting in the bearing of children – it does – but the process of sacralizing sex and childbearing is predicated on being loved by the divine and loving the divine within the sacrament of marriage. The process of sacralizing sex and childbearing in sacred marriages is dependent on the sacralization of love within the boundaries of sacred marriages. I also assert no normative value to the wide range of emotions that accompany sex and love, as they represent a rollercoaster of emotions and a potentially mixed bag of beneficial and harmful effects in relationships (Durbin 1998).

A great deal of some people's religious lives deals with sex and childbearing. Much of the lived experience of sacred marriages for devout Catholic couples I interviewed included an ongoing negotiation of elite religious discourse pertaining to sex and childbearing. Given Church teachings discouraging the use of many forms of contraception (West 2007), and the political divide among Catholics concerning the use of contraception (Burns 2005), it was not surprising that many Catholics in this study spent a great deal of time talking with their spouses and others about sex and childbearing as part of not only their love for one another but as part of what they perceived to be God's love for them. Likewise, some Protestant couples shared beliefs that erotic love and sex were "gifts from God" as a form of "blessing" within their marriages. Sex and childbearing can be two of the most sacred aspects of sacred marriages – even more important than love.

Religion's influences on sex have received more attention in the research than has childbearing. Studies show that most Americans believe that marriage is the appropriate context for sex, and many people believe that sex in marriage is sacred (Christopher and Kisler 2004; Jones and Hostler 2005; Rosenau and Sytsma 2004). Of the studies of religion's influences on sex, most have focused on concepts like frequency of sex, sexual satisfaction, and relationship quality (Bell 1974; Greeley 1991; Laumann et al 1994; Young et al 1998). Although some studies have examined religion's influences on sex in marriage (Wallin 1957; Wallin and Clark 1964), other research has examined religion's influence on the sex lives of young, often unwed adults (Burris et al 2009). There is also a body of research related to religion's influences on attitudes about premarital and extramarital sex (Koenig 2001; Thorton and Camburn 1989).

While there has been some scholarship concerning the sacralization of sex (Hernandez et al 2011; Murray-Swank et al 2005; Mahoney et al 2013), these studies do not include childbearing, which is a critical aspect of religion's effects in sacred marriages. Childbearing, the physical experience of giving birth, is a unique aspect of sacred marriages. Almost all of the wives described childbearing as an expectation of marriage and requirement for having a "good" marriage. Wives frequently described discussions with other women (e.g., their mothers, mother in-laws, sisters, friends in school, and friends in their congregation) during their formative teenage years as well as their early years as new wives and mothers concerning the bearing of children. Often, wives' values and attitudes about childbearing shaped their choices about whom they eventually married, how they spaced the births of their children, their participation in the paid labor force, and their day-to-day activities as wives and mothers. Clearly these choices entangle sexual practices, childbearing, and parenting processes within a multitude of social forces, but the physicality of childbearing is a unique contributor to the sacralization of marriages. In the entire sample for this study, only one couple had no biological or adopted children. The sacralization of love, sex, and childbearing are interdependent cultural and discursive processes in sacred marriages. The present study takes the examination of religion's influence on sex and childbearing in a new direction. Rather than analyzing the effects of the sacralization of sex and childbearing on people's attitudes, I examine how couples use sex and childbearing to discursively construct sacred marriages as part of religious culture, ultimately influencing their relationship.

Sacred sex

The sacralization of sex and childbearing begins with the widely held belief that sex and childbearing should be exclusive to marriage, and that sex serves a purpose in sacred marriages. As Keller and Keller (2011: 253) put it, "The Christian sex ethic can be summarized like this: Sex is for use within marriage between a man and a woman."

The manuals do far more than suggest that sex should be exclusive to marriage, sex is framed as a duty in sacred marriages because it strengths marriage and foreshadows the glory of the afterlife and communion with God. According to one manual,

> The Christian teaching is that sex is primarily a way to know God and build community, and, if you use it for those things rather than for your own personal satisfaction, it will lead to greater fulfillment than you can imagine. [. . .] Sex is a uniting act that renews the marriage covenant. Sex is a commitment apparatus causing marriage-like ties and feelings that the other person has obligations to you. Sex is a foretaste of being in complete union with God through Christ. Feelings of unity associated with sex are far less satisfying than the sensations of love felt when we meet God face-to-face. Sex is a duty in marriage.
>
> (Keller and Keller 2011: 255)

Sex between a man and a woman points to the love between the Father and the Son. (1 Corinthians 11:3). It is a reflection of the joyous self-giving and pleasure of love within the very life of the triune God. Sex is glorious not only because it reflects the joy of the Trinity but also because it points to the eternal delight of the soul that we will have in heaven, in our loving relationships with God and one another. . . . No wonder, as some have said, that sex between a man and a woman can be a sort of embodied out-of-body experience. It's the most ecstatic, breathtaking, daring, sacredly-to-be-imagined look at the glory that is our future.

(Keller and Keller 2011: 271)

Sheen (1996: 1) describes the distinction between the "glandular and spiritual" in the first paragraph of his popular Christian marriage advice manual about religion and sex, which has been republished several times since its original publication date of 1951. He draws upon imagery of love in marriage being in common with God, while likening the pleasure of sex to animal lust.

Love is primarily in the will, not in the emotions or the glands. . . . The *pleasure* associated with love, or what is today called "sex," is the frosting on the cake; its purpose is to make us love the cake, not ignore it. The greatest illusion of lovers is to believe that the intensity of their sexual attraction is the guarantee of the perpetuity of their love. It is because of this failure to distinguish between the glandular and spiritual – or between sex, which we have in common with animals, and love, which we have in common with God – that marriages are full of deception. . . . Marriage founded on sex passion alone lasts only as long as the animal passion lasts. Within two years the animal attraction may die, and when it does, law comes to its rescue to justify the divorce. . . . Animals never have recourse to law courts because they have no will to love; but man, having reason, feels the need of justifying his irrational behavior when he does wrong.

[Emphasis in original]

Sheen (1951) warns that sex must be framed within greater God-like love in marriage or people will fall prey to "decadent civilization" and allow their imaginations to embrace a culture of movies and magazines in which "unrestrained desires come to the fore." Like other manuals I analyzed, Sheen (1996) draws upon discourse laden with egoistic self-satisfaction and humankind's sinful nature as corrupting the sacred image of God's love in marriage. This juxtaposition of the sacred image of God and God's love against the glandular, unrestrained promiscuity of the "beast" is used rhetorically to draw connections between sex and the soul. The sacred act of sex "draws two souls together in the image of God's love in marriage." Ultimately, the manuals discursively construct sex as the embodiment of God's love in sacred marriages. "Just as the enrichment of the mind comes from the body and its senses, so the enrichment of love comes through the body and its sex." (Sheen 1996: 3). According to the manuals, the purpose of sex in sacred marriages lies not only in procreation, which is highly valued itself, but in the "quickening of love for one another through the embodiment of God's love" in the act of sex in marriage. The meaning of sex is not found "in the organs or the body itself but in the soul." According to the manuals, sex between husband and wife is a spiritual and religious act within their sacred marriage.

The sacralization of sex and childbearing in sacred marriage is further developed in the assertion that sex allows humans to "share in the creative process and purposes of God." The manuals draw a clear link between sex and religion because they assert that God creates new life through sex. The manuals describe an "awesomeness," a "greater purpose," and a "powerful, divine purpose" to sex in sacred marriages that is "far from the immoral act of sex for pleasure" outside of marriage to which they frequently make reference. Sheen (1996: 14) suggests that the fact that sex is not performed in public is evidence of the supernatural order symbolized in the "mystery of Christ and the Church in which married couples become co-creators with God." The sacralization of sex and childbearing in the advice manuals exhibits an ascension of sex and childbearing through imagery of God's love and power of and over creation. The argument in the manuals is that if sex is no longer merely part of the animal kingdom but rather part of the "Kingdom of God," then childbearing is a reflection of the "fatherhood that is eternally in God" (Sheen 1996: 141).

Broyles (1993: 15) describes the power of being a co-creator with God and the salience of childbearing as part of the sacralization of sex and childbearing through a gendered lens as a mother. She mixes images of the embodied experiences of childbirth (e.g., vernix-covered, slippery, pain, and a seven-pound and 14-ounce body) with powerful images of supernatural and transcendent connections to all motherhood in the past and present.

> My self-image altered. *I am one who gives birth,* I thought to myself. *The Creator God is in me, empowering and powerful* . . . I had been amazed by the primacy of birth. That basic urge to push came from across centuries of womanhood, not just from within me. I felt connected to all of life, but especially to all women who had ever given birth – prehistoric cavewomen, Anazazi (sic) cliff dwellers, French marquises – mothers in all times and places.
>
> [Emphases in original]

Broyles' (1993) word choice is important because it represents the way that the sex and childbearing are gendered in sacred marriages. She prays for God's spirit to be in her as she relates to her husband and family. Consistent with other gendered representations of women as receivers, the discursive construction of love, sex, and childbearing in sacred marriages frames women as recipients of power, emotion, and in need of sex and to be childbearers. In addition to being recipients, they are also nurturers and protectors. The advice manuals are filled with references to women as purveyors of companionate and compassionate love. Drawn from gendered culture in which women are nurturing and caring, the sacralization of sex and childbearing exalts everyday experiences in which "matriarchs share faith" "by osmosis" while participating in the mundane activities of "making candy or playing games." The sacralization of sex and childbearing are not predicated on extensive theological discussions but rather in everyday activities in which the sacred is introduced. According to the manuals, for women, childbearing is an opportunity not only to share as co-creator with God but to receive God's gift of life physically in their bodies with an implied responsibility to nurture the sacred, not just through religious practice but by imparting a sacred consciousness to that life. As such, the manuals discursively construct religious culture that incorporates a gendered embodiment within sacred marriages.

Gendered embodiment

The power of the gendered body to discursively construct religious culture and the sacred stands in stark contrast to the focus of much of the literature extant. While gendered embodied practices have been described as being structured through social forces (Brasher 1998; Griffith 2004; Griffith and Savage 2006), little attention has been given to the gendered construction of religious culture and the sacred. Bodies are not only discursively written upon, they establish difference and power relationships (Davis 1997). They are actively constructed within a contrast with the other. Bodies, like gender, are relational, not static, not normative, and not mere objectivities. Gendered bodies are not only constructed in but producers of religious culture and the sacred. Sex and childbearing are sacralized using gendered body practices. The sensate experiences of the body are key to the sacralization of marriage through the felt experiences of sexual intercourse and childbearing. The Bible is filled with sensuality in its descriptions of humanity's relationship with the sacred (Lawrence 2011). The Bible sensualizes the divine with a vocabulary of love premised on a familiarity with the divine that is full of love, desire, flames, sweetness, charms, and enjoyments. God is to be desired and is described in sensual terms as the sweetest, dearest, most beautiful savior who is the fairest of ten thousand. One may lie in his bosom and be filled with the fullness of his love. Sex and childbearing are sacralized through a love for the divine that is sensualized, gendered, and embodied.

Through embodied practices sex and childbearing are sacralized in a contrast with the other that empowers certain practices and ways of being. For example, the manuals draw upon embodied gendered expectations of women as nurturers to sacralize sex and childbearing through an intentioned exclusion of the profane. This exclusion is not intended to construct a certain type of sacred mother but rather to position mothers' embodied practices within the sacred through discursive practice. Fisher (2014b: 15) shares the story of being in her first week of pregnancy and using profanity.

> Then one day, about a week into my pregnancy, a casual f-bomb slipped past my lips. And it hung there in the air, sounding stupid and foul and poisonous. It sounded like a bomb for real, with the sickening thud and that dreadful ripping sound as the air is torn apart. I had never heard a word sound so ugly before, so disastrous. It sounded that way because I had said it in front of my

baby, my little one, this being who was, according to the books, the size of a grain of rice.

What was the big deal? She couldn't understand me, or even hear me. She didn't even have ears yet. But I was in the presence of someone who had never had any experience of ugliness of any kind. And I did not want – with my whole heart, I did *not* want – to be the one who started her out on that education.

[Emphasis in original]

Sex and childbearing are sacralized through an eschewance of that which is profane. Bearing children is the "ultimate gift from God," "a blessing," "a joy," and "part of a greater purpose and divine force in the world for good," as "children hold the potential to lead others to salvation and an eternity in God's love." However, children themselves are not described as sacred. The realities of rearing children are specifically addressed in the manuals. Children are described as "expensive," "messy," "hard work," "scary," "a hassle," and "part of the pancake-batter-encrusted day-in and day-out of it all." Fisher (2014b) contrasts the basest utility of children as "property in the culture of the sex slave trade," to the love parents share for their children that enriches the world and that gives sacred marriages "love, purpose, and strength."

Childbearing is further sacralized through gendered, embodied discourse with imagery of women physically lowering their bodies to their knees in the pain of childbirth, being up to their knees in the responsibilities of caring for their children, and on their knees in prayer for their children. God is feminized through gendered, embodied discourse as part of religious culture in sacred marriages when God lowers himself to earth to nurture and care for his creation as a mother cares for her children. God is equally engendered through a discourse of sacred masculinity found in fatherhood through imagery of God as a husband who is protector and defender as wives are at their lowest – physically on their knees – during childbirth.

Uebbing (2014: 83) offers yet another example of the gendered embodiment of the sacralization of sex and childbearing through a story of her own experiences after childbirth by juxtaposing health care culture with religious culture in her sacred marriage. After hospital staff asked multiple questions about plans for using contraception after the birth of their child, the author described her sacred love for her husband with the following story.

Finally, fed up, Dave summoned a hospital official to our room and explained patiently that we were practicing Catholics, that we were very much aware of the "risks" and "dangers" of contraception, as evidence by our mewling three-day-old son, and could somebody *please* make a note in my chart to stop asking us this silly question.

Lying there in my hospital bed swollen and emotional and clutching my new baby, I don't think I've ever been more attracted to my husband, or more grateful for his love for me. *All* of me. Dangerous baby-making parts and all. I wished I could explain that to the hospital officials who were so eager to sterilize that love that flows between us.

[Emphases in original]

The physicality of the female author's body "lying in bed," "swollen," "emotional," "clutching," with "dangerous baby-making parts" threatened with sterilization becomes sacred because it elicits the husband's masculinity in the form of protector just as "God protects His children." It is the symbolic flow of love between husband and wife to which the author refers that represents the physical flow of body fluids during sex and childbearing that create life. This type of imagery is persistent and frequent in the manuals. Even when theological bases are used as part of the sacralization of sex and childbearing through references to scripture and other sacred texts, the importance of the body and gender remain paramount in the sacralization of sex and childbearing within sacred marriages.

> Jesus is the Bridegroom who lays down his life for his bride, the Church (see Eph 5:25). He gives himself for her . . . He gives himself to her. Everything He does, He does for her. In return, the Church as His bride freely gives everything she is and everything she does back to Him. This exchange of persons is the New Covenant . . . Jesus desires intimate communion with us. He not only wants to come into our hearts: he also wants to come onto our tongues and into our bodies. That's how completely He wants to give himself.
>
> A similar gift of self takes place in holy matrimony. We give our very selves as gifts to our spouses, and our spouses receive us as gifts. In the process we become channels of sacramental grace to each other . . . We have become one body with Christ in a nuptial union as He enters us, the bride, with his divine life. Likewise, husband and wife are united in a one-flesh union as the wife receives her husband's life-giving seed.
>
> (Hahn 2001: 87)

Husband and wife are feminized as sacred vessels of God's penetrating love and are to be receptive to divine life, according to the manuals (Fisher 2014a). The imagery is further normalized by basing it on a religious culture in which men are protectors, and have natural desires for sex that women are expected to accommodate. Failure to accept those desires (i.e., being unwilling to have sex or bear children) is likened to rejecting God himself. Sex and childbearing are thereby elevated from the mundane to the sacred and empowered with sacred, sensate feelings. Whether referring to women's delivery scars serving as reminders of Christ's brutally scarred body on the cross, or husbands' will to restrain their concupiscence as a sacrifice to their wives in imitation of Christ sacrificing his life for humankind, the manuals repeatedly use gendered discourse to sacralize sex and childbearing in sacred marriages.

The sacralization of sex and childbearing is used to frame the way husbands and wives think, feel, and act through gendered discourse. One common theme within the manuals is that men are "angry and frustrated" when their sexual needs are not satisfied or have to be postponed for the purposes of family planning (Fisher 2014b: 11). Men's sinful attitudes and reluctance to follow – or outright disobedience of – Church teachings not to use contraceptives is described as causing wives to become "bitter and perplexed," leading to "misunderstandings, hurt feelings, and alienation." In their attempts to provide practical guidance in the application of Church teachings related to sex and childbearing, authors of Christian marriage advice manuals sometimes portray husbands as the cause of marital discord and conflict by pressuring wives into submission to sex, which leads to unplanned childbearing. Even on the night of the wedding, Marks (2001: 31) cautions the groom not to expect sex.

> With all that it takes to carry off a wedding reception, bride and groom may be exhausted by the end of the day, especially the bride, who generally bears the burden of preparation. Your first night is not, for this reason, a good time to apply pressure of any kind or to feel any sense of compulsion. The more sensitive the groom in this regard, the more he will merit the esteem and confidence of the bride. The greater also will be the chance for a happy honeymoon. . . . The physiological side of marriage is like a flower that takes time for all of its radiant petals to unfold. . . . The marriage act is only one mode of expression among many and not necessarily the most important. . . . Authentic love seeks intimacy in countless ways, and when this is the case, the sexual element has a way of falling into line.

The manuals overwhelmingly frame husbands as sexual aggressors. In his discussion of Natural Family Planning, Marks (2001: 23) contrasts a happy Catholic marriage with one child against a family of seven or more children with a tired wife whose husbands are clearly "raping their wives every night." Although Marks' intention is to highlight the harms and fallacies of what he refers to as "reading the hearts of couples" by offering what he refers to later as a "horrible accusation" that is "completely untrue" to make his point, his anecdotal reference to husbands raping their wives reifies the underlying gendered construction of husbands as sexual aggressors and wives as victims of their aggression who literally bear the results of husbands sinful, lustful behaviors. While Marks (2001) uses a hypothetical rape to discursively sacralize sex in sacred marriages, West (2007: 13) uses his actual witnessing of a rape in a Catholic college dorm to depict his own "sexual behaviors" and the way he should think about them in sacred ways as follows: I've never raped anybody. . . . But am I much different from that guy in the way I've treated women in my own thoughts and attitudes? Don't I use my girlfriend for my sexual kicks? When I was finally honest with myself, I had to conclude that I wasn't much better than the rapist."

Wives are described frequently in the manuals as withholding sex as a means of controlling husbands' behaviors. The resentment and bitterness some of the authors claim women feel towards their husbands is "because of other things in the relationship." As Marks (2001: 103) puts it, "if she's unhappy, he needs to put more effort into making her happier, and she needs to put more effort into being reasonable and contented." Marks further suggests that, if men make their wives happier, it will result in more sex. "If, on the other hand, she feels appreciated, cherished, admired and sought-after (in the best way), and generally like someone whose happiness matters, then it is amazing how much easier it is to overcome hormonally-based disinclinations and fatigue. 'Yes, my dear, I'm tired. *But not that tired!*'" [Emphasis in original]. This rhetoric reinforces a gendered religious culture of male-domination in which women's feelings are hormonally-based and unreasonable. The expectation is that women should want to have sex, even when they are disinclined and fatigued, and that husbands can and should control women's emotions and bodies.

Discourses of engendered embodiment in the sacralization of marriage require attention to the audience for which the discourse is intended. Christian marriage advice manuals are often written for specific gendered audiences. For example, in the introduction of her devotional guide, which is intended for an audience of wives, Schultz (2008: 1) cautions new wives about their new husband's expectations for sex.

> By the time we have an inkling of an idea that we are looking at the man of our dreams, hopefully we've done some adjusting. We've fine-tuned our expectations. We've figured out what matters, and what is fluff. We have matured. We've also probably been surprised by the intensity of our feelings for a man who is short or bald or nearsighted or allergic or underemployed. We feel powerful attraction to what we would not have guessed.
>
> We women also would be wise to keep in mind whom our prospective mate has been led to expect by the gorgeous woman scenario: She arrives at his door with cold beer. She is well-endowed, scantily clad, beautiful, fit, reasonably intelligent without being a grind, and smells really good. Yet she is a virgin. She knows when to be quiet, when to make noise, and how to seduce. She loves only him, and she is an attentive and adventurous lover. She can bring home a paycheck as adeptly as she can whip up a home-cooked meal that is heavy on the meat and light on the vegetables. Also, she understands the need for football.
> [. . .]
> Men must adjust and mature, too. They come to understand that the woman they desire for life may be fat or odorless or wordy or not blonde or may command a larger salary. And they, too, are surprised when the intensity of their feelings for her knocks them sideways.

Schultz's (2008) marital advice is filled with anecdotes that summon her intended audience of wives to abandon their expectations of husbands, see themselves and their husband's in light of real, lived experiences (e.g., trying to keep children quite during mass by giving them Cheerios, waltzing alone as a mother with a two-month old in the early hours of the morning, and her husband's exploits playing the cello to her distraction), and then bases the rationale for sex and family planning on scripture, prayers, and religious symbology, positioning her advice within powerful elite religious discourse. In this sense, many of the authors of the Christian marriage advice manuals blend culture, gender, and religion into a seamless discourse with tremendous power to proclaim a regime of male dominated oppression as a natural expectation that is divined and commanded as part of God's plan for marriage, sex, and childbearing.

Sex is further sacralized in the manuals through the assertion that sex mirrors God's love for humanity. According to Schultz (2008: 38),

> Sex is how we produce all those new Catholics. It is also hot, satisfying, and the most fun of all early pleasures. Sex is how we connect, how we unwind, how we relate, how we cherish, how we commune, how we express what we cannot always say. Marital sex . . . comes from a deep and abiding love, an almost unbearable closeness that mirrors God's love for us.

She follows this passage with quotes from the Song of Solomon describing sexual passion and love, which she describes as "reading like foreplay." Throughout her book, she intertwines direct observations about the sensate experiences of sexual intercourse with a religious language of sacred love and women's perceived expectation for a high degree of emotional quality for sex to be satisfying. For example, after a reference to climbing the palm tree in the Song of Solomon, she writes "I say I will!" She also describes her husband's cello being nestled between his legs, which is "a lovely place to be" according to the author. While the author's imagery is more direct than most of the other manuals, the blending of sacred text and religious symbols with sex and childbearing is a common discursive device they use to sacralize sex and childbearing in sacred marriages.

Gendered negotiation of sex and childbearing

At almost no other point in my interviews did I find more incongruity between elite religious discourse and people's lived experiences of marriage and family than when I queried couples concerning their attitudes and thoughts about sex, contraception, infertility, and childbearing. While almost all the couples in this study described sex and childbearing in their marriages with sacred imagery, this was the area of the study that elicited some of the most extreme opinions and responses from participants. The topic of sex and childbearing highlighted the greatest levels of variation between spouses' beliefs and adherence to Church teachings.

At times, the interview process with the wives revealed long-kept secrets and deep resentments. Some wives never told their husbands they used contraception to prevent pregnancies because they felt their actions were immoral. They relied on deceit to cover their family planning choices. Some wives described their resentment of their husband's lack of responsibility for bearing children, which they believed freed their husbands from family planning responsibilities the wives felt they shouldered alone. Although these were retrospective accounts of events that happened decades previously, given that many of the wives had long past their childbearing years, their stories of resentment recalled old hurts like fresh emotional wounds. Several wives dismissed these feelings as selfishness and unfairness towards their husbands, whom they never told about their feelings. Some wives described resentment directed at the Church and the male power structures that they believe placed them in positions of conflict with their husbands, as well as feelings of resentment towards the Church's promotion of large families as a sign of God's blessing but with what some described as little or no concern for the physical, economic, and emotional resources necessary to bear and rear children.

Husbands' narratives were widely divergent concerning religion's influence on sex and childbearing. The foundation of this divergence was largely based on husbands' familiarity with Church teachings about sex and childbearing. Most husbands could easily be classified into one of three groups. The first group of husbands perceived little to no influence of the Church on their sex lives and childbearing practices. The second group of husbands shared religion-based philosophical perspectives on sex and childbearing practices in marriage but claimed little practical impact in their lived experiences. The last group, which was by far the smallest, held a thorough understanding of Church teachings concerning the sacralization of sex and childbearing, and while some fervently practiced these teachings with their wives, others believed that sex and childbearing were sacred but did not agree with Church teachings and intentionally acted in ways contrary to those teachings.

The first category of husbands claimed that beyond a general condemnation of premarital sex as sin, they were unfamiliar with any sermons, workshops, books, or discussions of sex and childbearing in their religious experiences. When I asked Simon about religion's influences on sex and childbearing, he said he didn't understand my questions. However, when I asked the same questions of his wife Gladius during her individual interview, she described several Bible studies for women and Methodist women's conferences she had attended that addressed the topics of sex, contraception, and childbearing openly among women in the church. When I asked her if there were similar opportunities for husbands to engage in these topics or if men were welcome at such events, she shared her feelings of general trepidation to discuss these topics with men, even her husband Simon. Gladius believed other women would share her feelings. She also explained that she and Simon never practiced any family planning and were simply "blessed" with three children. The first two were born within their first two years of marriage and another was born ten years later. During their interview together, when I asked about Christian marriage advice manuals their church might have in a lending library, Simon told me he would be uncomfortable asking if the church had books about sex and childbearing. "Well, I really wouldn't know. Pastor Anne's a woman," he explained. But before I left, and separately from her husband's earshot, Gladius volunteered to retrieve some titles of books that the "women's group" has for new wives.

The second category of husbands described their church's philosophical perspectives on sex and childbearing as the foundation of God's plan for rearing new Christians. The intensity of their descriptions of this philosophy ranged from a relatively minor assertion that children are part of God's plan for procreation to one Evangelical Baptist husband's militant labeling of rearing an "army of Christian warriors who will proclaim God's word." Although these husbands exhibited varying degrees of agreement or disagreement with Church teachings concerning sex and childbearing, their lived experiences of implementing Church teachings in their sex lives was almost nonexistent. On the whole, these husbands did not know about their wives' use of contraception, feelings about infertility, attitudes or practices concerning the spacing of their children's births, thoughts and feelings about adoption, or, in some cases, wives' use of fertility treatments to conceive. The most extreme example of the latter was a wife who stayed with her sister in another state under the auspices of helping care for her mother, while in actuality she underwent a surgical procedure to repair an irregularity in her fallopian tube to increase her chances of becoming pregnant. She never told her husband about the procedure.

The third category of husbands' shared narratives that were often filled with frustration, blame, and remorse, even when they practiced Church teachings because they felt their "lustful" and "immoral desires" were unfair to their wives. These feelings often stemmed from physical sexual frustration and what they perceived as a lack of caring for their wives' physical needs due to their biological sex drives. They shared feelings of remorse for their perceived lack of self-control for pressuring their wives to have sex and bear children. In contrast, other husbands in this group sometimes blamed the Church and family members for intruding in what they believed should be private decisions about when to have children. After his prolonged description of the importance of sex in marriage, that included a thorough and thoughtful reflection on changes in sex associated with the aging process, I asked Hank about the use of contraception and the Catholic Church's views on matters of sex and childbearing. "You know," Hank took a long pause and drew a deep breath, "those men – and they're just men, and they are all men, by the way [laughter] – they need to consider what it costs the woman's body, the pocketbook, and the soul – you know what I mean – the soul to have children. Sometimes you just can't afford to have more children, and I don't just mean in your wallet."

"So, did you and Heather decide to use contraception rather than one of the approved options the Church offers?" I asked.

"What? The handshake? You mean the handshake? That's what I call it. What an unnatural bunch of [Unintelligible guttural vocalizations]. That is so unnatural. We tried that and that's just such a perversion of sex between a man and a woman. That's unnatural, unfulfilling, and just [unintelligible guttural vocalizations]. We call it the handshake, well at least I do. [Laughter]."

Effects of the sacralization of sex and childbearing through time

For one of the most outwardly devout couples I interviewed, the sacralization of sex and childbearing and the way they thought, felt, and acted before they married shaped the meaning they ascribe their lived experiences of marriage. The impacts of the sacralization of sex and childbearing influenced their decisions about dating, marrying each other, their decision for Katherine to stop participating in the paid labor force, and "the blessings" they have received for following Church teachings in their present lives and the lives they believe they will have in the afterlife. They strongly believe they will remain married in heaven when they die.

Katherine and Scott were both raised during the Great Depression, and they were looking forward to celebrating their 60th wedding anniversary a few weeks after our interviews. Their use of elite religious discourse in their narratives was far more extensive and direct than almost any other couple I interviewed. Their narratives are typical of many couples who found sacred meaning in their marriage through abstinence before marriage and their openness to having children during their childbearing years. While Protestants tended to focus more in their narratives on abstinence before marriage as an important factor in sacred marriages, Catholics were more likely to focus on a willingness to have children. This is not surprising given the Catholic Church's prohibition on many forms of contraception and its focus on a willingness to procreate as an essential component of all Catholic marriages. Being unwilling to have children is one of the few grounds for annulment of marriages in the Catholic Church (Blackburn 2011; Foster 1990).

When I asked Katherine how she knew that God had chosen Scott for her, she replied, "I knew that God sent me Scott because I prayed for him. I was lonesome in my childhood." Katherine's father was an alcoholic which forced her mother to work long hours in several part-time jobs. Compounding her father and mother's absence was the age difference of 15 years between Katherine and her next youngest sibling.

> I prayed for babies. I prayed for a nice guy to marry, and I just thought Scott was a nice kid. At first, I thought he'd be just like the other guys that took me to a dance. They would buy you a pop, and then they expected something in return, and I just wasn't that kind of person. You know what I mean when I say, "They expected something in return?" I'm not going to say it. Do you know what I mean?

"Yes, I assume you mean sex," I nodded.

"Oh, please don't say it. I just don't think that's something that should be said." I apologized and asked her to continue.

> Scott never was like that at all. In fact, he could not have been nicer. Most of the girls he went with were Protestants, and Protestant girls did anything

in those days. Catholic girls didn't, and I was a good Catholic girl. He knew what he was getting when he married me. He knew that if he didn't marry a Catholic girl, there would probably be problems down the road.

I know you think I'm probably some silly old woman when I say that I prayed for a nice boy and that's how I knew God sent me Scott, but that's how God's miracle came true in our life. I had four children in four years, so that kept me pretty busy. Then the last one came a year and a half later. I wanted to go to work, but Scott said, "Why don't you give yourself some more time to think about it?" I was about ready to go to work, and I thought, no, the most important thing in my life was babies. I love babies. I wanted to have as many babies as God would give me. So when Scott gave me the okay to go to work, I decided I didn't want to go because I wanted to take care of my kids. I always stayed at home, and I never went back to work. I taught them their religion once a week. They also attended religion classes at the church.

If I hadn't prayed for a good boy, and I hadn't been a good girl, God wouldn't have blessed me with my kids, and I wouldn't have had the chance to raise them for his glory . . . I would have never even dreamed of leaving Scott because we were raising future saints.

During Scott's interview, he offered a similar rationale for their enduring marriage.

We both prayed to find each other. Every day in boot camp I would serve at the mass, and I would pray for a wife. Just pray. [. . .] When we were dating, she and I never had sex before we were married. We decided both that we were to do it this way. If we were going to date each other, we were not going to be involved that way. That wasn't the way I was raised, period. After we were married [we saw] the beauty of all these things culminated in our marriage. Our love life was so intense and so beautiful for both of us that I think that was the most important thing that really intensify our love for one another. We both really loved family, and we did everything we could to raise saints for the Lord. She just loves babies. We both wanted a family, and we knew God would not bless us with children if we had sex before marriage. We had a common goal with our marriage. We wanted to have a nice family that God would be proud of, and that's what we did.

There are two things that keep a marriage together. Two prominent things. First thing is the physical aspects of marriage. The first thing that people do now is go out and jump in bed. Wrong. They're so emotionally attached to one another with those kind of things that they do not recognize the strengths and weaknesses in each other that can complement each other for a very wholesome and fruitful marriage. The second thing is that the couple have a similar religious theology. I think having that allows them to work together to pray together to ask the Lord's help for the extra strength that they need to be able to raise their kids for him. That they are able to meet that goal and that challenge head on and not succumb to some of the pitfalls that some couples get into because they don't have the gift of his additional strength. And it's because the physical act of sex is attached to the emotional part of love.

This extra strength comes from prayer. Praying together for many years the couple not only becomes emotionally and physically attached to each other through love, but they also become attached in a spiritual way. That spiritual level of attainment is the additional strength you need, and it is not going to be gained unless the couple works at it starting before they get married. They have to have help from the Lord himself to get to that point. Those are the things that make a long-lasting marriage. Very simply.

I pressed Scott to expound on the connection he believed existed between the "physical aspects of marriage" and "similar religious theologies."

It's love, marriage, and family. Love, sex, and marriage are designed by God for one thing, and that's for the purpose of continuing the human race. Very simply. That's the teachings of Jesus and the apostles. Both the man and the woman have the full realization that at any time they're united in a physical bond of love, they can take part in starting a human life. I'm saying take part in, but only partly so. It's up to God to do the rest. I think that very same thing gives a spiritual depth in marriage that keeps a couple together because they have prayed for that and they have practiced what God has taught about sex. Our current way of thinking, where sex is only pleasure – which is total, brutal nonsense – is an affront to real human nature. Consequently, that kind of thing puts lovemaking on a purely physical, sexual plane. It becomes a mechanical thing. A man and woman are not generous enough to each other to be completely and totally fulfilled without that spiritual dimension in their lovemaking. So, it's not completely and totally fulfilled without the knowledge that they are furthering God's kingdom.

At the conclusion of his interview, Scott shared what he described as "a miracle" that his wife didn't like for him to discuss. He shared with me, that they had not been completely forthcoming with me concerning their children. He explained that their daughter and their granddaughter had died recently in an automobile accident. Because of their deaths, Katherine and Scott were raising their two great-grandchildren, despite being in their 80s. He shared that his wife had a sight impairment, which was obvious to me due to the thick, black glasses she wore in the house during the interviews. Scott told me that God had performed a miracle in his wife. He said that because she had prayed for babies, and she had been faithful to God's teachings concerning sex before and after marriage, that God allowed her enough sight to see her great-grandchildren. "God is still blessing us with babies because of our prayers, and we're still raising saints for his glory," Scott said.

Katherine and Scott believe that their marriage has endured to a large extent because they prayed for babies, prayed for spouses who share their religious beliefs, abstained from premarital sex, and had an active sex life without the use of contraception. Throughout both of their interviews, and especially when I interviewed the two of them together, they offered numerous practical relationship maintenance behaviors they practiced throughout their marriage. They had taken classes through their church and had traveled to several churches and religious conventions across the country where they were first participants and later teachers. These included training in communication skills, conflict resolution skills, parenting skills, and religious instruction of various types for premarital instruction, marriage instruction, and instruction for religious converts. Despite the many skills they possessed and their active religious lives, they reported the sacred nature of their sex life as the primary influence on their long-term marriage.

However, when I asked Katherine if she had ever used contraceptives, she immediately responded, "No!" But after further consideration, she offered that, "My mother had problems having babies, so I went to the doctor when we first got married, and he gave me some pills to help regulate everything."

I asked, "Are you referring to your menstrual cycle?"

"I don't know what they did. I just know I took them and God blessed me with five babies right away." I asked when she stopped taking the pills and she replied, "After my last baby was born. I knew I didn't need them because God gave me five babies already and I knew He'd give me more if it was his will." I asked if she had discussed the pills or her decision to take them with her husband, and she replied, "No, the doctor said they were ok, and he went to our church."

"Have you ever told Scott about the pills?" I asked.

"No, why?" Katherine replied.

Links between discourse, religious culture, and the sacralization of sex and childbearing

Most of the couples I interviewed ordered their experiences of sex and childbearing within shared culture characterized by moralized sex and childbearing using gendered discourse and embodied gendered experiences. However, their lived experiences were often different from the idealized sacred marriages in which they believed. Wives like Katherine used various methods to control their fertility, sometimes without their husbands' knowledge, and husbands largely left family planning decisions to their wives, almost without regard to Church teachings, except in a small number of couples. Even when husbands held strong views, family planning was negotiated in tandem between husbands and wives.

Regardless of the degree to which participants espoused the sacralization of sex and childbearing in their stories about their marriages, their thoughts and actions were often in conflict with elite religious discourse. At other times, couples' narratives shared significant consistencies with the manuals. For example, Bennett and Bennett (2014: 7) begin their book with a reference to the marriage scene in the pulp classic movie, *The Princess Bride*, in which the "solemnity" and "majesty" of a wedding is interrupted by the "wholly incongruous" speech impediment of the clergyman, "Mawwiage – that bwessed arrangement, that dweam within a dweam." They contend the quote has become part of the "cultural lexicon" because it violates the dignity of the "serious business" of marriage. They argue that the fairytale wedding and "Happily Ever After," are possible. "The 'Happily Ever After' of marriage is doable, and not just doable, but incredible, and far more common than the world would have us think. . . . Marriage *is* the best" (Bennett and Bennett 2014: 8). Many of the participants in this study noted the fragility of marriage in their stories but overwhelming suggested that sex and childbearing within marriage was sacred and superior to sex and childbearing outside of marriage.

Consistent with the manuals' elevation of marriage to a plane beyond the mundane through the sacralization of sex and childbearing, participants like Scott and Katherine frame their lived experiences of sex and childbearing as sacred using similar language. While their focus is almost uniformly on the challenges, hardships, and trials of marriage, marriage itself is always described in superlatives (e.g., Katherine's vision loss is a miracle because she retains enough sight to see her great-grandchildren). Scattered throughout the interviews, couples used phrases found in the manuals like "wealthy of joy," "unending bliss," "holy sacrament," "blessed arrangement," "gratitude beyond belief," and "exponentially expansive love." Elite religious discourse clearly influences the way people think, talk, feel, and act in their sacred marriages.

Sacred marriages are discursively constructed through religious culture by elevating the most common aspects of marriage (e.g., love, sex, and childbearing) to the realm of the sacred. The advice manuals discursively sacralize marriage within the will and determination of the individual through a discourse of control and regulation of the body through feelings of love, sex, and childbearing focusing on the sensate.

> Muscles of all kinds must be exercised. There will be times we can't wait to get to the next rest stop. There will be breathless treks wherein we can't fathom crossing a river or climbing a mountain without the companion at our side, the one we're holding onto so tightly. There will be memories and great story-telling. And there will be exhilaration when the final destination comes into heart-stopping, glorious view.
>
> (Edmisten and Edmisten 2014: 13)

The manuals not only draw on the lowest levels of mundane cultural constructions of marriage in comparative contrast to the superiority of sacred marriage, they frequently infuse cultural imagery into the sacred consciousness they wish to create. Edmisten and Edmisten (2014) use superlative, embodied experiences of breathlessly crossing rivers and climbing mountains on a trek that ends in a heart-stopping grandeur to describe marriage itself which mirrors rhetorical devices used in popular culture to describe love.

Religious culture is discursively produced and adapted through the sacralization of the mundane, drawing on the sacralization of love, sex, and childbearing. Lived experiences become sacralized because they occur within sacred marriages. This is not to suggest that sacred marriages are purely religious, as they encompass both religious and nonreligious spheres. However, lived experiences of marriage are sacralized within sacred marriages by positioning them within all other contrasted forms of relationships.

While people use cultural repertoires to form strategies of action based on the cultural tools available to them, the discursive sacralization of love, sex, and childbearing by drawing on the sensate not only orders marriage processes, it uses marriage and family as an analogy for the divine, producing sensate gendered experiences of the sacred common to everyone. This two-fold processes not only sacralizes marriages, it connects specific sacred marriages with the broader community of those who believe that marriage is sacred. While the meanings and reactions to sacred marriages may be shared widely, they may also be shared only between two people.

Sacred marriages may develop over couples' lifetimes together. This is evidenced in the numerous accounts of the transition of love from lust to a deep, abiding love that is not "gushy and touchy feely" as one husband explained. Instead, both the manuals and the couples I interviewed described a sacred consciousness about their love for one another and their everyday experiences. As time passed, the experiences of their lives became infused with emotional ties to their interactions, and they drew upon the sacred consciousness they shared at different times to give meaning to life events. Just as most of culture is rejected in the development of cultural repertoires, sacred marriages are discursively constructed using different cultural tools (e.g., sacralized love, sacralized sex, and sacralized childbearing) that allow people to hold concurrent, conflicting cultural meanings. The sacralization of everyday experiences holds tremendous power in sacred marriages, but it is not without its pitfalls, as I describe in subsequent chapters.

4 Blending religious and secular

Marriages are strengthened when couples seek out religious culture and religious discourse that aligns with their lived experiences in their sacred marriages. In this chapter, I examine seeking and controlling behaviors that occurred when couples' experiences of lived religion, marriage, and family were at odds with elite religious discourse and religious culture. Couples sometimes disagreed with Church teachings and sought out new churches and religious discourses supportive of their views on politics, diversity, and use of contraception. When couples were in agreement about seeking and controlling religious discourse and social contexts, the changes tended to strengthen their marriage. However, when couples were not in agreement about the changes, or when the new social contexts did not align with their lived experiences of religion, marriage, and family, couples tended not to see benefits from seeking and controlling behaviors.

In this chapter, I am interested in how families use the sacralization of marriage to respond to challenges they face. There are several factors that affect family resilience, which refers to the successful coping of families during life transitions, stress, or adversity (Allison et al 2003; McCubbin et al 1996). There are a variety of maintenance behaviors that couples exhibit in attempts to be more resilient, although their effects are inconsistent in successive iterations (Canary et al 2002; Weigel and Ballard-Reisch 1999). Families that successfully deal with problems incorporate both protective and recovery factors that work synergistically to respond positively to stressors. Protective factors are those that allow the family to continue to function during adversity. Recovery factors allow families to adapt to their new circumstances and navigate crises. But more than survival, protective and recovery factors work together to grow through adversity.

Resilient families are able to experience stressors and more than just recover, they become stronger families that are more loving and better able to deal with stressors in the future (Walsh 1998; White et al 2004). As Black and Lobo (2008) suggest, the most resilient families are those in which repertoires of coping skills are exchanged within the family. Although all families deal with problems differently, and there is no recognized set of key attributes of resilient families, Black and Lobo's (2008) meta-analysis of family studies suggests that a positive outlook, family member accord, flexibility, communication, financial management, time together, mutual recreational interests, routines and rituals, social support, and spirituality are the most recurrent and prominent attributes of resilient families found in the literature.

According to Marks (2004), religion can help couples construe a future together of triumph and hope during crises. Shared beliefs give meaning to the challenges couples face together. Rather than feeling isolated and alone during critical times in their relationship, shared meanings associated with religion and spirituality can provide a sense of connection to the family and the community. Spirituality can help families unite, understand, and overcome stressors through prayer and supportive social networks associated with religious involvement (Mahoney et al 2001; Mullins et al 2004; Rew et al 2004).

Religion does not always result in positive outcomes in marriages, even when it promotes resilience. Often, shared meaning is not easy to find. When couples attempt to navigate elite religious discourse and their lived experiences of marriage and family, they attempt to seek and control religious discourse. Religion's influence on family resilience may lie not only in providing shared meaning and connectivity in times of crisis, but different religious discourse and religious culture may provide families options to be more resilient by abandoning, rejecting, or temporarily setting aside religious cultural repertoires and religious regimes – potentially returning to them later in life to promote stability or leaving them indefinitely – through efforts to seek and control religious discourse supportive of solutions to problems of action they face. Religious discourse is not a one-size-fits-all proposition. Instead, religious discourse and the cultural repertoires couples employ in their sacred marriages can be dynamic and may afford them more options for dealing with stressors when they eschew strict adherence for a period or indefinitely depending on their needs, their circumstances, and their social context. The following describes the blended ordering of religions and nonreligious spheres in participants' lived experiences of sacred marriages.

A culture of caregiving

Mildred and Harry's interview together exemplifies the pragmatic approach they take to family resilience without the influence of religion. They, like many couples I interviewed and several Christian marriage advice manuals I analyzed, stress the importance of give-and-take and placing the needs of relationships over individual interests.

Mildred explained,

> Don't believe what you hear. Marriage is not 50–50. You have to give a lot more than 50 percent to make it work. You've got to put your husband first and your kids first, and sometimes you have to convince each other to put the kids first, even when it isn't what neither of you wants to do. That means you come last, if at all a lot of the times.

Harry echoed this sentiment.

> Never ever keep score. Never keep score means that when the other person
> does something they don't come to you and say, "Well, I did this for you."
> You never keep score. You do it because it's the right thing to do or because
> you genuinely care for that person and you don't keep a little score, so
> that you can remind them of that when you want something. That is verboten.
> The other thing is no matter what you do in life you put that person ahead of
> yourself. In all the decisions you make and all aspects of your life. It's a real
> simple formula. And everybody ought to be able to remember that. But for
> some reason they don't.

A superficial reading of Mildred's and Harry's narratives suggests they are simply advocating self-sacrifice as an important characteristic of enduring marriages, and they are. However, they have a child that is physically and mentally disabled, and they are the primary caregivers to their adult, disabled daughter. Their focus on self-sacrifice is not surprising, given their pragmatic approach to religion. They intertwine practical aspects of being full-time caregivers to their daughter with religious meanings in their sacred marriage.

Mildred and Harry find religious discourse most meaningful in their marriage when it supports their needs to care for their daughter. When asked about their frequency of attendance, how often they prayed, and similar questions, their responses conveyed a sense of duty and responsibility to their daughter's care, with little focus on specific aspects of religious involvement. They explained that they often could not attend, pray, or participate in religious activities and rituals because they had to care for their daughter. One of their primary criterion for selecting a church was handicap access for their daughter's wheelchair.

They were also pragmatic about Church teachings. Although they are Catholic, they did not believe they could care for a second child given their daughter's disability, so Mildred talked to several priests and decided a tubal ligation was appropriate for her. Harry supported her decision. Mildred laughed about the number of priests she spoke to in search of one who could understand the demands of caring for a severely disabled child, and their shared social imaginary of a future in which they continued to care for their daughter for the rest of their lives. They sought a priest who supported their decision to have a tubal ligation for the practical reasons they described. Although she and Harry expressed no disagreement with the Church's stand on contraceptives, they sought out a priest who supported the creation of a different perspective on the interpretation of elite religious discourse in which their actions where "appropriate" and "moral" because they wanted more children but knew they would be caring for their daughter their entire lives.

Because religious discourse and culture are malleable, Mildred and Harry were able to support elite religious discourse in the Catholic Church and at the same time find deep religious meaning in their decision to violate Church teachings to adapt to the challenges of caring for a disabled child. Their marriage was more resilient because they sought out and controlled elite religious discourse by finding religious meaning in rejection and modification of dominant discourse to produce religious discourse supportive of their resilience needs. They, along with their priest, rationalized the decision to have a tubal ligation as being aligned with Church teachings because they were not opposed to having more children, but were choosing not to have more children to focus on their daughter's needs. In so doing, they found sacred meanings in caring for their daughter.

As Harry put it, "There's nothing more sacred than giving yourself completely for the love you have for another. I wouldn't change anything. We have been given a blessing others will never know or understand."

Mildred and Harry reframed elite religious discourse within a culture of sacred marriage based on caregiving in the way they talked, thought, felt, and acted. They found authenticity and legitimacy in their rewriting of religious discourse through the approval of a priest. They moralized their decision to violate Church teachings and Catholic culture through the sacralization of parenting, caregiving, and love in their relationships.

Political discourse and a culture of social justice

Unlike the majority of husbands in this study who began their narratives by describing their work-history – while wives typically began with descriptions of their families of origin and childhoods – Bruce's narrative began with his military service. Bruce was a Vietnam veteran, and was raised in a Catholic family, attended Catholic schools, and spent a lifetime as a practicing Catholic. His wife Rose described herself as "a practicing Catholic."

Bruce shared why he and Rose attend St. Ignatius:

> I think when I came back from Vietnam and before I went over to Vietnam I was very strongly conservative. I was a member of the Young Americans for Freedom, which was a junior John Birch Society founded by Darren Buckley, and very conservative. When I went to Vietnam I said this is ridiculous. This country is being run by the military. The people had no interest in freedom. They didn't comprehend it. They were a bunch of people who just wanted to be left alone. So when I came back it was more my politics than anything else. I went to different churches and we were dating back then. We went to St. Ignatius which was the only church protesting the Vietnam War. Admittedly there were a lot of people there, especially the pastors, that were very pacifist including Patrick Mulligan. He was an assistant priest there. I was a little bothered by that. I definitely was not a pacifist. I carried guns in Vietnam. I was there a year after the bunker we were guarding was overrun by VC. If I had been there a year earlier, who knows, I might not even be here. I certainly was not a pacifist, and I still am not.
>
> We went to St. Ignatius only because we, well I, was attracted by their position on Vietnam. They had different music. They were a maverick. And

it was kind of fun. And then eventually we really got involved there. I got to know Father Patrick really well. [. . .] In that sense I would say we were shaped more by Father Patrick and the social justice message purported by the church.

[. . .]

Everything I do is kind of a result of my belief in the social gospel, and that comes from being around Father Patrick. In that sense it influenced me more and Rose more than the overall dogma of the church. I was less interested in what the church had to say. [. . .] I think it was a relationship I developed with Father Patrick, and admiring what he was doing and trying to emulate him – although I can never emulate his role because he was a pacifist. Because of my background I could never make that jump.

While Rose avoided the discussion of politics by saying, "I've never been political like Bruce," it was clear that she sought out supportive elite religious discourse and religious culture in their decision to attend St. Ignatius.

We actually got married at St. Ignatius, but before that we were looking around to find where we were going to be because we go past a few other parishes that are a lot closer. It's the feeling of family and everyone making you feel welcome at St. Ignatius. It's a smaller community, and it's, well, not homey but more family oriented, I guess you'd say. We agree with the people there about right and wrong and the way people should live their life.

Despite her professed lack of interest in politics, Rose was clearly aware of the impact of Bruce's political convictions in their choice of church early in their relationship.

After returning from the war, Bruce wanted to marry immediately, and Rose was concerned that they did not "know each other anymore." She insisted that they date for another year, and that they "try out" several churches before committing to one. She wanted to marry in the church they would attend together. She took her ques for selecting a church primarily from Bruce's political motivations. Like many couples in this study, Bruce and Rose sought out religious discourse within a religious culture that aligned with their lived experiences, and for Bruce those experiences were political. For Rose, their choice of church was one based on a family-oriented, community service focus, within a social justice culture that both Bruce and Rose found appealing.

Bruce and Rose are the one couple in this study who do not have children. Although they are self-described, devout Catholics who are expected to be open to having children as part of the sacrament of marriage, their political interests played a strong role in their decision not to have children. Bruce had significant misgivings about having children because of population overcrowding. Although they support the Church's position that childbearing should occur exclusively within marriage, they have volunteered with unwed mothers and pregnant women in different ways throughout their lives. Both politically and financially – they are one of the wealthiest couples in this study – they support social welfare programs aimed at improving the lives of single mothers and their children. They find deep, sacred meaning in their political involvement through volunteerism and social activism in their church. They blend political discourse with religious culture in the way they talk, feel, think, and act in their sacred marriage.

A culture of support

It would be hard to imagine more different religious upbringings than Teri's and Otto's. As far back as Otto could remember, his relatives were Catholics. He was born into a large Catholic family with nine siblings attending parochial schools, not eating meat on Fridays, confessing on Saturdays, and attending mass on Sunday mornings. In contrast, Teri's father professed no religious beliefs, and her mother died the day after she was born due to childbirth complications. Teri and her two older brothers and older sister were raised by her alcoholic father and her grandmother. Teri's grandmother sent the children to the nondenominational church nearby, but did not attend with them.

"The house was quite most of the time," according to Teri. "You didn't dare make a sound, and there wasn't much to talk about anyway."

Teri described her active search for a religious culture supportive of family that began in her childhood.

"The neighbor girl was Catholic, and I knew her from school. I went with her to church when I was a kid, and I just said to myself, I want this when I get married and have a family."

At the time of their wedding, Teri had not converted to Catholicism. When I questioned the timing and motivation of her conversion, she shared that she did not convert when she married Otto because she wanted her conversion to have meaning beyond the perception that she converted just to marry Otto.

"Converting is something sacred between you and the Lord. It's not something you enter into lightly, just so the Church says your marriage is okay," she explained.

Because Teri was not Catholic, they were not allowed to marry in the church. It was not until their first child started parochial school that she converted to Catholicism. During that time, she and Otto attended faithfully, but they "tried out" different churches in the community traveling over an hour one-way to attend a large church they both liked. Eventually, they moved to be nearer this church, which they ultimately joined.

Otto was blunt, "I didn't care which one she picked, as long as Teri was happy. They're all the same to me. It's all the same God."

But Teri's decision-making process was far more complex. She sought out a church that was heavily involved in local child welfare programs. She investigated the academic quality of the church's parochial schools. Mostly, she sought out a large congregation she felt could provide both physical and social support should she ever need it. Otto was a retired steeplejack, and Teri was concerned that given the risky nature of his career, he could be seriously injured or die. She wanted a church with a "culture of caring," as she put it.

When I asked about the importance of the theology and beliefs of the church in their decision-making process, Teri agreed with Otto. "We all pray to the same God. I wanted a church that practiced what they preached. Actions speak louder than words, and I was searching for a family kind of atmosphere. The homilies are all the same in the Catholic church. It's what the people do with it that matters to us."

Teri and Otto sought out a culture of family and support in which to experience religion. For them, the consistency of religious experience was important, but they believed they could find that experience in many churches. They placed little value on the theological meanings of elite religious discourse. To them, the church's positions on politics and family support were the most important aspects of their sacred marriages, so they controlled their religious experiences by seeking out churches they believed would strengthen their family's resilience to adapt to changing circumstances.

A culture of diversity

Mike and Agnus both grew up in rural farming communities. They pursued college degrees in education, and retired as a school system administrator and university professor, respectively. Both shared their interests in social justice and lifetimes of activism related to issues of race and ethnicity. Mike was a leader in early bussing initiatives and school realignments for the district to promote ethnic diversity in the classrooms of the 1970s. Agnus taught in predominately ethnic minority schools before becoming a professor.

Mike experienced a great deal of transition in his religious experiences as a child and early adulthood. His mother was a Christian Scientist and his father was agnostic. With no Christian Scientist congregation in the small town in which Mike was raised, he and his siblings rarely attended any church as young children, other than during Boy Scouts. As he entered his teenage years, one of his neighbors invited him to a "Quaker church." Over the next approximately decade and a half, he attended Quaker churches, a Presbyterian church, an Evangelical United Brethren church, and a United Methodist church. In contrast, Agnus' entire extended family belonged to the Church of Christ. Since their marriage, they had always attended the same church with their children, although the Protestant denominations of the churches varied. For most of their children's lives, they attended a Methodist church that was within walking distance of their home. When I asked about the importance of denomination and religious teachings in their choice of churches, their narratives shifted quickly to an individualistic and personal tenor that stood in stark contrast with their otherwise family-focused stories.

Agnus shared how she chose her church:

> For me faith is personal. That's my personal basis and no one else's. I've never even asked Mike about what he believes. That's none of my business.

[. . .] So I don't know that what the church teaches has helped me in my marriage or in how to be a mother, except that I am faith-based. We share the same faith, although we come at it from different angles. We go to the Methodist Church [. . .]. It could have been the Presbyterian Church, if they had been more friendly. It could have been any church in our proximity, but Methodists accepted us being a biracial family. My husband and I are both white and so are our two biological girls, but our three adopted sons are not white. I have to have a church that encompasses and is inclusive due to the racial differences with my kids. But at the same time I want the church to accept anybody. My church is real open. We have gay members. We have members with visual impairments. We have a few, but not many, people of color. That's the kind of church I want to belong to. I want a church that shows me acceptance the same way that I want to be accepting of others. In some of the churches we went to our kids were the only people of color. I did not want that here. When we went to our church here the first time, I saw three families who had adopted children of color. So, I felt that we would be accepted before I really knew.

Mike confirmed that he and Agnus do not discuss their personal beliefs, only that they have "shared faith." Both of them are aware they disagree in significant areas with Church teachings, but they do not discuss those differences with each other. Rather, they sought out ethnic diversity and acceptance in their church. Both Agnus and Mike wanted the church to be close to their home, and Mike's primary interests were in the quality of their youth group and choir, so he could share these experiences with his children.

They had attended different denominations of Protestant churches throughout their lifetimes. This occurred due to different childhood experiences, residential moves associated with their undergraduate and graduate school experiences, and later moves due to changes in their careers. Mike and Agnus have largely abandoned denomination-specific religious discourse and rely on their own individual understandings of their faith to the point that they do not discuss their beliefs with anyone. Rather, they seek a culture of acceptance for the diversity of their family within which they negotiate their personal faith. They consistently dismissed my questions about the importance of specific Church teachings in their marriage. Both had strong faiths, but almost completely rejected elite religious discourse, that they said had little influence in their marriage. Yet, church involvement played a salient role in their marriage. In fact, Mike said he would have stopped attending church when their children went to college, but it was important to Agnus to continue being involved. They weren't seeking Church teachings through their involvement; rather, their marriage was strengthened by being part of a religious culture that embraced diversity.

Agnus' unsolicited, last words encapsulate their approach to religion in their sacred marriage, "Religion is made by man. You have to take it all with a grain of salt. It's faith in whatever you believe in that matters. It's about what's sacred to you."

Sacred meanings in engaged encounter and marriage encounter

Riley and Gertrude have been married 50 years. Their son Robert was molested by a priest at the age of 14, leading to a complete breakdown of their family with effects lasting into adulthood for their children and their children's families. Riley shared stories of a happy childhood in a large Catholic family with 10 brothers and sisters on the farm, while Gertrude summed up her childhood by describing her mother and father as follows: "She was poor me, and he was self-absorbed in his beer. I'll just say that my mom was a happy widow when dad finally died. No, no, I didn't have a happy childhood. I don't have any pleasant memories."

While Riley described a "wonderful Catholic upbringing" with consistent and regular attendance at worship services, confession, parochial schools, and Church-related activities like square dances, movies, and roller skating parties, Gertrude was raised in a household with what she described as a "denominational mixed bag of religion." Her father expressed no religious beliefs or affiliations, while her mother "bounced" from one church to the next "to find anyone who would listen to her self-absorbed, sob story. As soon as one church got tired of her complaining about her husband and kids, she'd move on to the next." Gertrude shared that her mother would take her and her siblings "on parade" to new churches she visited "to show them how bad she had it with five bad children." It was Gertrude's paternal grandmother who insisted that Gertrude and her four brothers and sisters attend the local Catholic church. Her grandmother arranged for Gertrude and her siblings to attend St. Augustine school, which was located across the street from their house. Later, two of her brothers attended the seminary, and one eventually became a priest and taught in the same seminary he and his brother attended in their youth.

Initially, during her individual interview, Gertrude cried openly as she described her husband Riley as a saint. "I take everything out on him. He is a saint. So forgiving. He is a saint. He's all good. He prays at the office every day. He prays the rosary every day. He goes to mass every day. He is a saint, and I mean that literally." But soon her demeanor changed, no longer crying and becoming sullen as she blamed Riley for the dysfunction in their family.

> He was a workaholic when the kids were little. He came home at six for supper but went back to work after the kids went to bed until two or three in the morning. Then he went out with people from work on Friday nights drinking after the kids went to bed. He was the vice president of Main Street Bank. He had several departments that he was over.
> [. . .]
> He was raised on a farm to be a good boy who worked hard. He tried to be a good dad, but he didn't learn that from his dad. His dad was abusive. Riley was very strict, but we were that family everyone wanted to be like

when they came in the church. The perfect family. It exploded into the most dysfunctional mess you can imagine. Our son went to the seminary. It was a very unhealthy setting there. He came home just terribly, terribly a mess. It was a bad place for him to be.

"Why was the seminary an unhealthy setting?" I asked.

It's made me grow stronger in my faith instead of turning away because I feel for the 98% of good priests like my brother and how they take this bashing. They are carrying the cross and the bad guys are still out there. Our son will never admit that he was abused by the priests in seminary, but he was both physically and mentally abused. He was molested. It was a sick place. So when he came home our daughter became alcoholic and bulimic. He had 12 years of nightmares.

"Gertrude, do you blame the Church?" I asked.

I blame Riley! When he wasn't working, we led Marriage Encounter together. I told you, we were the perfect family. We taught marriage classes, led Sunday School, and never missed anything the church had going. We were the perfect family everyone wanted to be. But, our kids felt like orphans at times because of Riley's long work hours and our involvement in Marriage Encounter and Engaged Encounter.

Gertrude then described the many challenges she and Riley faced with their children. Throughout her narrative, Gertrude described the problems her children faced in terms of how they affected her, with no mention of how they potentially impacted Riley or the children themselves. Gertrude's narrative echoes her description of her mother as "self-absorbed." According to Gertrude, the attention given to her son in coping with his abuse in the seminary led to one of her daughter's alcoholism and bulimia. However, after questioning for clarity, she affirmed that her son's abuse occurred after her daughter's initial development of alcoholism and bulimia, although she forged on with her story when I unintentionally pointed out the inconsistency in her timeline. Their other daughter married a "sex addict," according to Gertrude. "That girl, she was a nightmare. She took us down roads that other people never get to go. She was pregnant at 14."

"Given the challenges your marriage and family have faced, why do you believe it is sacred?" I asked.

God kissed them all on the cheek with a perfect family. They had it a lot better than I ever did. None of them are really strong in the church, but they have good jobs. The oldest boy [the son who was abused], he has such negative attitudes towards the church. Sometimes I wonder why this happened to me.

When I spoke with Riley during his individual interview about the influence of his work and involvement in the church on his wife and children, he shared the following almost as though he were talking to himself.

> I have three sisters who are nuns. They took their vows right out of high school. They only come home about every three years. All of my brothers and sisters are still Catholic. They pretty much all married Catholic people and are raising children in the Catholic faith. There was very little conflict when I was a kid. Demonstrative? There was very little of that in my parents' relationship. My dad was always outside working and mom did everything for dad. She would get a saltshaker for him once dad got seated to eat. Whatever he needed, mom went up and got. I think I saw them kiss each other on their 25th wedding anniversary. Other than that, I can't say. But I got my ideas about love from them. It was not a lot of touchy-feely, but there was never any doubt that they loved each other. We didn't even think of love when we were kids. No. No. We did not.
> [. . .]
> Love is an action. It's not a feeling. You can have a feeling of romance and closeness and we call it love, but love is doing. Doing what's good for the other person is love. How to determine that I don't know. You have to make a conscious decision. It's doing what we think is best for that other person. That means you work hard and you lead a life for God before anything else. Yes, I worked a lot of hours, travelled all the time, and worked three to five hours a night after working all day because that's when the computers were available, but that's what I had to do, damn it! So I had to miss some ball games. I'm still here. I still make her coffee every morning. What was your question?

"I asked you how your work and involvement at church influenced your marriage?" I replied.

> It did take away from the family by being gone so much. No question about it. And I strayed at times from our marital bed, but I never broke my vows. I said forever, and I'm still here. That's what love means. You argue and fight and dislike each other, and you can do lots of things, but you know that you know you're together. You are not splitting up. You also know that if you're not splitting up there are bridges you cross going away from each other and you have to come back. There is no question you are coming back. We're of the same faith, and that's very important to me.

During their interview together, Riley and Gertrude stressed the importance of praying together, attending worship services, confessing, and forgiveness. They described religion's influence on their lives in terms of the tasks and activities they taught others in the Encounter sessions. They shared their attempts to write a letter to each other daily, as encouraged in Marriage Encounter – although they never completed this task consistently due to their involvement in the Encounters,

Riley's work, and their children's problems, which "took that time away from us," according to Gertrude.

When I questioned them together about religion's role in conflict resolution in their marriage, they shared that, according to them, Marriage Encounter teaches participants to "let go of everything after 24 hours," but both admitted they were not able to forgive that easily. Instead, they described a standing history and tolerance in their marriage for yelling at each other and long periods of anger, distrust, and resentment towards each other's actions and words.

Gertrude shared that, "If people will just follow it, Marriage Encounter has all the answers for them." Riley added,

> We actually started Engaged Encounter with the priests here at Blessed Heart. For five years we led workshops and all the couples and the priests in the diocese went through it. We gave talks. They gave talks. We told the priest what to put in their talks and what not to put in their talks. It was incredible. It lasted 20 some years. We so wish that we would've had Encounter before we got married. Our marriage was really strengthened through Marriage Encounter big time.

"Could you share two or three specific ways that Marriage Encounter strengthened your marriage?" I asked.

"It just teaches you everything your marriage is supposed to be." Riley said. "But people just don't live up to it sometimes. But it's all in there."

Despite their self-admitted turbulent marriage, as evidenced through infidelity, angry outbursts, frequent yelling and arguing in front of their children, and emotional and physical intimacy issues that began prior to their marriage, Gertrude and Riley find solace in their shared faith and their shared belief in their experiences leading Engaged Encounter and Marriage Encounter. They portray their marriage as one to be emulated by others, and they lead others through the activities in the Engaged Encounter and Marriage Encounter manuals. They believe the actions outlined in the Encounters are the foundation of sacred marriages, despite the fact they were most often unable to succeed in completely those activities. So why do they cling to these texts, and the suggested behaviors include in them, as a means to explain the endurance of their marriage, when they have clearly failed at meeting the expectations of the Encounters?

The answer lies in their faith in cultural scripts. While at first their narratives may seem confusing and conflicting, they exemplify the power of religious discourse to imbue cultural scripts with sacred meaning. The very essence of the story of Christianity is that humanity is flawed and requires divine intervention to overcome human failure. Many of the couples I interviewed continue to persevere in their marriages despite poor conflict resolution skills, despite emotional outbursts, despite an inability to forgive, despite infidelity, despite infertility, and despite their inability to adequately support the needs of their children or spouse when they faced serious problems like abuse, addictions, or eating disorders. It might be tempting to question the efficacy of the advice within the Encounter workshops and literature because Riley and Gertrude failed to implement the pre-scribed activities in their marriage and their marriage is fraught with problems. However, it is the very fact that Riley and Gertrude share the belief that humans are flawed and unable to succeed without divine intervention that sustains them through the hardest times in their marriage. According to Riley and Gertrude, the endurance of their marriage despite their shortcomings is evidence of God's sacred love for them and the divine origins of marriage.

When Riley describes and admits his inadequacies as a husband and father who "cheated" on his wife, "worked too much," and "went out drinking instead of being at home" with his wife and children who "needed" him, he juxtaposes those shortcomings against a sacred discourse of forgiveness and God's intervention in his life that he believes sustains his marriage. Likewise, when Gertrude decries her husband for their problems but almost simultaneously extols him as a "saint" for tolerating her "irrational behavior," she too uses the sacralization of marriage to situate her and her husband's weaknesses as spouses and parents within a reli-gious culture of God's forgiveness of their behavior.

While it may appear that they are sharing a conflicting narrative, the reality is that they are situating their experiences within culturally approved religious discourse. This is striking because they both contend that their involvement as leaders of the Encounters took time away from their marriage and their children. While one might view them as failures as spouses and parents, they actively pro-duced and reproduced religious discourse in a controlled, approved, social context of the Encounters. They portrayed themselves as "the perfect family" and led oth-ers in religious schema to acquire that same status. They are able to position their own marriage within the broader religious context of having nuns and a priest in their extended families. At the same time, they distance themselves from the Catholic school where their daughter developed her addiction and eating disorder and the Catholic seminary where their son was abused. They illustrate the situ-ational existence of the sacred as discursively positioned within blended religious and nonreligious spheres.

Like many couples I interviewed, they ignore inconsistencies in the telling of events that make the sacred meanings they have ascribed the events illogical. When the inefficacies of these religious schema are pointed out, they quickly turn to their own weaknesses and shortcomings as the reason for the failures of these religious schema. Their weaknesses and failures are forgiven and ignored because failure is part of elite religious discourse and the cultural script of the Encounters. If they did not fail at times as spouses and parents, they would have no need for divine intervention which nullifies the very essence of their belief in God's redemptive power.

Resilience and religion

Religion is not a fixed, external reality. In contrast to the perception of religion as a social institution that systematizes, orders, and consistently structures and organizes the way people talk, think, feel, and act, people's experiences of religion are incoherent, confusing, inconsistent, and contradictory. Yet, there is power in religion to promote resilience in marriage. Religion promotes resilience through its fluidity. It fills the relationships it creates with meaning because life is unpredictable. The multiplicity of religious meanings that people ascribe events in their lives allows them to remain open to change, to adapt, to survive, to protect, and to recover when their marriage is threatened. Through religious discourse, people are able to choose between different social practices and to investigate possible lines of action that bring new ways of classifying their experiences and linking those experiences to sacred meanings. Through seeking and controlling behaviors, people are able to create new versions of realities that reproduce sacred meanings within different religious cultures supportive of what is sacred to them (e.g., caregiving, politics, social justice, support networks, diversity, or the Encounters).

The power of the sacred is not passive. People actively seek out and align simultaneously competing and contradictory sacred meanings as part of their lived experiences. Religion is powerful when people are able to read sacred meaning into their behaviors by the way they talk, think, feel, and act. Resilience was promoted for the couples in this chapter because they produced sacred meanings as bricoleurs. Rather than being constrained by elite religious discourse, people sought out contexts and networks supportive of their particular needs.

Mildred and Harry used religion to promote resilience as parents of a disabled child by crafting personalized sacred meaning in the contradictory stance of undergoing a tubal ligation while still advocating the Catholic Church's position on contraception. Bruce and Rose used religion to promote resilience by finding religious meanings in the politics of social justice. Mike and Agnus have shared faith and a desire to integrate their biracial family into a supportive religious environment, although they do not talk to each other about their individual beliefs. Gertrude and Riley produce religion, and elite religious discourse in their case, through their leadership in the Encounters, despite the dysfunction in their marriage and family, and the deleterious effects of over-involvement in the Encounters.

People's use of the sacred is not structured or rational in the promotion of resilience. The sacred is malleable and plastic. Sacred meanings are contingency-based and unique to each couple. The sacred is equally not a choice of nonreligious and religious discourse that promotes resilience. It is a blending of discourses to form sacred meanings and strategies of action through religious repertoires. Seeking and controlling processes demonstrated by the couples in this study allowed for the production and modification of religious discourse supportive of their unique resilience needs.

Sacralizing marriage through blended secular and religious discourses and cultures

In the *Free Methodist Handbook*, Slider (2011) addresses the differences in religious culture and elite religious discourse found in the Bible. In recognition of the various forms of marriage throughout the Bible, which spans multiple millennia and multiple cultures, the pastor of a Methodist church who authored this self-published Christian marriage advice manual suggests that not all marriages in this sacred text were healthy. He specifically refers to bigamous marriages that included multiple wives and concubines that resulted in "tense familial relationships, to say the least." Slider argues that the Bible does not offer a specific "blueprint" for marriage that can be transplanted directly into contemporary culture. Instead, he argues that the Bible is the basis of the principles of equal value of all persons before God, and that the Bible provides "guiding principles through which God will bless our marriages." Elite religious discourse found in the scriptures then is not sacred for its performative value as a code or checklist ensuring marital bliss. Rather, the sacralization of marriage lies in the elevation of the potential that marriage has through the "story of God's offer of abundant life – of which marriage is a part – and the efforts of persons to respond to that offer by faith within the context of their world."

If the Bible and similar sacred texts do not contain a specific blueprint for a blissful marriage, as Slider (2011) suggests, just how are people to glean useful cultural tools from these sacred writings? The answer lies in the discursive construction of sacred marriages. While the exact wording of sacred texts may not address contemporary problems of action, the manuals discursively construct a sacred consciousness that can and is employed by some Christians to address crises of culture.

In a common technique I found in the manuals, in which authors emphasize inconsistencies in the translation of sacred texts from the original languages in which they were written, Slider (2011) offers a quote about marriage from what he describes as "a source that most scholars date in its current form from around the tenth century BC or about 1,000 years before Christ and approximately 3,000 years ago." The quote from Genesis 2:21–24 is accompanied by an uncited religious icon of a haloed man, appearing to be from the Middle Ages, holding large books with a scroll draped over his opposite arm. This iconography conveys sacred imagery by blending a divined halo with the texts the man holds. Slider then teases apart specific words in the modern text by making reference to the intended meaning in the original language in which the text was written. Finally, the original meanings of the words in the language of origin are used to construct new meaning to sacralize marriage in modernity.

> As the translation displays there are two words for *Man* used. The Hebrew word *adam* (man or mankind) is based on the root *ADM* and is closely related to *adam* (soil, earth). Adam can be understood to mean *created man or being*. It is Adam who is created in the image of God.
>
> It is this Adam who is separated by God to create mail (*Ish*) and female (*Issa*) . . . In addition, though verses 21–22 say that from Adam woman is formed; verse 23 suggests that from *Ish* comes *Issa*. The word for *rib* can also mean *side*. . . . The original unity of the created being is separated into two parts.
>
> The two parts of the whole are reunited. This reuniting of the created being suggests that the relationship between husband and wife is more than a social

institution. It is part of the re-establishment of the wholeness of a human being. Man is incomplete without a permanent and intimate relationship (emotional, spiritual, and physical) with Woman. The same holds true for Woman.

[Emphases in original]

Through this discursive process, Slider (2011) eschews what he perceives as impractical language in which Eve is created from Adam's rib, and discursively constructs an image of humankind first in Adam, that is only later separated into males and females. He suggests that God did not create men before women, but rather God created humankind in Adam as one being that was later divided into two sexes. The union of husbands and wives therefore reestablishes humans into the original, whole being God created. Ultimately, this rhetorical device is constitutive of a sacred consciousness in marriage that ties a sacred sense of wholeness, completeness, and normality; in which, marriage is a natural state of existence for all humankind designed and created by God.

Just as the original text from which Slider (2011) quotes is widely accepted among scholars – ancient, and sacred of its own accord as mirrored in the accompanying religious iconography – the implication is that the sacralization of marriage includes a timelessness and endurance reflective of Christian's believe in God's omnipotence and omnipresence. There is meaning and power in the discursive construction of sacred marriages that rises far above the culture of religion and the specificities of elite religious discourse that may not address problems of action in the contemporary world. Rather than detract from the meaning and power of the sacred consciousness being discursively constructed by Slider (2011), the unfinished, incongruent, fragmented, incomplete thoughts present in the manual actually add to the sacralization of marriage the author strives to construct. This discursive process can be likened to the discursive construction of imagery and meanings in Haiku poetry. With short phrases and evocative word choices, the author constructs sensate meanings and draws distinctions from the mundane that people can use as a touchstone for sacred meanings when culture fails to solve problems of action in their lives. Thus, that which is sacred is socially ordered above religion although constituted from religion. The sacred at once evokes the sensate in religion and orders specific cultural scripts through a sense of belonging to the broader community of sacred marriages.

While at times the Christian marriage advice manuals use specific elite religious discourse drawn from sacred texts to construct sacred marriages, the preponderance of these manuals use stories from people's lived experiences and draw on images from common culture in their production of sacred marriages. Even Cardinal Müller applies the words of another producer of elite religious discourse, Pope Francis, by drawing on common cultural themes to explain the meaning of sacred texts and elite religious discourse (Grandos 2014). Throughout *The Hope of the Family*, Cardinal Müller makes references to the sexual revolution, including pets in the definition of family, the privatization of marriage, individualistic families, and the failure of parents to provide religious instruction as failures of culture and antithetical to sacred marriages.

In each of these examples, Cardinal Müller discursively constructs sacred marriages using imagery of marriage as a "state of natural grace," the "core of the Church," "enlightened by the living God," the "reality of God the Father," emboldened by "the cross and the resurrection," part of the "mysteries of salvation," and a "perpetual covenant with each other and God eternal." Cardinal Müller cautions believers not to focus on specific language in sacred texts, or even basic principles found in elite religious discourse, because in so doing there is a disruption of the "sacramental order." Thus, the sacred consciousness is powerful and meaningful only in its entirety based on lived experiences and interaction. "[Instructors of religion] lack the real-life foundations and the intellectual capacity to present the Christian message clearly, coherently, and, above all, attractively" (Grandos 2014: 66). Rather, Cardinal Müller contends that there are connections between sacred writings and the Magisterium of the Church that are constitutive of sacred marriages that extend beyond specific verbiage found in sacred writings. "[T]he faithful know that they must examine their conscience, which also obliges them to *form* their conscience continually " in their "*search for the truth*" (Grandos 2014: 59) [Emphasis in original]. Cardinal Müller, like many of the authors of the manuals and the participants in this study, construct sacred marriages from stories about the sacred and people's lived experiences negotiating religious and nonreligious spheres by drawing on the sensate aspects of religion found in the sacred and the community of sacred marriages.

Popcak (2008: 21) eludes to the complexities of applying elite religious discourse in everyday life by drawing the reader's attention to the application of a sacred consciousness in marriage. After several pages of rhetorical devices used by the author to discursively construct the powerful imagery, emotionality, and meanings inherent in sacred marriages, the author writes, "Pretty words, Greg, you may comment. But what do they mean for real life?" Only then does he offer prescriptive advice using the consciousness of sacred marriage he so carefully crafted. These include "doing more romantic things for your mate" in the absence of feelings of romance because it is "through these gestures you participate in God's plan for letting your partner know how special she is to God." When women fail to express romantic love the author frames this behavior as a "barrier to God loving her husband the way God wishes to love him" and "the way the husband needs to be loved." The refusal of affection is contrasted with "Christ's endless supply of love." Here again, the sacralization of marriage is gendered, and in this case promotes the gendered expectation that men need sex, that women withhold sex, and that women should submit to sex because "God may or may not have felt like it [loving humanity], but, oddly these issues never came up" (Popcak 2008: 21).

Often, the manuals use the shortcomings of gendered culture as a recursive tool to think, talk, feel, and act in ways congruent with their sacralization of marriages. For example, Popcak (2008: 22) enjoins men to be supportive of their wives' ambitions when he asks, "Do you hide out behind that 'Men are rational, women are emotional' nonsense, or do you seek to exhibit the *whole, rational, and emotive personhood* that God himself does?" [Emphasis in original]. Authors frequently refer to the inadequacy of the secular cultural tools in people's cultural toolkits to address problems of action in their lives, although they did not use that specific terminology. In contrast, they advise readers to employ the sensate, sacredness of their marriages in their lived experiences. "For the Christian, being a master of marital skills has little to do with being a good earthbound companion and everything to do with being a collaborator in God's plan of salvation for you and your mate" (Popcak 2008: 22).

Accomplishing sacred marriages

Sacred marriages are sociological forms that are discursively and cultural constructed and accomplished. Therefore, substantive changes to their discursive and cultural content are accompanied by changes in the form of sacred marriages.[1] Given that religion is discursively constructed by drawing upon cultural tools in blended religious and nonreligious spheres, sacred marriages are neither wholly constructed of specific religious or nonreligious scripts. Equally, people who believe their marriages are sacred are not passive recipients of religion; but rather, they are bricoleurs who do cultural work in the production of their sacred marriages.

Their sacred marriages do not stand apart and independent from the rest of their cultured lives. Instead, sacred marriages penetrate religious and nonreligious spheres within sometimes competing cultures (e.g., caregiving, ethnic diversity, politics, and social justice). The power of the sacred in sacred marriages to produce resilience is dependent on being positioned within a contrasted state with the other. The sacred exists in the contrast of lived experiences of Church teachings about contraception and the decision to pursue a tubal ligation as part of sacred love in a caregiving culture as parents. The sacred exists in the contrast of lived experiences of conservative and liberal politics about the war in Vietnam within the culture of social justice. The sacred exists within the contrast of lived experiences of "a dysfunctional mess of a family" and the "perfect family everyone wants to be" within the discourse and culture of the Encounters. There is no certain type of sacred marriage, rather sacred marriages are accomplished through discursive practices that are relational between religious and nonreligious spheres and ordered within competing cultures.

Note

1 See Alexander and Sherwood (2002) for a fuller discussion of the relationship of form and content within culture.

5 Rituals

I do. Two simple words – a pronoun and a verb. They could be used in conversation with relatively little significance – uttered almost passively, with no important meaning. Do you like the book you are reading? I do. Do you want a tissue? I do. However, in the context of a wedding, some would argue that they are the two most sacred words anyone can ever speak. Although religious dialog can be found almost anywhere in people's lived experiences, it takes on special meaning and unique power during rituals bounded by religious culture. The power of religious rituals to sacralize marriage lies in the blending of secular discourse and religious discourse in the negotiation of strategies of action. Religious rituals structure and order religious and nonreligious discourses and cultures through gendered embodiment in the sacralization of marriage using everyday spaces in which sacred marriages are lived.

Embodied rituals and sacred marriages

Rituals structure group solidarity through loyalties and memberships (Riis and Woodhead 2010; Swidler 2001). Everything from the guest list to where people sit in the church signals a hierarchy of relations. Religious rituals also instill obligations and expectations of role transformations on participants. These roles and memberships are variable, as are the social hierarchies, prestige, and power they represent. Religious rituals also allow participants to negotiate these relationships. Rituals focus participants' attention on religious and sacred meanings and how people are supposed to think, talk, feel, and act in regards to those meanings. Religious rituals allow people to organize competing, conflicting, incoherent, and often incomplete discourses into meaningful strategies of action. Sacred meanings are shared through ritual and are also recalled and used to negotiate relationships in the future.

Religious meanings associated with sacred marriages are a response to the fragility of marriage with the underlying recognition that modern marriages – and love itself – endure primarily through personal choice. Sacred meanings unfold through time and arise from within the lived experiences of marriage. Religious rituals offer a space in which diffuse, fragmented cultural resources can be structured into more coherent strategies of action. People can use religious discourse found in rituals to orient themselves to and reproduce sacred meanings in their marriages as they face problems of action that threaten their marriages. At the same time, rituals can be the source of conflict within sacred marriages.

Sacred marriages are embodied processes that are reproduced in the social context of rituals. The public settings in which rituals occur signal religiously approved sacred meanings embedded in cultural strategies of action. Public religious rituals also produce sacred meanings by making people's actions known to others. While religious meaning may be private, illogical, and inconsistent in the minds of individuals, they become coherent and directed in the performance of religious ritual. Decisions not to follow religious rituals can lead to privatized, sacred meanings in which the participants construct new or altered meanings to the ritual based on their lived experiences. Sacred meanings are located at the nexus of lived experiences and the cultural strategies of action people use to solve problems as they negotiate blended religious and secular spheres.

Through religious rituals, sacred meanings can be discursively written upon, and rewritten by, the body (McGuire 2008). Embodied religious rituals are symbolic referents of transformational discourse associated with sacred marriages. Weddings need not have religious meanings to provide powerful cultural scripts and social approval of dominant discourses about marriage. Kalmijn (2004) suggests that weddings are surrounded by culture as exemplified by expectations that one should marry, the appropriate timing of marriage, and the type of person one should marry. These cultural expectations are, in part, negotiated publicly through wedding rituals. More importantly, weddings – regardless of religion's influences – link characteristics of the couple being married with cultural scripts, which in the case of religious culture often includes the sacralization of marriage.

These connections and networks between the social and the couple are symbolically represented through material objects. As an example, Carol is a school bus driver who is Catholic and attended her granddaughter's wedding a week before her and her husband's interviews. She shared pictures of her granddaughter and her husband dancing, smiling, and dressed in a wedding gown and tuxedo, respectively. She then turned to a nearby curio cabinet and handed me an old photograph from her parents' wedding in the 1920s. Her father's face was stoic and somber. Her mother wore a large cross on a necklace and a veil that covered her face. Carol commented on the differences in her parents' wedding picture and her granddaughter's. In comparing the photos Carol shared, her father and mother were pictured seated next to each other in large, Gothic style chairs – they did not hold hands. There was no photo of them kissing, smiling, or hugging, although Carol shared several photos of her granddaughter and her new husband in embracing poses. The importance of the body in religious rituals cannot be overlooked in the examination of sacred marriages.

As McGuire (2007) points out, human bodies matter because religious practices involve people's bodies (e.g., kneeling to pray, making the sign of the cross as a means of prayer, submerging the body in water during ritual baptism, and genuflecting in front of the alter). Religion is filled with embodied practices that emphasize rituals in which sacred meanings are discursively rewritten through embodied practices framed in religious culture. While embodied rituals often occur in religious institutional settings such as a church, embodied practices are present in a myriad of ritualized everyday experiences ranging from the mundane to the sacred. People use their bodies to accomplish religion by blending their lived experiences with cultural problems of action to construct sacred meanings. Not all embodied practices have the same effects on sacred marriages. As McGuire (2007) explains, some embodied experiences are more conducive to and evoke more and different sacred meanings.

Holy communion is an example of a sacred, embodied ritual that is often repeated with regular frequency throughout a Christian's lifetime. Holy communion is an embodied experience in which the body and blood of Christ are symbolically eaten and drunk through a communal experience that occurs with sacred objects, in a sacred space, and using culturally scripted religious language. It is typically conducted by a religious leader and accompanied by prayers, sacred music, and the reading of scripture. Although the mechanics of participation differ denominationally, and by local practice, the dialog and embodied experiences share commonalities in all of its performances (see United States Conference of Catholic Bishops n/d; and Vanderwell and Malefyt 2010). Local variations might include the body of Christ being represented by bread, crackers, or a wafer, while the blood of Christ may be represented by red wine or grape juice. The embodied experiences of approaching the alter, standing, kneeling, or the order in which participants partake in the wafer and wine may differ as well. Although the order of events varies, typically participants are reminded of the theological centrality of Christ's crucifixion and incarnation, and thus Christ's humanity and corporeal existence. Participants are encouraged to participate and unite together in the symbolically larger "body of Christ" representing the amalgamation of all Christians. Participants are cautioned of their unworthiness to receive the body of Christ, and that they need to be prepared to receive the sacrament by not being conscious of unrepentant personal sin. Embodied rituals, like holy communion, can play a salient role in the sacralization of marriage, as the following couples can attest.

Lived experiences and the embodiment of sacred marriage

Riley described periods of conflict with his wife Gertrude that included yelling and occasionally throwing. Riley offered that, "Before [their son was molested], that would've included profane language, but not anymore because we don't use that language anymore. That has to do with receiving holy communion. I told Jesus that I wouldn't use that kind of foul language and then receive him in my mouth." For Riley and Gertrude, holy communion sacralized communication within their marriage. And while embodied religious rituals often occur within formal religious contexts and sacred spaces, like holy communion, the couples I interviewed frequently engaged in private, embodied religious rituals in their everyday lives. Several participants in this study described a variety of embodied religious experiences they claimed enhanced sacred feelings they held in their marriages. Examples of these embodied rituals range from a wife who ritually prayed while doing the dishes, to a despondent couple who, during a period of infertility, knelt together in prayer after every time they had sex, asking that she become pregnant. As McGuire (2007: 198) states, "Individuals' religions become *lived* only through involving their bodies (as well as minds) and their emotions (as well as their cognitions)" [Emphasis in original].

The embodiment of sacred meanings is not only cultural; it is discursively embodied. Following McSwite (2001: 243), my intent is not to reify or normalize the body itself as an object in ritual practices, but rather to position the body within discourse and culture used to sacralize marriages.

> The body is seen in rationalistic discourse as an object, a reified thing. The consequence of this reification is that the body is effectively located outside discourse. The idea of the body functions as a limit to discourse or as an objective reference point beyond which discourse cannot move. In other words, the body is employed to serve as an objective boundary for thought itself. To me conceptualizing the body in this way impedes and distorts discourse rather than acting to enhance or ground it.

The examination of religion in sacred marriages, and specifically the embodied practices associated with rituals, requires not only the consideration of embodied practices but the ways that cultured embodied practices are constitutive of religious discourse. The role of the body in discourse, and specifically religious discourse, has not been considered in social science research to any significant extent (McSwite 2001).

In one way, the body represents the subjectivities of the human being beneath it. Others interact with the body as representative of these subjectivities. As example, the deceased body is viewed and people talk, feel, think, and act with the deceased during a funeral as a representation of the subjectivities the body symbolizes (e.g., mother, friend, and wife). On another level, we can perceive our bodies symbolically through the perceptions of others and not as an autonomous physical object. The body is an imaginary of the human subject. Thus, the body is discursive and religious embodied rituals are constitutive of sacred discourse. When it becomes problematic to use particular cultural tools to solve problems of action in marriages, people sometimes turn to their sacred marriages to find meaning in competing strategies of action.

Consider Riley and Gertrude, who struggled to reconcile their son's molestation by a priest with a culture of religion and their Catholic identity. Facing this problem of action, their discourse became more elaborate and regulated with a greater number of rules. This is evidenced by Riley's and Gertrude's incorporation of more embodied practices into their discourse. Riley and Gertrude's rules of discourse are regulated not by elite religious discourse or religious culture alone, but rather through embodied discourse framed within sacred meanings in their marriage. The power of the sacred to act in their lives comes not only from the social institution of the Church, which they support but do not trust. It comes not only from elite religious discourse, which has failed to result in the reality they envisioned together. Instead, they also turn to the embodiment of the sacred body of Christ to guide their interactions. There is power in the blood and the body of Christ. Christ's body is not a reified object, but rather it is a representation of the sacred meanings of which it is constituted as subject. The body of Christ is socially constituted and a representation of sacred power practiced in discourse within sacred marriages. Embodied rituals are not passive objects shaped only by external religion or religious culture; but rather, they are a discursively constitutive element of some sacred marriages. They find belonging in the Church through communion as part of the larger body of believers (Dodaro 2014), despite their lived experiences of religion.

Public vs. private sacred spaces

Place is an important aspect of embodied religious rituals because sacred or special places provide a religious social context that fosters and fuels religious discourse and the use of religious culture to sacralize marriage. Some religious rituals take place in special places set apart from the daily routine, the mundane, and the secular world, and when they do not take place in sacred spaces people may question their sacredness. Sometimes it is this very detachment from the everyday world in which people live that causes a ritual to be deemed sacred and religious. It is a perceived detachment because, while sacred spaces may be public (e.g., churches, consecrated ground, or public venues adorned with religious iconography or symbolic objects), individuals may also sacralize private spaces (e.g., a chair used for daily prayers, a hospital bed in a living room where couples read scripture with a terminology ill parent, or a nightstand jewelry box used to store a Bible and daily devotional guide). Social context and place are important dimensions of religious rituals. These sacred spaces provide religious context in the form of religious discourse through religious iconography and symbology that typically accompany religious rituals. Religious rituals are embedded with religious discourse that occurs within sacred contexts.

Often, religious discourse and cultural scripts are ordered and structured during religious rituals to sacralize marriage. The Christian marriage advice manuals offer several examples of structured dialog associated with religious rituals designed for public use in shared public spaces. Here, I offer three examples of manuals for wedding ceremonies that regulate these religious rituals and spaces. Slider (2011) describes the Methodist wedding rite, Champlin (2012) the Catholic ceremony, and Biddle (1974) describes wedding ceremonies for multiple denominations ranging from Baptist, to Lutheran, to Episcopal. More than providing scripted language that sacralizes marriages to be used during wedding ceremonies, these manuals use religious discourse to regulate and control the sacred spaces in which the rituals take place.

For example, according to Slider (2011: 76), "The pastor may conduct weddings at locations other than sanctuaries. Homes, gardens, and wedding chapels may be used. The pastor shall not conduct a worship service in a location that is not conducive to worship of God or consistent with the Christian witness." In contrast, Champlin (2012: 3) states that "Catholics are required to celebrate their wedding in a Catholic Church, before a priest and two witnesses." For Catholics, use of the church by non-Catholics marrying Catholics is governed by the diocese. Even the terms used to describe the wedding ceremony have specific meanings within Catholic culture (e.g., rite, liturgy, or liturgical celebration).

Biddle's (1974) prescriptive text for wedding ceremonies describes the regulation of almost every aspect of any wedding ceremony including when and where people sit and stand, how they enter the space in which the ceremony is conducted, specific music to be played and when, the order in which candles are lighted and by whom, costs and fees, the consumption of alcohol, allowable decorations, and policies governing photography. Biddle's (1974) service for "blessing" civil marriages offers a particularly powerful perspective of the sacralization of secular marriages within religious culture through the use of religious discourse in the sacred space of a church to sacralize a civil marriage. The manuals also sacralize embodied practices that accompany weddings (e.g., placing the wedding ring on a finger, holding hands, kissing, and kneeling together).

Sacred rituals are not always performed in shared, public spaces. Often these rituals occur in private spaces that individuals construct as sacred by using religious discourse and religious cultural repertoires. Many devotional guides and prayer books are specifically written to sacralize marriage through the use of quotidian spaces for the performance of ritualized religious discourse. Manuals like Bartkowski's (1989) *Prayers for Married Couples*, offer specific scripts for couples to pray to strengthen their sacred marriages in their homes. Devotional guides and prayer books are often gendered, as is the case of O'Boyle's (2013), *Catholic Mom's Café: 5-Minute Retreats for Every Day of the Year*. Lindsey's (2003: 7) imagery of transcendent aspects of nature typifies the use of private, sacred spaces for the sacralization of marriages.

> Some have made it a habit to pray upon awakening, before the morning sun peeks over the horizon. The faint light of dawn can make praying from a prayer book difficult. The illumination of the spirit through prayer should not depend on the illumination of our homes and churches. . . . Our poor earthly vision cannot possibly compare to the all-knowing Father's view. . . . Prayer connects us to loved ones seen and unseen, present and departed.

Religious culture is used to sacralize private spaces for rituals designed to sacralize marriages through religious discourse. These manuals are intended to be used in private spaces for the performance of ritualized prayer and devotion in the sacralization of marriages. They represent a blending of religious and secular spheres through rituals that produce sacred marriages.

Blending of religious and secular discourse in rituals

Both public and private spaces in which religious rituals occur can serve as contexts for the blending of sacred and secular spheres (Munson 2007). While the scholarly separation of the religious aspects of religious rituals from the nonreligious aspects of religious rituals is arbitrary and artificial, it highlights the way people weave a tapestry of sacred marriage using religious rituals. Religious rituals are bounded, but porous, allowing a blending of sacred and secular spheres through a juxtaposition of the secular with the sacred. As example, consider a wedding in which the Church formally recognizes the marriage, but the religious officiant signs the state-issued marriage license. Religious rituals may simultaneously hold powerful secular and religious meanings.

It is because religious rituals are polysemous – meaning they have multiple and competing meanings simultaneously – that people are able to blend secular discourse and religious discourse in them, seamlessly and without questioning from which domain the discourse originates. The blending of religious discourse with nonreligious discourse allows people to incorporate religious emotional regimes into their cultural toolkits to form strategies of action. People can incorporate these multiple meanings of religious rituals into the way they act, think, talk, and feel about their lived experiences of sacred marriages. People are comfortable not separating religious and secular meanings in their lived experiences of sacred marriages.

The polysemous nature of the sacralized spaces in which religious and nonreligious discourse overlap in religious rituals results in a blurring of domains that gives these events power through positioning that is reflective of the other. For example, some people may attend a wedding and find only secular meaning in the event, while others may find deep religious meanings in this religious rite. Everyone participating need not accept the religious meanings of the wedding for them to have sacred meanings. Likewise, secular rituals carried out in sacred spaces may carry sacred meanings for some people because of the sacred space and context in which they take place, while others may ascribe no sacred meaning to the space or the ritual. Some of the power of the sacralization of marriage lies in the very fact that some people find little to no significance in the religious aspects of the ritual. Sacred marriages are socially ordered above secular marriages because they are positioned within sacred spaces that do not accompany weddings taking place in nonreligious or non-sacred spaces. The challenge for the couples I interviewed is that polysemy and ambiguity associated with religious rituals sometimes results in an uneven distribution of sacred meanings and power.

Weddings and the sacralization of marriage

I offer four stories of weddings that exemplify the conflict that can occur in sacred marriages due to the polysemous nature of religious rituals. The first is a story of a couple in which the husband was Methodist and converted to Catholicism 17 years after their wedding. In the second story, a Catholic husband insisted the priest change a marriage document to remove references to "being open" to having children. In the third story, a wedding ignites a longstanding conflict about one Catholic husband's degree of extended family involvement that has troubled his wife throughout their marriage. Finally, in the fourth story, I describe a married couple who is neither legally married nor married in the eyes of the Church. In each story, the couples face problems of action they solve by blending religious and secular discourse in the context of their sacred marriages.

Henry is a retired railroad engineer, and during his working years that meant leaving suddenly to drive an arriving train and being gone unexpectedly for weeks at a time. He grew up in a Methodist home and converted to Catholicism 17 years after he married. Amelia was a "stay-at-home mom," to use her words, and occasional employee at the public school in a clerical support position. Her mother completed suicide and her father was an alcoholic. Amelia shared, "I know this isn't something you say, but part of me was glad [God] took her when she was young, so she didn't see what dad became."

Henry and Amelia offered similar stories about their wedding ceremony, but vastly different narratives concerning the context in which the wedding occurred. This is Henry's account.

> Our priest, he was going to marry us, and my wife said, "I've heard you never do mixed marriages," and he was a no-show. He didn't show up for the ceremony. We took classes with him a few times, and we just didn't get along because he said my folks was going to go to hell. He had a different priest who came in to do the ceremony. The deal was that we weren't allowed to go up to the altar and had to stand down in front of the rail because I wasn't Catholic. That's the only way the substitute priest would do the ceremony. We didn't know the first priest wasn't going to show. We had never even met this substitute priest. He just showed up for the ceremony. It really wasn't a big deal to us. It took longer for the three bridesmaids to walk down the aisle than the service took. Bang, it was done. [Laughter]. But that was all right.

It was Amelia who gave context to the wedding.

> My dad had some real problems with my husband because he wasn't Catholic. He is the one who told the priest not to marry us. When dad was drinking he would talk terrible about my husband and his family who are wonderful Christians. Wonderful Methodist people. When he wasn't drinking everything was wonderful. He never said it to Henry. Just mom and I could hear it . . . I'm lucky my husband finally became Catholic.
> This priest said he was known for never officiating at a mixed marriage. So I asked him if he would, and he said, "Of course." He lied, but dad told him no. So, I guess the Church would say we're not even married.

During their interview together, I questioned Henry and Amelia about the religious authenticity of their marriage within the Church and whether they felt their marriage was sacred. They recognized that their marriage was not officially approved by the Catholic Church, but that did not matter to them. During their interview together, Amelia shared with Henry for the first time in their 52 years of marriage the arguments she and her mother had with her father about their wedding. Amelia was heartbroken for the first few years of their marriage and blamed her mother's death and her own infertility for the first five years of their marriage on her decision to marry a man who was not Catholic.

Although they claimed the Church does not recognize their marriage, and the wedding ceremony was embroiled with conflict, it is within these conflicts and where they physically stood in the church that they find sacred meanings in their marriage. Both Henry and Amelia said they would not change their wedding because it typified their struggle to marry and remain married as they dealt with Henry's absences.

"We had everything going against us," Henry shared. "But we're still here together."

They raised the topic of their wedding ceremony early in their interviews, and they referred to it frequently. They find sacred meaning in their wedding ceremony through a combination of religious and nonreligious meanings, but mostly they argue it is sacred because it is unique. When I asked about the reasons they thought their ceremony was sacred, they both said that the ceremony was sacred because it was in the church. They make no distinction between the religious and nonreligious meanings they ascribe their marriage. The wedding was a sacred event to them because its discursive and embodied contradictions inform their sacred marriage within a contrasted other.

Burt and Blossom have been married 44 years and are retired teachers. They both hold master's degrees and provided me several references to Christian marriage advice manuals as well as other texts they thought might be beneficial to this study. They are self-described "cradle Catholics" who find sacred meaning in their marriage through service to others.

> We liked Father Bill because he's all about helping others. You know, he and I started the soup kitchen downtown. We were walking to the rectory for lunch, and we saw some guys hard on their luck and said to ourselves, "We've got to feed them." So, we made some sandwiches and invited them into the rectory out of the cold. The soup kitchen has been feeding people every day since then. That's the kind of religion that makes marriage sacred. Blossom supports what I do there, and she helps out from time to time. That's sacred to us.

Burt and Blossom do not agree with many Church teachings. Blossom explained,

> We left St. Martin's where we grew up as children – which was like a family compound for our two families – we left because we wanted something more progressive like Father Bill. [. . .] We started with Father Bill because he and Burt are old friends. He needed a wheelchair ramp for a choir member, and

Burt built it. That's religion to us. Those kind of things are sacred – the soup kitchen and building someone a wheelchair ramp. That's what marriage is all about.

After several questions in which I attempted to illicit how they could find sacred meanings in their marriage given the degree of their disagreement with so many Church teachings, Burt stopped me and abruptly interjected the following.

Look, it's like this. There are actually books you're not supposed to read according to the Catholic Church. Can you imagine? The Church tells you what you can and can't read? To have everything all spelled out? That was one of the things I had problems with in the seminary so many times in different classes. I would bring up the idea that this Church is not interested in truth. It's more interested in uniformity. Look at all the scholarly theologians that have been absolutely obfuscated.

[. . .]

The Catholic University is an oxymoron. How is it that you have a person who specializes in religion and man's place in the world, and his relationship with that being, and because you come up with different conclusions than the hierarchy of the Church you are obfuscated? How can we do that?

[. . .]

Father Bill's . . . emphasis was get out and take care of people in need, those that need soup, that need education, that need clothing. [. . .] Our goal in life is not to let Catholicism interfere with being a good person and not to let the Church tell us what religion is and what makes our marriage sacred. Our marriage is sacred because we practice our religion, and not because the Church tells us it is, while it obfuscates the scholars who challenge its "truths." [Burt used his fingers to make air quotes around the word truth].

Despite their disagreements with many Church teachings, their home is filled with artifacts of religious rituals. During the course of several hours in their home, they showed me religious iconography that one of their grandchildren made, keepsakes from their children's confirmations and first communions, and a digital picture frame with a continuous loop of photos of their family participating in various religious rituals. It happened to be near Palm Sunday during the interviews, and their dining table was covered in palm fronds their grandchildren were weaving for Palm Sunday services.

Near the end of their interviews, Burt said in jest, "And to think, you've spent all this time talking to two people that the Church would say aren't married." Blossom explained Burt's comment.

When they brought out the big paper for you to get married at our wedding, where you have to sign, it does say, at that time, that you're getting married only for procreation. And Burt said, "That's not right. Strike that out. It's not the only reason to get married anymore because you've got an old paper there. I'm not going to sign something that's an old paper because I don't believe that."

In response to my questions about her feelings and perspective on Burt's insistence that the document be changed, which the priest ultimately agreed to do, Blossom referred to her miscarriages in an attempt to explain her feelings about Church teachings concerning marriage.

> I lost two babies in miscarriages. From that point on we tried the Church's way of the rhythm method, but that didn't work for us. So, we went to the cervical thing, and that was against the Church law. But I wasn't going to ask Burt to just give up sex and his rights in that situation. [. . .] When I had my first child I . . . had to take medication shots to keep the baby. They decided to take it C-section. [. . .] When we had the third baby, the doctor decided that I should not have any more, so he tied my tubes and that's against the Church too. [. . .] That's what the doctor decided would be better, and I was asleep and I never knew it. So, that's how that went. Sometimes the Church isn't in touch with what happens to people and how they have to live. We see it with the gays, and the prostitutes, and the addicts every day at St. Martin's.

People use disjointed and conflicting narratives to articulate their sacred marriages to others. Burt and Blossoms narratives reflected their lived experiences of religion in their sacred marriage. They drew few distinctions between the religious and nonreligious aspects of their lives. They blend religious and nonreligious spheres to produce their sacred marriage. They – like all the couples in this study – are active agents in the construction of their sacred marriage. Their lived experiences of serving others, miscarriages, disagreeing with Church teachings, regulating their sex lives, forced sterilization, and altering Church documents during their wedding ceremony are constitutive of the sacred meanings they find in their marriage. The circuitous nature of their logic and its many conflicting elements and tangents are not problematic to them. It is indicative of their process of sacralizing marriage by positioning it in reference to the other. They pick up and reject aspects of religious culture as they negotiate religious discourse in light of their lived experiences. It is the sum of these experiences, not the individual elements of their lives together, that gives their marriage sacred meanings.

As Blossom explained, "These rituals have to mean something more than just strict adherence to Church law. You have to look at the whole of your marriage and what you did together to serve others to understand the sacredness of marriage."

Veronica and Jason have been married 48 years. While extended family relationships are important to both of them, they each view extended family relationships differently. He was born and raised in a large, Catholic family with an active religious life. She only attended the Peace on Earth Christian Church, a nondenominational church, on average about once every other month and on Easter Sundays.

Veronica's mother died the day after she was born, so, according to her, "My grandmother and older siblings raised me." She is 15 years younger than her next oldest sibling. Her father was an alcoholic and was largely absent from her childhood. Veronica converted to Catholicism as a teenager because she "liked all those big families," and she shared she had feelings of loneliness as a child.

It is easy for Veronica and Jason to stay connected to Jason's side of the family because they all live nearby, but Veronica 's side of the family lives quite a distance away. She did not know how to drive when their six children were younger, which resulted in them not visiting Veronica's siblings or her siblings' grandchildren who were close in age to Veronica and Jason's children, except every other year for Christmas. Veronica longed for closer relationships with her siblings and their families because she "felt like an orphan" as a child. She viewed her older siblings as "surrogate moms and dads."

Religious rituals (e.g., christenings, baptisms, confirmations, and first communions) have always been accompanied by large extended family gatherings, but primarily by Jason's side of the family. Since Veronica's extended family only includes one brother who is Catholic, she has faced a significant amount of anti-Catholic sentiment concerning their Catholic religious rituals. "They don't mean any harm. They just never understood." Veronica explained. Their disinterest and misunderstanding of Catholic rituals, coupled with the distance they have to travel, has further weakened the bonds between Veronica and Jason's children and their maternal extended family.

I interviewed Veronica first, and she shared that she and Jason were "having a big argument" when I arrived. Veronica explained that the source of the conflict lay in Jason's refusal to attend her nephew's wedding. She cried while she shared feelings of hurt, betrayal, and anger towards Jason, all the while reiterating her love for him. "You can be mad at someone and still love them more than anything in this whole wide world," she explained.

In his interview, Jason said that he refused to attend the wedding based on the initial invitation they received in the mail. He confirmed his decision after calling his wife's nephew.

> In the announcement, they wanted you to send money to the gay and lesbian and whatever organization in lieu of wedding presents. I don't believe in any of that. [. . .] He even said he doesn't even believe in God when I called him up and challenged him on that right there. [. . .] You know, I bet if you read Ann Landers she would say you should go for the sake of the family. But no, that man has to understand that he is insulting and upsetting people. [. . .] The bride dropped the F-bomb during the ceremony. What kind of a crap wedding is that? I'm not driving all that way and paying for a hotel for that mess right there.

Jason insisted his refusal to attend was an expression of his "faith," and others should view it as a "testament" to his willingness to "stand up for what I believe." "It has nothing to do with family," according to Jason.

Veronica raised the topic of their disagreement during their interview together. For her, "It opened old wounds. I never had a family when I was a kid, and we've always put your family first. My family didn't always agree with what we did with our kids, but they showed up when they could. You're treating them just like you say they treat us."

"Do you think disagreements about religion like this one have hurt your marriage," I asked.

"I can't think of anything that we ever ran into that really hurt our marriage," Veronica quickly replied. Jason agreed and said,

> If you hold it in I think you hurt your own heart. [. . .] I think what really hurts people most is when they quit going to church. [. . .] She knows when I'm mad, and I know when she's mad. Basically we've got six good kids. We got some good grandkids and great-grandkids. [. . .] You get past the conflict by voicing your opinion. It's easier for me to voice mine than hers. But I give in too. You have to give in every now and again. If it weren't for our religion, we would've divorced a year out, and I'm serious on that right there.

"I know Jason is sticking by what he believes, and I respect and love him for that. I just wished we could have had a closer relationship with my family for our kids' sake. Our grandkids don't even know all their cousins" Veronica shared.

Veronica and Jason's experiences of the wedding ritual are interesting because they were able to negotiate their conflict using a cultural script of love and forgiveness to reaffirm their sacred marriage by rejecting lines of action they perceived might lead to problems in their marriage. But they never resolved the source of the conflict. Veronica continues to have hurt feelings, and Jason continues to distance himself from her side of the family. Nonetheless, Jason feels justified by feeling, thinking, and talking about his actions as part of his religious beliefs about sacred marriages. Veronica uses a similar religious regime to feel, think, and talk about her hurt feelings toward Jason by framing them as part of their sacred marriage. While this has not always resolved the sources of their conflicts, it has allowed them to overcome the conflicts in their marriage. They would agree it would be better if they did not experience this conflict, but they also argue that their marriage is more sacred because their beliefs about marriage allow them to disagree and even dislike each other at times due to their understanding of sacred love in their marriage.

Esther and Adam have been married 48 years. They are Catholic, and Esther has been married before.

> We were married June 5, 1964. I was 16 when I got married. I was married ten days after my 16th birthday, and this young man and I eloped. It lasted about six or seven weeks, and he decided to enlist in the Army. When he did that, I think he acted like he didn't even care. So, when he came back, I said I wanted divorced – which I didn't. But then he said okay, so I thought well that's that.

Esther spent her childhood without parental figures. She didn't meet her biological father until she was ten, and later she learned he was not actually her biological father. Her mother was a prostitute who rented rooms to other couples and did not know who Esther's father was. Esther said she had no "religious experiences" until she was in her early teens, when she joined a Catholic youth group and later converted to Catholicism.

Adam grew up in a home where "there wasn't any love" but there was a high degree of structure and consistency in their religious lives as Catholics. To Adam, "The Church was the only thing that held us together because no one divorced in my family. Catholics don't do that."

Esther never divorced her first husband out of apathy. "I just didn't care. It wasn't no real marriage, so I didn't bother with any papers." Adam and Esther never filed legal documents with the state to marry because the state refused to issue them a marriage license given Esther's existing marriage. Adam shared that their wedding took place in the Catholic church by a priest. Adam's sister "got into where she worked and typed up a marriage license" that they showed the priest. "He never even took it out of my hand. I showed it to him kind of leaning back in the chair, so he couldn't see it good."

"Is your marriage sacred since it's not a legal marriage and you deceived the Church?" I asked.

Esther explained.

> Look, we got four kids that's all pains in the ass. They always have been. Adam and I don't argue much anymore. We both just shut up. If we argue, it's about our children or our grandchildren. We have one child that's the biggest pain in the ass. So, we argue about how much of her bills to pay. We still own another house in Wingate, and she lives in it. We are constantly seeming to be paying for something for her. Our marriage just works. When we ran into problems, we conquered each one as it came. Now we've got a whole history of conquered problems so nothing seems impossible. We just keep adding to our relationship through our experience and it grows stronger.
>
> I don't know why some people's marriages don't work. [. . .] It's like divorce wasn't an option for us. No matter what happens, it's going to work. [. . .] I've walked out of the house before and didn't come home for three hours. I sat with a friend at her house and calmed down and came back home, and Adam and I talked later on. Divorce crossed my mind only for a minute. It's like your kids. You say to yourself, "I wish the hell you didn't live here," but in the next moment you're ironing their clothes.
> [. . .]
> Adam came from a traditional Catholic family. I came from a traditional nothing. He was determined to have a good, strong family, and I was determined to have a family. It's what we wanted, and we worked at it. [. . .] Unfortunately the Church is not raising children. They don't help financially or anything else when it comes to your kids. But, they sure have opinions. We just made it work. [. . .] I didn't feel the Church ever had the right to tell me

what to do in regards to our personal lives. I said money is money. You can only have so much to spread around, and kids aren't cheap.

"Esther's right about shutting up," Adam added.

> Even at the wedding, my parents knew. I told them, come to the wedding or don't. But, keep your damn mouth shut. I had gotten her pregnant. We did get married before the child was born, which was what I thought was right given my religion. That kept their mouth shut. They came to the wedding and everything else, but they weren't happy.

"Why is your marriage sacred?" I reiterated after they both had finished speaking.

Adam spoke first this time. "Our religion teaches that you do the right thing when a man gets a woman pregnant. You work, you make the kids fall in line, and you stay married. That's what we done."

Esther added,

> Look, the Church and anyone else can say any damn thing they want. It's not them. It's us. Who cares? What are they going to do now? Take our kids? They can have them, just as long as they pay their bills. [Laughter, then a pause]. Marriage isn't sacred because the Church says it is. I never cared what the Church said. It's sacred because God wants you to live a good life, and do the best you can, and that's what we did and are going to keep on doing. We're going to keep loving one another, just like God wants.

"We kept it together and hope to stay together. We don't have any foreseen problems that would cause us to divorce," Adam concluded.

Esther and Adam are clearly an outlier in this study. They are the only couple who are not legally married and knowingly deceived the Church to get married by their priest. They faced a multitude of socioeconomic challenges in their childhoods. They abused their children physically and emotionally, just as they had been physically and emotionally abused themselves as children. They believe they provided their children a better life than they had as children, and that they did then, and continue to do now, what they think is best, given the challenges they have faced as parents. Nonetheless, their wedding and their marriage is filled with sacred meanings to them.

Rituals as producers of blended embodied memories and social emotions

Many couples in this study imbue religious rituals with sacred meanings that are incongruous with elite religious discourse. They blend their everyday experiences of life (e.g. "making it through the hard times") and their religious beliefs (e.g., "live a good life") to give sacred meanings to their marriage. It is the polysemous and ambiguous meanings within cultural scripts and religious regimes that can be filled with people's lived experiences that give sacred meanings to marriages. Riley and Gertrude use the sacred elements of holy communion to regulate their communications as part of the sacralization of their marriage. Henry and Amelia find sacred meaning in their marriage, in part, because they were not allowed to stand on the alter during their wedding. Burt and Blossom have sacralized their marriage through a life of service to others based on changes they made to their wedding documents because the documents were inconsistent with their beliefs and lived experiences, thereby setting the tone for their futures together in a sacred marriage. Jason's failure to attend a wedding based on his beliefs caused significant discord with Veronica, but they believe their marriage is sacred because they can have disagreements and continue to love one another, emulating God's divine love. Esther and Adam are not married legally and deceived the Church at their wedding, but they sacralize their marriage by blending the secular pragmatics of the problems of action they have faced with a sacred construction of their marriage premised on its endurance and "doing the right thing." Each of these couples offer a glimpse into the ways people sacralize their marriages through embodied religious rituals in which they discursively blend secular and religious spheres to address problems of action.

By abandoning a dichotomous perspective of the religious sphere and the non-religious sphere as being opposed to each other, the myriad individual ways people put their stories about religious rituals into practice to produce sacred marriages. In this chapter I have focused primarily on weddings as religious rituals because they are embodied religious experiences that some people draw on throughout their lifetimes to find sacred meanings in their marriages. They accomplish this not through an abstract body, but in their actual, real bodies. They wear wedding rings, weave palm fronds, build wheelchair ramps, write on Church documents, hold wedding invitations, and fill their living spaces with photos with which they share their stories of their sacred marriages with others. Sacred marriages are one of many ways to make sense of their worlds.

According to McGuire (2008), memory is not just located in the brain, but throughout the biological body. And, Bourdieu (1977) concludes that all senses – both physical senses and social senses – are involved in remembering embodied practices. Among other ways, people's embodied experiences play a part in the development of learned social senses like a sense of justice, sense of good taste, sense of right and wrong, common sense, and a sense of religious morality, and a sense of the sacred. The body plays an active role in rituals not only as recipient of sacred meanings but as forger in in the production of sacred meanings from the available cultural tools and spaces at hand.

6 Religious dissonance

Recent research indicates that dyadic religiosity influences relationship quality (Goodman and Dollahite 2006; Rostosky et al 2008.). When couples pray together, serve on church committees together, participate jointly in religious worship or rituals together, and even when individual spouses engage separately in different types of religious activities but perceive themselves as participating in them together (e.g., one spouse serves as an usher while the other plays piano for the choir) there can be mutual benefit to the couple's relationship. A perception of sharing in religion, in all its many forms in people's everyday lives, can form the basis of transformative processes that provide meaning to sacred marriages resulting in relationships with shared futures and shared meanings in their socio-cultural histories. However, not all shared experiences of religion are beneficial to couples, and what might seem minor or irrelevant to one spouse can be a source of significance to the other, especially when behaviors violate the sacred consciousness of their marriages resulting in religious dissonance. Religious dissonance and the compromises it promotes can play a salient role in self-regulation (i.e., mediating distress without external intervention from a professional and continuance of the marriage) associated with change in sacred marriages.

Ordering discourse and culture in the sacred marriages

A recent trend in the study of religion and marriage focuses on transformative processes and the bridging capacity that religion can play in linking everyday events to sacred meanings (Fincham et al 2007; Goodman et al 2013). This scholarship represents a significant shift in the study of relationships in marriage. Rather than focusing on conflict as a form of distress in which couples' aversive and ineffectual reactions to disagreements harm their relationships, transformative processes scholarship takes into consideration social forces that effect relationships along with individual behaviors. By considering the effects of external forces like religion in relationships, the transformative processes they promote can be examined in the production of remission of marital distress. According to Fincham and his colleagues (2007: 277), the examination of external forces that shape transformative processes in relationships allows us to 1) consider the meanings of the interplay between conflict and other processes, 2) move beyond the behaviors of individuals to a broader view of contextual forces that affect couples, 3) take seriously external motivations and meanings affecting behavior, and 4) reposition the focus of research from distress to change that may not be monotonic or linear.

Religion facilitates transformative processes within marriage bringing couples closer together, improving relationship quality, and improving marital satisfaction beginning as early as the wedding ritual, if not before that during courtship. Religion may provide a cornerstone of consistency and congruency to competing cultures and strategies of action to stabilize marriages through compromising by helping couples delineate roles, commit to marriage, and be better parents while supporting each family member's unique identity. In their study of sacred marriages, Goodman and his colleagues (2013) found that couples spoke of prayer, scripture study, and other religious practices as being beneficial in coping with challenges.

Given the potential of transformational processes to promote self-regulation associated with change in sacred marriages, a fuller understanding of these transformational processes may provide insights into relationship self-regulation associated with change in sacred marriages. Because marriage is an institution in which spouses negotiate various cultures and strategies of action – for example, embracing a culture of romantic love or rejecting a culture of divorce – the cultural strategy they select as individuals and collectively as a couple can affect their responses to changes in their marriages. Extending Swidler's (2001) description of institutional forces on culture, I suggest one possible explanation of religion's influences on self-regulation associated with change within sacred marriages – which are comprised of individuals who regularly operate in diffuse, incomplete, and contradictory cultural scripts – lies in sacred marriages' propensity to order disperse cultural scripts in the production of collective social agency.

Religious emotional regimes

People in sacred marriages orient the ways they think, feel, talk, and act towards institutional demands, thereby continually reproducing structured sacred understandings and meanings among disjointed, fragmented, unsystematic thoughts and feelings. If, as Swidler (2001) suggests, social institutions like marriage exert an organizing effect on individuals who are actively choosing to remain in their marriages, Riis and Woodhead's (2010) model of the links between religious emotion and agency are particularly powerful in explaining the effects of religion's influences on transformational processes in sacred marriages by creating a sense of wholeness and consistency within disparate religious discourse and strands of religious culture.

In part, religious emotional regimes are founded on the idea that emotions are not just private, personal, and subjective. More than simply inner states accessible to individuals through introspection, emotional regimes are located in the interplay between social agents and structures. Emotions are both biological and cultural – personal and social. Individual agents are capable of resisting, changing, and producing emotions, even in conditions that are not of their own choosing.

People's emotional lives are framed within encounters with the living, the dead, the imagined, and the transcendent. Emotional regimes incorporate culture, discourse, places, and symbols. Religious emotional regimes include super-social relations and experiences of the sacred (e.g., sacred sites, sacred landscapes, sacred artifacts, and sacred beings). By attending to self and society, culture and self, and culture and society, religious emotional regimes speak to couples' collective sentiments, personal resistance, selections of cultural scripts, and the emotional dimensions of their agency. Religious emotional regimes take seriously the sensate experiences and social senses in people's lived experiences of religion in sacred marriages.

In an extension of Riis and Woodhead's (2010: 8) description of religious emotional regimes, I suggest that individuals shape and modify religious culture and discourse in ways that give purchase over their lives, and at the same time relate religious culture and discourse to wider social forces. In this sense, religion is not a hegemony over individuals that is uncritically internalized, but rather religion sets parameters and continuities open to change through manipulation of discourse and culture. Religion influences how people think, talk, feel, and act by positioning different elements of discourse and culture within either the religious sphere or the secular sphere. This structuring of different elements of discourse and culture within a dichotomous dialect of either religious or not religious holds tremendous power to legitimize or delegitimize as religious the way people talk, think, feel, and act. Religious emotional regimes can call people's motivations and logic into question. Despite people's ability to seamlessly blend religious and secular spheres in their lived experiences, when the ways they talk, think, feel, and act are cast as religious or nonreligious – whether by insiders or outsiders – their relationships may be affected. By ordering strategies of action through claims about religion and the nonreligious, relationships can be restructured. While each individual spouse retains agency within religious emotional regimes, the couple together exhibits a collective social agency as well. The sacralization of marriage advances a structured system of power relations found at the nexus of the individual agency of each spouse and the collective agency of the couple.

Disconnection and harms can occur when individuals do not agree with aspects of religious culture or discourse but fail to reject them in favor of the power of religious emotional regimes. Equally harmful can be the failure to support the institutionalization of the ways they talk, feel, think, and act as legitimate and authentic aspects of their sacred marriages. The detrimental effects can be exacerbated when the person's spouse or others outside the marriage attempt to control religious emotional regimes, promoting individual doubt about the religious correctness or sacredness of the way they talk, feel, think, and act. Religious emotional regimes may cause people to feel that what happens in their sacred marriage is beyond their own control, effectively feeling trapped and dispossessed in religious culture.

At different times in their lives, most of the couples I interviewed questioned the efficacy of their religious emotional regimes in their sacred marriages. Religious dissonance between spouses sometimes resulted in power imbalances when spouses perceived their everyday experiences as not reflecting shared religious meanings in their sacred marriages. At times, individual spouses simply accepted these imbalances as part of a new construction of a sacred consciousness within their marriages. But for many couples, these were opportunities to focus on when their religious emotional regimes were actualized in their everyday lives as they gave greater or lesser significance to religious culture and religious discourse in their cultural repertoires and strategies of action. When couples disagreed about the subjugation of cultural scripts in favor of religious emotional regimes it caused conflict and longstanding rifts in their sacred marriages.

While couples often framed their experiences of marriage within elite religious discourse of self-regulation, it was the suppression of individual agency in favor of the collective agency of the couple through compromises that held import in their sacred marriages. Many participants in this study shared stories in which religious emotional regimes suppressed their individual agency. But, at the same time, they described their actions as though they were of their own volition. For example, Lizzy shared that she wished she had received a college degree, but she married immediately after high school and began bearing children. Her husband Ted used profanity as he vilified Lizzy's father for supporting all of her siblings in completing their college educations, but not Lizzy. Nonetheless, when I asked Lizzy whether she felt like she had sacrificed anything to be a wife and mother, she replied, "I didn't give up anything. It was all in God's plan, and I'm just blessed that he led me to choose his plan over my own." The influence of religious emotional regimes on individual agency often go unnoticed by people in sacred marriages. More than being invisible to individuals, the suppression of their agency through religious emotional regimes in favor of the collective agency of the couple was frequently reframed as supernatural agency with sacred purposes.

Compromise and agency

Several of the Christian marriage advice manuals proclaimed the benefits of not only sharing in religious experiences but also in shared secular experiences in their sacralization of marriage. Garascia's (2007) pre-marriage manual suggests in its first paragraph that these shared experiences should begin before couples marry. He suggests couples in the courtship period of their relationships should be actively engaged individually and together in reflecting on their expectations of the sacrament of marriage. However, togetherness often brings changes requiring compromises. At times, differences about religion can require compromises that not only suppress individual agency, but also inhibit the incorporation of the individual into the whole of the symbolic framework of religious culture in sacred marriages, effectively alienating and isolating them as marginalized subjectivities in their own sacred marriages.

These shifts in discourse or culture can result in a fracturing of the processes that give sacred marriages their shared meanings. While religious culture may organize discourse, in so doing it may delegitimize people's emotions and label them as evil or dangerous to their sacred marriages. This is one of the most dominant themes present in the Christian marriage advice manuals when taken as a whole. Placing the "good of the marriage" for religious reasons over the interests of either spouse individually is the primary theme in the authors' attempts to sacralize marriage. The authors of the manuals promote increased dialog, dyadic religiosity, lowered expectations of marriage, self-denial, and compromise as means of sacralizing marriage (Blyth 2011; Bosio 2008 and 2012; Clinton and Trent 2009; Cloud and Townsend 1999; Coleman 2006; Ford 2010; Guarendi 2011; Morse and Kerekes 2013; Popcak 2008; Popcak and Popcak 2013; Richardson 2010; Worthington 2005).

In her prayer book for married couples, as an example, Bartkowski (1989: 78) provides a culturally scripted prayer that couples are encouraged to pray together seeking divine intervention to promote compromise.

> O Lord, we have a problem that we just can't seem to handle. We've tried so hard to decide what to do about it, but we just don't know how to cope with it. Show us how to deal with this problem, Lord. Help us solve it. When you were on earth you promised to help and guide us in our daily lives. You promised us your constant and loving care. We believe in your power, Lord, and in your desire to give us your aid. We know that if we ask for your help and have faith in it, you'll eventually show us how to handle our difficulties. We know that if we wait patiently for your guidance you'll eventually give us the wisdom we need to resolve our problems. So come to us, Lord, and join your helping hands with ours.

Bartkowski's (1989) prayer demonstrates the impasse that couples may find themselves in at times when they struggle negotiating competing choices and power structures within their marriages. When couples experience contradictions in religion and their lived experiences, they attempt to seek balance between religious and secular spheres to solve problems of action. In the process of seeking compromise, they make choices together through collective agency that may subjugate the individual agency of either or both spouses. Supernatural intervention, at least in part, is the force of collective social agency couples create through discursive relational dialectics to solve problems of action. The contradictions couples experience between religious and secular spheres is at the heart of the construction of the sacred consciousness in sacred marriages. And, although compromise and the suppression of individual agency may have negative effects and promote conflict, compromise plays an important role in promoting self-regulation associated with distress due to changes that result in new or altered discourse and cultural strategies of action. In this transformative process, that which is deemed religious or sacred may be altered to solve problems of action in people's lives.

As Riis and Woodhead (2010: 95) explain,

> Dialectics refer to formative two-way processes in which the *realta* are affected and shaped by the relation. An implication here is that novel processes emerge from the interaction of the parts that are irreducible to those

parts. This is more than mere "interaction" and covers more than mutual actions between agents: it also embraces relations between agents, community, and symbols. Dialectical relations form an entity, which is something more than the sum of its parts.

Couples reflect on their expectations of marriage, their social imaginaries of a shared future together, and the realities of their lived experiences of sacred marriages. At the same time, religious meanings direct couples in canalizing their experiences towards shared expectations by ordering the way they think, feel, talk, and act into new cultural strategies of action. Religion can bring approved emotions and discourses to the forefront, clarify which emotions and discourses should be suppressed and form collective social agency through religious transcendence constituted from everyday experiences. These social processes often go unrecognized and are articulated as supernatural intervention, when they are in fact examples of the couple's collective social agency. While most of the couples I interviewed attributed supernatural intervention in their lives to God, supernatural intervention was also attributed to the secular sphere in references people made to "luck," "fate," "karma," "destiny," and "Mother Nature." This suggests that the sources of perceived supernatural intervention in sacred marriages exist through the discursive blending of religious and secular spheres framed within culture.

While many couples attributed the longevity of their marriages to supernatural intervention, religious emotional regimes played a significant role in the continuance of their marriages. In the remainder of this chapter, I offer examples of couples who experienced religious dissonance in their marriages and the effects religious emotional regimes had on transformative processes that promoted the continuation of their marriages.

Providing support

Lance and Emily took me to a small den in their home where they sit together on a love seat during their shared daily devotions at the beginning of almost every day. They have created a sacred space within their home where they pray together, read scripture out loud together, and take turns reading from various religious books ranging from Bible study texts, to prayer books, to daily devotional guides. They pray about "everything that happens in our family." The room takes on special meaning as a sanctuary from the quotidian, secular aspects of their lives, although it is filled with mundane, secular objects. For both Lance and Emily, these shared experiences have a biography of their own beyond that of the experiences themselves. Emily intertwined her stories about her family and marriage with references to kneeling in prayer with her husband by the coffee table in front of the love seat upon which we sat when their son was almost killed in a motorcycle accident, when their daughter was in labor with their grandchild who was in a breech position, and when they read together about coping with infidelity when Lance's brother "cheated on his wife," so they could "give godly counsel to them."

More than simply discrete expressions of dyadic religiosity, these experiences took on sacred meanings for both Lance and Emily. The communication between them and the feelings they shared during these moments in this room took on a transcendent reality of its own beyond the experiences themselves. These shared experiences enhanced their personal and collective associations and are the basis for a litany of shared memories and sacred meanings in which they organize their agency as individuals and as a couple. They, like many couples in this study, organized the choices they made using religious language. In so doing, their actions took on sacred meanings and understandings they asserted were beyond their own choices.

They believed the decisions they made together as a couple were no longer of their own volition but rather the result of God's intervention in their lives because of their shared dyadic religiosity. As an example, they believed their decision not to allow their sister-in-law to move into their home with her children after Lance's brother's infidelity was "God's will" because they prayed together about their decision and studied religious texts about infidelity. Lance was convinced, "That's what God wanted. Otherwise, we'd have loved to take them in. But that wasn't God's plan."

The power of religious emotional regimes in their marriage played a salient role as a transformative process in the continuation of their marriage and their perception of supernatural intervention in the face of their exhibited collective social agency. Lance and Emily modified cultural expectations of supporting their sister-in-law as a means of solving a problem of action when Lance's brother engaged in extramarital sex. While Lance and Emily wanted to support their sister-in-law, they did not want to play a direct role in the dissolution of a marriage because they believe marriage is sacred. Recognizing the conflict that could arise between them and with their extended family, they reframed their collective decision as supernatural intervention. In so doing, they were able to accept religious culture while rejecting cultural scripts suggesting they help their sister-in-law by discursively constructing their collective social agency as supernatural intervention. At the same time, they suppressed their agency as individuals.

Parenting

While the focus in contemporary sociology of culture lies in the importance of strategies of action associated with people's cultural repertoires, inaction is also a form of social agency. Often, couples faced what they felt were insurmountable challenges, and they almost always turned to religion in the broadest sense of the word to adapt to these challenges. Many couples shared that the greatest sources of conflict in their marriage stemmed from differences about parenting. Frequently, couples described situations with their children in which they turned to religion for guidance. In these cases, couples struggled with finding solutions and ended up doing little to nothing to actually resolve their problems. Instead, as Cyrus, a retired Methodist construction worker said, "We put our kids in God's hands and things just turned out – sometimes good and sometimes bad." In their retrospective accounts, self-blame for working too much, being too involved in church activities, not being directly involved in youth group activities to know what their children were being taught or experiencing, and generally feeling inadequate at times as parents were common elements of the stories these couples shared.

Many couples dealt with feelings of shame and failure at times as parents through their belief that their dyadic religiosity produced supernatural interventions in their lives. As they described "God's will" and "God's plan" using religious discourse comingled with secular advice from secular marriage counseling books or stories from people they knew, they often stressed the importance of their shared religious experiences as a means by which they claimed they took no actions through phrases like "let go and let God." It was their shared faith, attendance and involvement in their churches, and shared prayers that they argued were indirect means of being involved as "good Christians" while still "staying out of God's way" to solve their problems of action. The underlying theme in their narratives was that through reliance on individual and dyadic religious practices they yielded to supernatural forces beyond their control. Despite their claims of not understanding these forces, there was a sensate aspect to invoking these sacred interventions in their narratives that brought them a "sense of peace and calm" in their shared knowledge that what they perceived as an insurmountable challenge was "in God's hands."

Randy and Betty are Lutherans who have been married 52 years and their narratives illustrate the impact of collective agency in their sacred marriage. They have three adult children, two boys and a girl. All three of their children have experienced at least one divorce and a remarriage and relationships outside of marriage that have resulted in children. Their daughter is in her fourth marriage. Randy described raising his children as teenagers as "a living hell." One son almost died due to an overdose, another was convicted of rape, and their daughter was pregnant at 16. Their children's lives remained complicated as adults, and their grandchildren have experienced multiple family disruptions. Their daughter and her three children now live with them, and they have not been able to realize their retirement dream of traveling the country visiting their children in a recreational vehicle because they cannot sell their home or their daughter and their grandchildren will have nowhere to live.

Like many couples I interviewed, Randy and Betty indicated that they learned most of what they knew about marriage from their parents and not from their church. They attended church most Sundays, but otherwise were relatively uninvolved. They described a sense of shame and inadequacy as parents as their children aged, and when they attended church services and activities they said there was a heightening of these feelings. They shared numerous hypothetical situations in which they could have acted differently as parents in hopes of better outcomes for their children and grandchildren. But they are fervent in their resolve that the events of their children's lives were beyond their control as parents, and they framed their experience as parents in their "steadfast belief in God's plan." They share a faith that they believe has sustained them through the most difficult times in their lives. Betty described the power of prayer and shared faith as a quintessential element of sacred marriages.

> The thing that holds us together is faith. [. . .] How do you deal when a child comes home? How do you deal when you're raising your grandkids? [. . .] I think religion and faith is the most important thing in a marriage. And if you marry somebody like that you are working together. If you're marrying someone who doesn't want to work together, it's just easy to say, "Don't worry. It'll be okay." But no, you can't take care of it. You both have to work together in that strong faith together. That's what's kept us together. If we didn't have our faith, I don't know what we'd do. [. . .] And we both have common faith. When things get rough [Randy] just always says all we can do is pray about it. And that makes me remember too. [. . .] When we had it hard with the kids, he just said to me, "You know you can't do anything about it, so don't worry about it. Just pray about it, and let God take care of it."

Randy echoed Betty's sentiments about prayer and shared faith, but shifted the focus to his own responsibility as a parent.

> The secret is that you have to work together and stay in your faith and pray. You got to pray a lot. It all goes back to the values of what you think is right and wrong, and you learned that from your parents. I had my plans for raising the kids, and they weren't the same as Betty's plans. We prayed about it, and God did what was right. Thinking back, we could have done things differently as parents.

Betty interrupted, "But that wasn't God's plan. All we can do is pray and let his will be done. All these kids have to make their own way in life. It's not what God wanted. We stayed in our faith together and let God work in their lives."

While Randy and Betty's narratives relates to their experiences of parenting, several couples identified what they perceived to be weaknesses or mistakes they made in their relationships as supernatural interventions unrelated to parenting practices. While all the challenges people felt they could have "handled differently" that threatened their marriages are too numerous to list here, and they were sometimes not specified by participants, some examples include drug and alcohol addictions, a motorcycle accident, loss of employment, berating a spouse, infidelity, mood swings due to menopause, excessive spending of shared money, and lying to a spouse. The specific challenges people faced are less important here than the power of religious emotional regimes to externally organize the way they thought, talked, felt, and acted. In the face of these challenges, often they did not talk or act, which many claimed exacerbated the distress caused by the challenges they faced. Their discursive construction of new or modified sacred marriages in which they legitimized and normalized their own social agency as supernatural intervention allowed them to use religion as a transformational process to promote self-regulation and continuation of their marriage.

Prayer

Shared prayer can be an important reinforcer of religious emotional regimes couples use to sacralize their marriages. The manuals suggest that shared prayer is necessary to strengthen contemporary, fragile marriages.

> When people marry, they have the choice of building a union that is as flimsy and collapsible as a straw house or as strong and sturdy as a brick edifice. But even a structure made of bricks cannot stand for long if the builders don't use mortar and cement to hold it together and support it. This is what shared payer can be in your life – the mortar that holds together the bricks of love, understanding, and concern for one another. Shared prayer is often the cement that gives a relationship foundation that makes it strong, solid, and enduring.
>
> (Bartkowski 1989: 8)

The manuals suggest that shared prayer promotes dialog between spouses, effectively sacralizing communication in their marriages.

> Couples who pray together often find that their prayers become more than just conversations with God. The prayers become a means of communicating for the couple. The prayers act as windows through which husband and wife can see each other's needs and desires. Shared prayers serve as doors opening the way to the sharing of each other's hopes, concerns, and dreams. The prayers in this book can help make it easier for a couple to pray aloud together and can promote a more open and expressive sharing of attitudes and feelings. Such sharing can lead to better understanding between spouses and also to deeper insight into each partner's responsibility in building a successful relationship that includes God as a third partner.
>
> (Bartkowski 1989: 7)

Some of the couples I interviewed shared stories of disagreements and compromises they felt they "had to make" because of shared prayer. In the case of Angie and Ben, their prayer life was an essential component of their early marriage. They are Methodists who prayed separately, prayed together, prayed publicly at prayer meetings at their church, and they hosted Bible studies and prayer groups in their home and attended similar prayer groups at the homes of others. They have known each other since childhood and were raised in the same church and attended the same schools. They married the summer they graduated high school, and other than Ben's military service, they have never been apart since they married. Soon after they married, they traveled to Washington, DC, for a week-long prayer event where "thousands of people" met and spent the week praying for "the future of this country and its leaders." As I left their home at the conclusion of my interviews, they told me they would be praying for me and the success of my study.

Their experiences of shared prayers have not always been positive. A few years into their marriage, they disagreed about the content of public prayers. At one public prayer meeting, the husbands separated from the wives, and each group took turns praying out loud for their spouses in the other group. They were praying on opposite ends of the church sanctuary, but, if they listened closely, they could hear the prayers of the other group. During his prayer, Angie overheard Ben praying publicly about something she felt was private between them. She felt betrayed.

When I asked her about where she got her ideas about marriage during her childhood, she shared her early interest in romance novels and romantic movies. She was drawn to story lines in which men were chivalrous, protectors, and providers for objects of their love.

"I always wanted a godly husband who would take care of me and make me feel safe," she said.

Angie embraced a culture that aligned masculinity with intimacy and protection. Ben's prayer was, therefore, particularly hurtful because it occurred in a "sacred place" and with "sacred words more powerful than any words man can speak," according to Angie.

From Ben's perspective, he failed as the religious leader of his family. "We never really recovered from it." He explained he was trying to be a good husband and "lift Angie up" in his prayers to "support her through something difficult in her life. [. . .] I never thought in a million years that what I was praying about was that personal."

"Do you regret the prayer?" I asked.

"I regret the hurt it caused, and in hindsight I would never have said that prayer at a prayer meeting. But, no, I don't regret the prayer itself. I just didn't know it was such a private matter to her," Ben replied.

Although they have "moved past" Ben's prayer, it was obvious they still negotiate feelings of betrayal and guilt in their marriage of 54 years as evidenced by their unwillingness to share the topic of the prayer with me, and each prefacing the sharing of the story with me during their individual interviews by insisting that I not mention it to the other spouse. They did not raise the topic during their interview together.

The example of Angie and Ben is illustrative of several couples' stories of the subjugating of cultural scripts by religious emotional regimes through shared religiosity that ultimately proved stressful in their marriage. While Ben embraced a religious discourse and culture of his role as religious leader of the household who was responsible for supporting his wife through prayer, Angie valued a culture of romantic love in which intimacy and the privatization of interactions and communications remains within the marriage. Sometimes, couples struggled with the negotiation of religious emotional regimes within their sacred marriages and the subjugation of one religious emotional regime in favor of another was at the core of the dissonance.

The religious dissonance Angie and Ben experienced was not necessarily harmful to their marriage. While the scholarship of religion and marriage frequently calls for further research into the negative influences of religion in marriage, framing religious experiences as negative or positive promotes a power discourse that judges the lived experiences of religion in people's lives. While Angie and Ben both felt badly about their experience of that one shared prayer, they continue to pray together in their sacred marriage. What did happen was that they and their relationship were changed. They experienced changes in how they felt, talked, acted, and thought about prayer in their marriage that led to modifications of the way they communicated in their marriage, producing altered cultural repertoires of religion in their sacred marriage. Marriage is no less sacred to them, and their marriage did not end. Their relationship changed, but they do not moralize the change as either good or bad. Rather than reinforcing a power discourse that moralizes religion's influences in sacred marriage, I turn to an examination of associations in religion that influence transformative processes in sacred marriages.

Associations in religion

While the sociology of culture has made tremendous gains, it is important not to reify culture as an object. Culture is constituted through discourse. It is not an external reality; rather, it is the result of academic discourse and the academic categorization of that which is and is not culture. Culture is reproduced through discourse that regulates ways of taking, thinking, feeling, and acting towards the experiences of humanity. In contrast, emotions can be real, and couples' relation to their sacred marriages have a dialectical character that unfolds in their strategies of action. Rather than thinking of individuals interacting with an external social institution called religion, the people I interviewed expressed a lived experience of religion in which they merged cultural schema and scripts as husbands and wives, sons and daughters, and fathers and mothers with religion through dialectical bonds between objectification and subjectification within their sacred marriages. The people in this study each ascribed unique meanings to religion's influences in their marriage, but they all shared in religious associations and sacred meanings they associate with their marriages. It is not the meaning itself that is of paramount importance in religion's effects in marriages, but rather it is the shared associations between religion and marriage that matter most. These associations between sensate emotions, social emotions, unique sociocultural histories, and cultures are the basis of the unique plasticity in sacred marriages that orders transformative processes.

The shared associations people have in common within all sacred marriages are part of religious culture and are transmitted among members of groups through discourse. People are emotionally tied to these shared associations and react in similar ways when they observe religion's influence in their lives and relationships. This shared emotional response to religion's potential effects in their lives and relationships promotes an emotional bond that grows when it supports the ordering of their experiences in ways they construct as sacred in the ways they talk, feel, think, and act in their sacred marriages.

At the outset of this study, I wanted to examine how religion effects marriage. Like any sociological study, I began looking for direct variables and indirect variables in an attempt to seek causation. What I found is that it is the associations people share between variables that gives religion its power and sacred meanings in their marriages. A reductionist perspective fails us in the examination of religion's influences on marriages because religion is more than the sum of its parts.

To illustrate this concept, consider attending a concert. I have often been emotionally affected by a symphony. Aficionados, of which I am not, know the qualities of a good performance and the physical structures that produce the best sound quality. They know when to applaud a performance and when not to clap as the music transitions from one movement to another through social cues like the placement of the conductor's hands and baton. They feel the movement of the music as it moves from the clarinets to the flutes and from the trumpets to the trombones. They sense the rhythm of the beat in the percussion without any one section of the symphony overwhelming another. But the power of the music is not in one violinist's hand or bow or violin any more than it resides in the mouthpiece or spit valve of a tuba. The power of the music to move people emotionally and influence the way we talk, think, feel, and act before, during, and after the performance lies in the associations they share with others. Everything from parking, to refreshments, to the comfort of the seats becomes associated with the performance. Music can be transcendent experiences evoking emotion in response to the *Hallelujah Chorus*, or when memories of attending previous concerts with deceased love ones evoke simultaneous feelings of joy and loss.

Similarly, individual spouses may disagree about religious interpretations, meanings, Church teachings, and even sacred meanings, yet still find tremendous power in religion in their marriages. While they each approach religion in a unique way, they share in the associations inherent in religion found in the past, present, and perceived future. It is the associations between the constitutive elements of religion that matter. There is no guarantee that religion will have power in marriages, and that power may be more effective at certain times in couples' lives. Just as music has different influences on different people, the shared associations in sacred marriages will have different effects in transformative processes in different marriages.

Each newlywed sacred marriage begins anew with its own unique future, but it shares patterns of similarity with other sacred marriages in the past. Each couple must fulfill the need to make sense of their marriage and find security and comfort in the face of changes. Cultural tools provide people the resources to discursively construct their sacred marriages, not from scratch, but from existing religious meanings and understandings existing as pre-fabricated links within the religious and secular spheres from which they are drawn. But cultural tools are discursively constructed and shaped based on what is meaningful and valued in each sacred marriage. Rather than definitely and externally limiting people's individual and collective agency in sacred marriages, religious discourse and religious culture offer strategies of action towards the production of other ways of being, serving specific social contexts. As people face problems of action in their sacred marriages, they engage in an endless production of meanings to the strategies of action they pursue. It is a never-ending ordering of the ways they talk, feel, think, and act. Thus, committing to supernatural intervention is a means by which people commit to a particular way of ordering meanings in sacred marriages. When religious dissonance exists in sacred marriages, there is a disordering of meanings eliciting masked collective agency of the couple through which they construct a new ordering of meanings based on compromises that produce new and altered realities of their problems of action. Religious dissonance is therefore neither good nor bad for sacred marriages. Instead, religious dissonance requires compromises that are the basis of the production of new and altered meanings in sacred marriages that can serve as transformative processes to overcome stressors.

Masking agency in lived experiences

Religion is not a dichotomous objective reality that stands against the secular world (Green and Searle-Chatterjee 2008). Instead, religion is discursively constructed from the resources found in culture which are embedded in power discourses. Much of religious discourse (e.g., sacred texts, stories, and iconography) is labeled as passive sources of religious knowledge that shed light on sacred meanings as bridges between this world and the other worldly. But religious discourse and religious culture have power to move in people's social worlds and to reshape them. Religious discourse amplifies voices at the centers of power in relationships that influence practices and approved and accepted meanings. These voices legitimize supernatural interventions as separate from individual and collective social agency. Given the power of religious discourse, people begin to expect and look for supernatural interventions to belong and continue belonging to the religious communities to which they aspire. By silencing alternative discourses and meanings, individual and collective agency can be masked. Supernatural interventions are one means of silencing competing discourses and agency through power relationships embedded in religious discourse and culture in sacred marriages to help reclassify and link experiences couples face into new versions of reality that mask competing realities.

7 Belonging

Beyond the obvious selection effect – I only interviewed couples who were married 40 years or more – the couples in this study exhibited a strongly pro-marriage culture. Almost all of the couples in this study married by the time they were 22, and most of them married by the age of 19. The presence of this pro-marriage culture is, at least in part, due to a generational effect and the intergenerational transmission of a pro-marriage culture from the study participants' parents' generation which was highly pro-marriage (Elder 1999). And while many couples expressed differences of opinion with Church teachings in different aspects of religious culture, few participants favored non-marriage relationship structures to marriage. Given these characteristics, coupled with their belief that marriage is sacred for religious reasons, it is not surprising that the couples in this study highly value marriage as an institution. Their pro-marriage stance supports many of their perceptions that adherence to "God's will" through prescriptive religious behaviors concerning marriage resulted in what they believe are "blessings" in their relationship and families. In this chapter I examine perceptions of the links between couples' religious adherence and their perceptions of outcomes in their marriages and families.

Marriage formation

There are both secular and religious cultural expectations for people to marry, especially during the period that most of the couples in this study were dating. The manuals describe preferences for singlehood as "selfish" and an "inability to love." According to Wrona (2004), there is not only an expectation for most people to marry, but God chooses whom one should marry. Given the importance of the expectation to marry for the couples in this study, many felt that their decision to marry was the first act in the formation of their sacred marriages. They described the decision to marry as not only an expectation of entering into adulthood, but a form of obedience to religious teachings. They juxtaposed their decision to marry against "living together," "the risk" of participating in premarital sex during their courtship, or "tempting God" that a woman might become pregnant before marriage.

While the men overwhelmingly favored marriage, their reasons for marrying often differed from the women I interviewed. Some men described what one husband referred to as "strictly sex within marriage," by which he was referring to a culture in which sexual relationships should occur exclusively within marriage. One husband from a rural community of only a few dozen people explained that, "You didn't dare have sex without being married. Everyone in town would have known." Another husband was blunt: "I married for the same reason any man does: sex!" But, most men described their decision to marry as a matter of what they perceived to be a normal process, not recognizing the influence of cultural hegemony in their lives. Marriage was less an achieved status but more an ascribed status to which they did not object. To them, marriage was a taken-for-granted expectation no different than graduating high school, enter the workforce or military, and eventually having children. There was no sense of urgency to marry in most men's narratives, and they were more likely to describe their decision to marry in terms of a logical outcome of courtship related to approved dating practices (e.g., dancing with enough room for the "Holy Ghost" between the couple), school and church-sponsored venues for dating (e.g., roller rinks and sporting events), and within group mate selection (e.g., social class distinctions and religious denomination homogeneity).

Several men described their decision to marry almost as though it were beyond their control and the purview of the woman they were dating accepting their proposal followed by the woman's parents' giving approval to marry. Men often described themselves as shy, quiet, or as one man put it, "just dating around when she found me." Some men claimed they "didn't know much about girls," that they "never really dated," or that they were "naïve about women in general," having attended seminary, all-boys Catholic schools, or having been raised in rural areas on farms where they had little interaction with girls.

Although George's case may appear extreme due to his physical disability, the feelings he expressed about his inadequacies to communicate with women echo many husbands' experiences. George and Anne are retired foreign language professors.

> I knew I wanted to marry Anne because she was marvelous. First of all, she shared my interest in Portuguese. She was truly dedicated to the study of Portuguese. To be able to talk to somebody about what it is that you are interested in is, from my point of view, a really attractive feature. To be able to communicate about intellectual things where both parties are well-informed about the area of discussion, it's not like I know a little bit about this or a little bit about that, but we can always talk about Portuguese. We were also in courses together at the same time and studied the same things in graduate school.
>
> [. . .]
>
> I always thought that it was rather serendipitous that a very good-looking woman like that would be interested in a rather plain person like me who was also a uniplegic gimp. That doesn't seem right, but who am I to say.

Somebody is making this happen. We just seem to hit it off in every respect. But the bottom line was that we had common interests right from the beginning. It's not like I had to find some area of interest that the two of us could share. I really didn't know anything about anything else other than Portuguese. Who knows why she married me?

For wives, the pro-marriage and pro-motherhood culture was particularly prominent, and a clear process of socializing girls to value a culture of marriage and motherhood was evident in their stories. There was no question in the minds of many of the women I interviewed that they would be wives and mothers. Although some couples adopted children when they were unable to bear children or when they preferred adoption over biological childbearing, the wives in this study clearly valued marriage and motherhood. Almost all of the couples in this study had multiple children rather than having only one child, and only one couple had no children.

Mary, a Methodist housewife who never worked with any regularity outside the home for pay, described the socialization process associated with the culture of marriage and motherhood for women in her generation with the following story.

Some people want careers, but all I ever wanted was to have a happy home with a good husband and kids. That's just what everybody did back then. It was the inevitable back then. It was just the pattern of life. My family may have had more influence on me than I realize because I don't know why I think what I did. I think it just came from observing other people and knowing that I wanted to be happy. I read a lot of magazines about marriage. Through high school, if I saw a marriage article – this is weird – I cut it out. And I started a file on just good things that I wanted to take with me into my marriage and my family. I don't know if other girls did that. I thought I would need some help along the way. That really was a goal for me, to have a happy home.

Several wives described a socialization process within the culture of marriage and motherhood in similar terms. Daisy is a retired bank teller who attends a nondenominational church. In her narrative she intertwines elite religious discourse with the culture of marriage and motherhood that was prominent in her generation. Her first words on the topic of religion and marriage are a rejection of singlehood.

Some of these women are selfish and just want to do what they want to do on their time and their terms. I never gave up a thing to be married. It's what I had chosen. It's just what I always wanted to do. I never regretted a minute of being married or having kids. When I was growing up there were so many other people around to learn from – good solid families – and to communicate with them. We had dances. We had church. We had school. We were around a lot more people. I think that rubbed off. You learn how to be a wife and a mother. You learn how to be a family.

[. . .]

I don't expect anything for my husband because something or some area belongs to me. It's all ours together. It's our story, not my story or not his story. It's our story. God didn't make us to be alone. He created Eve as a help-mate to Adam. It's like you're not whole as a woman until you get married. That's God's plan, and it's what you saw when I was a kid in all the families.

Several women described their decisions to marry their specific husbands as the result of "God's plan." One Catholic couple, Sid and Linda, explained that after growing up in the same parish, then going their separate ways through college and their early adulthood, they returned to the same parish to be closer to family. Then, through the intervention of their extended families, they were provided the opportunity to begin dating. Eventually, they married. Both Sid and Linda described these events as a natural progression of "God's plan" for them, although they were "unaware of his plan" at the time. They organize events leading up to their marriage within religious and sacred meanings by silencing and masking social forces.

One of the most pronounced descriptions of "God's plan" to marry someone is found in Claire's description of the moment she first knew for certain she wanted to marry Earl through a "miracle." Claire is a retired nurse who is Catholic. Throughout her narrative she shared stories of her "love for the iconography" and the "beauty of Catholic churches." She and Earl have traveled to many countries to see Catholic churches and religious icons in their 45 years of marriage. Claire has a strong personality and was rarely equivocal in her responses to my questions. Claire was an only child after her mother had five miscarriages. She was raised with her parents and grandparents in the same home due to her grandmother's stroke. Claire claimed she felt no pressure to marry or have children, which she attributed to the number of miscarriages her parents experienced. Her mother was Catholic but was "not a believer." Although Claire's mother rarely attended church, "she made sure dad and I were always ready Sunday mornings." Claire engaged in marriage and motherhood planning early in her teenage years. "I'm a list maker" she explained.

I didn't want what my parents had. I wanted someone who was Catholic. I married with a list in mind. I wanted someone of the same faith. I wanted someone smart, moral, and ethical. I really went into relationships with my little list.

[. . .]

I knew Earl was the man for me when we had gone out with his mom one time. We had a great time. We took mom home. He walked around the car, and I saw a halo around him. It was probably just a light from somewhere, but I actually saw a halo around him. There was no doubt in my mind then, he was the one for me. That was definitely a confirmation for me.

"Do you believe God put a halo on Earl?" I asked.

"It's all the same. It doesn't matter where the light came from, God made that halo. He chose Earl for me, and that halo was a bona fide miracle. It was a sacred sign. I knew I had to marry him," she said.

While Claire recognizes that some light source created the effect of a halo on Earl's head, she is convinced that the timing of the light shining around Earl's head was supra-human. Religious discourse allows people to ascribe religious meanings to events in their everyday lives. Through this combining of scripts, they are able to talk, feel, and think about marriage in terms of religious discourse that incorporate the transcendent. They are sometimes unaware of the conflicts in their narratives, but at other times they are keenly aware of these irrationalities and inconsistencies. Religious discourse can organize and give sacred meanings to these conflicting narratives because religious culture embraces the concept that "God's plan is beyond human understanding. That's why we need faith," as one husband explained.

A culture of family

Some of the couples I interviewed, although they represent only a small minority of the sample overall, shared stories of their lived experiences of religion in their marriage and family that directly paralleled elite religious discourse in which they purported to have attained culturally and religiously expected positive outcomes in their lives. Their narratives were filled with loving relationships that began in their childhood with large, supportive, extended families. They differed from other couples, in that they organized their family lives around religious involvement. They were typically well-versed in various religious scripts and scripted religious language about sacred marriages. They drew on their experiences to reflexively construct and employ religious regimes. For example, they volunteered in soup kitchens and clothing banks, listened to religious radio, watched religious television programming, actively engaged in committees in their churches, served in leadership positions in their churches, and taught and mentored younger couples in their churches.

Their involvement represents both social and physical spaces in which religious discourse, religious culture, and religious emotional regimes are practiced. They had some of the highest exposure to elite religious discourse and communities that extolled the benefits of religious culture. They were often involved in the production of elite religious discourse and religious cultural practices. Some served as lay speakers in their churches. Some helped write marriage counseling and pre-marriage counseling workbooks. One couple wrote a blog with thousands of followers. And, another husband and wife host a talk radio program about marriage and family issues on a local "Christian radio station."

At the outset of this study, consistent with the sociological paradigm of *seeking* religion's effects in people's lives, my focus was on identifying where religion existed in the everyday lived experiences of the people I interviewed and the texts I analyzed. What became apparent was that for this small group of couples, who exhibited some of the most outwardly successful marriages and families, there was little separation between religious and nonreligious spheres. For these couples, their religious social worlds and secular social worlds were interwoven and informed each other.

For example, Kathleen and Wayne have been married for 48 years. They have 12 children. They grew up in the same Catholic parish a few doors down from each other in large Catholic families. They, and their siblings, played together in the park across the street as children. She became a nurse, and he worked for the city. They both have siblings who became Catholic priests, Catholic Brothers, and Catholic Sisters. Their religious lives are monitored by their adult children and extended families, and they likewise monitor the religious lives of each other, their children's families, and their friends and extended families. By monitoring, I am referring to what Kathleen referred to as "checking in on how they're doing in their faith." They ask others about attendance at church. They ask others about their prayer lives. They are overt in their involvement in the religious lives of the people they know, and they expect others to question them and be overtly involved in their religious lives as well.

Kathleen and Wayne are not unique in their monitoring behaviors. Noah, a Protestant husband, referred to this monitoring process as a "command" by quoting a passage of scripture. "You use steel to sharpen steel, and one friend sharpens another. Proverbs 27:17," he proclaimed. Most of the couples in this study sought connections to the larger body of "the faithful," as Ruth put it, and wanted others, especially family and friends, to know why they missed church, why they missed a Bible study, or why they were not participating in various church-sponsored activities.

Almost all of Kathleen and Wayne's immediate and extended family attended the same parish they did. Every Sunday after mass, their house was filled with children. Their garage was stacked from ceiling to floor with outdoor toys, games, and bicycles for the over 50 grandchildren and great-grandchildren that came to brunch every Sunday. Even when Wayne was hospitalized and Kathleen stayed with him, their children brought their families to the house and the adults took turns visiting Wayne while their siblings cared for the younger children.

Both Kathleen and Wayne used the word "faithfully" when they described the integration of religion into the ways they acted, talked, felt, and thought about their sacred marriage. Their social imaginaries of a shared future together began in childhood and was premised on a culture of marriage and familism organized in religious culture.

When I asked Kathleen to explain how religion shaped her understanding of marriage, she shared the following:

> I always knew that I would get married and have children. I got that idea from my aunts, and my uncles, and my cousins, and my parents, and my grandparents. I think that's where the background was. It was definitely not movies, or television, or books, or magazines or anything like that. [. . .] The priest knew Wayne and I all our lives, so he wasn't going to feel bad about marrying us.

You know what I mean? In those days you got married in your parish by your parish priest. Monsignor Alfred had known us for years, and years, and years. So he knew us very well through all those years.

[. . .]

I've known my husband my whole life. We dated about five years. We enjoyed the same people when we were dating. A lot of the things we did were with the youth program. It was a group of friends that did a lot of things through the Cathedral with father Stan Laramie. Within that same group one would be dating one and pretty soon another one would be dating one within that group.

[. . .]

They were just all from the same Catholic background. I was never thinking 12 children. We always said, even when we were dating, that we would have 12 kids as a joke. I think the Lord took us for our word.

[. . .]

You asked about how religion influences marriage, but that's not how I see it. The Church doesn't support marriage. Marriage supports the Church. That's God's plan and why we need to make sure we're teaching these kids about God's plan for their marriage and how to make it work.

[. . .]

You have to pick out somebody to look up to, to direct you as a role model. We have had role models. My parents were Catholic and married 50 years and so were Wayne's. It's not like we had to look very far to see God's hand in things.

Rather than offering a retrospective account – like Kathleen's response – to my question about religion's influence on marriage, Wayne shared the following:

I don't know whether it's God smiling on us because we've made religion a part of our life. I can't commit to that because there are people like us who are not blessed like we are. I stopped saying that you can have this too. I don't know why it works so well. Our kids are all in town. They come back every Sunday for brunch. And nobody could plan that.

[. . .]

I decided I would just do what I could, say my prayers, and turn it over to God, and let him figure it out. That has helped me through a lot of things. That's one thing we have taught all the kids. Any time they come to us with an issue, we say spend some time in the chapel; get it worked out. Put your time and effort into it saying your prayers, and after you have done that there is nothing more you can do. So, just relax and be comfortable. It may not be what you thought it was going to be, but it's going to work out. It really does.

The couples I have described so far in this chapter claim to be blessed, although in general they do not know why they are blessed, what they did to be blessed, or why others have not been blessed. While they attributed their successes to the effects of religion in their marriages and families, they could not articulate why they were blessed when others were not. In general, they described mundane events that are not particularly religious. They dated. They married. They had children. They enjoyed time with family and friends. There is nothing uniquely religious about these mundane activities that many people experienced without giving them religious meanings. Even they, while claiming divine blessings in their lives, attribute their successes to positive role models of strong marriages and families as children, the pro-marriage politic in which they were raised, and shared interests in married lives together raising children – none of which required supernatural intervention or organized religion. These couples were able to use religious culture and religious discourse to frame their lives through stories that support their experiences. They were able to embrace religious traditions and assimilate them into new ways of being while facing life's challenges. That was not the case for all the families in this study. In fact, one family in particular experienced significant separations due to changes in religious discourse and religious practice. By examining the struggles they faced, the effects of religion in their sacred marriage becomes more evident.

Utility of religious culture in sacred marriages

Neither religious discourse nor religious culture remains constant. In the following example, I describe the influence that changes in Catholic discourse and Catholic cultural scripts associated with the Second Vatican Council had on one family in this study. "Vatican II was a uniquely Catholic experience in the mid-1960s; no other American faith group experienced the anticipation, formulation, and implementation of such drastic changes" (Davidson et al 1997: 116). Vatican II represented a shift in the Church's place in the world. "The council initiated dramatic changes in Catholic religious practice, most of which were on display at mass every Sunday morning" (O'Toole 2008: 199). The discontinuity and incongruence in the acceptance of this altered religious discourse and the new religious scripts that Vatican II effected, changed family relationships and shaped the marriage and family of Gary and Marie. From an analytic perspective, the question is not simply whether changes in religious discourse and religious culture produced changes in their sacred marriage – they did – but rather, what are the processes by which these changes occurred?

Gary and Marie were one of the most outwardly devout couples I interviewed. They had a life-sized carving of a crucifix in their front yard. A large, old tree had been struck by lightning and they commissioned a local chainsaw artist to carve the crucifix into the remaining vertical trunk and two large, horizontal branches. The artist used a clear stain on the carving and accented the crown of thorns and wound in Christ's side with a dark stain to represent blood. The carving was visible in most of their open-concept home through a large picture window.

Gary and Marie are the eldest children in large Catholic families and were born in the mid-1940s. Gary spent seven years in a cloistered seminary preparing for the priesthood after high school, and Marie spent four years in a cloistered convent preparing for life as a nun. They and their elder siblings were raised in the Catholic Church before Vatican II. Marie indicated her parents and siblings adjusted to the changes associated with the practice of Catholicism related to the Second Vatican Council "without any trouble."

But, Gary said, "It tore my family apart. In effect, it created three families that still can't get along, and it made everyone take sides like some kind of three-part civil war."

Gary's mother was vehemently opposed to the changes that occurred in the Church after Vatican II. After a lifetime of high involvement, she denounced Catholicism. Gary's father, on the other hand, insisted that the children continue to attend with him. Gary and three of his siblings continued to practice Catholicism just as they had prior to Vatican II. His father attended a parish that conducted services in Latin, they went to confession on Saturday, and they "stayed just like we were, as much as we could, even though the Church changed," according to Gary. Later, after some of his siblings were adults, Gary's father began attending what Gary referred to as a "schismatic Latin rite church." With the youngest children, Gary's father attended a mainstream Catholic parish. Gary described these events as follows:

> Us older kids were strong Catholic, and when mom and dad started to waver and drop off and join the schismatic church because of what the bishops were doing, the older ones have stayed solid Catholic. Some of the middle kids have no religion because mom and dad were wavering. Three or four of the younger ones joined the schismatic church. So you have three different religions in the family. They wavered in their attendance, their beliefs, their commitment. They flip-flopped and didn't have any strong beliefs in anything. Right now, one or two of my brothers and sisters have no religion. Two or three are of their own religion. Some are of the Latin group, but the rest of us older ones are still strong Catholic.

Gary later described the effects he perceived of the changes in the local parish that his parents attended on his relationships with them and his siblings.

> We mainly severed relationships with family due to terrible, terrible fights with mom and dad over religion. That severed our relationship with them. My brother and I made our faith very, very strong because we were fighting mom and dad in their beliefs. It is rock-solid hardened. The fights were about the authority of the Church to run things the way they want to. Mom and dad felt no. No, they did not have to believe in the authority of the church. That made us all the more firm in our beliefs and them more firm in their beliefs. We did not invite them to any of our religious activities like first communion.

We did not get invited to any of my brothers and sisters' religious activities either. Vatican II split our family apart terribly.

When I asked Gary about the effects of his strained family relationships on his marriage, he shared a story about his first kiss.

> I told you I was in seminary and Marie was in a convent right after high school. Neither of us had ever kissed anyone else. I hadn't officially proposed yet, but we both knew we'd get married. When I leaned in for that first kiss, I stopped myself. Marie looked really surprised. And I said, "I have to tell you something if we are going to get married. There was a division in my family, and I won't have that. If we raise our kids exactly the opposite of how I was raised, we will have a very normal family."

In Marie's interview, she raised the issue of Gary's split with his family over "religious differences." I asked about the impact Gary's views had on their religious life. She explained that they shared the same views about religion and faith as fellow Catholics, "so there was never a problem." Then, she paused, and began telling me about her childhood in a large, Catholic family with two parents who also came from large Catholic families.

> When we were growing up, we would spend one weekend a month in Cincinnati with my mom's family. And, we would spend a couple weeks in the summer visiting with my dad's family. That way, we got to see our grandparents and aunts and uncles. We went so often the car could go on its own. [Laughter].

Then she shared stories of her father falling asleep during long rosary services in their home. She talked about the photos she has of her and her siblings surrounded by extended family during important religious milestones. "I remember the incense and things for adoration and the blessed sacrament and how much that was an important part of my life and my family being together. Even the family in Cincinnati and Milwaukee came up for big things."

Then she explained the impact of the conflict on her and Gary.

> I had a very happy childhood. I thought I lived in a very normal family. I didn't realize how normal it was until I met my husband's family. We . . . just had a very normal family. My husband, on the other hand, had a lot of conflict in his family. You marry the whole family. Unfortunately, it comes that way. [Laughter].

> I loved his dad. If we could just go and visit his dad it was fine. But when his mother was there, well that was another thing. When we first started going, somehow the subject of religion would always come up. When it did, it would always cause conflict between my husband and his mother. So we would end

up leaving on a sour note. Then we would come home, and we would start arguing. Finally, we said this is not worth the hassle. So, we will either A) just not go over there, or B) if something does come up we're going to leave. That is what finally worked.

There were other things too. With his brothers and sisters, the younger ones, as soon as they would turn 18, they would move in with us because there was so much conflict with their mom. It was just in the strictness of being raised and some of the unrealistic things that were expected of them. They were expected to wear the long dresses and skirts even to school, even though they were in public school. They felt very odd. They had to where the veils to church. The conflict was mostly about religion but also about house-work and things.

[. . .]

Just trying to put things into perspective with his mom, I would say it was so foreign to me not to get along with his mom, especially where you grow up in a family that embraces your Catholic faith, and everything is just fine. Then you go to that extreme as our children was growing up that we never asked his parents to babysit, ever. And, they were not allowed to go over to their grandparents if we were not with them because of the religion issues. You have to pick and choose your battles, but for the sake of the marriage, that's the way we decided to do it.

Later in her interview, Marie offered an explanation for her children's divorces.

We have seven kids and four of them have divorced. What the Church tells you is how to get married. It doesn't tell you how to be married. Do you know what I mean? When it comes to knowing what love is everyone has lots of role models. You see how your parents love each other. You see how your grandparents loved each other. You see aunts and uncles and older cousins. You see your friends who are married and that love each other. So you have an idea what marriage is like and what love is like as opposed to the fairy book stories. I don't think it's a real rude awakening when you get married then.

Having God as part of your marriage is the most important thing. Without our faith there are days that I'm sure we would have said, "Forget it. I'm not going to do this anymore." But you know that you've got more behind it than just us because God is with us. God wants to work with us. We pray together, and I still think that's the biggest thing. Having God in your marriage, he's the third-party. He's the only one worth having. . . . you have to bring your kids up in your faith. For us, that meant being Catholic and living it. Even if it came at a cost with our family.

Entrenchment in the sacred

Wayne and Kathleen were most committed to their religious culture because their lived experiences of marriage and family reflected that culture. They found utility in religious scripts, religious rituals, and the power of their religious emotional regimes which supported their culture of familism. For them, religious discourse and religious culture provided solutions to their problems. In contrast, Gary's extended family held different and competing secular and religious cultures. Gary and Marie's experiences of religious discourse and religious culture did not fit their lived experiences of marriage and family. The differences in their religious cultures held little utility in solving their problems in their everyday lives. Gary and Marie drew upon religious traditions to find connections between their Catholic identity and their lived experiences. By changing the style of Catholic practice, they remade religious meanings within their marriage. They receded from a culture of family that highly values extended family relationships in favor of their preferred Catholic religious practices. They remained entrenched in Catholic tradition and rejected changes that their extended family supported.

The stories couples shared have to be examined in light of what people do with religion. While some of the couples in this study relied on a culture of theistic discourse to describe the influence of religion on marriage and family, their level of pursuing theistic discourse fluctuated drastically. They intermingle religious associations and mundane associations within their sacred marriages. They sought out religion's influences in their lives through the telling of their stories to themselves and to others, and thereby positioned outcomes of their marriage within an ordered hierarchy of cultural strategies of action. For most couples in this study, there are gaps between religious culture and their lived experiences. They did not abandon religion completely when faced with these gaps, but rather they drew more or less upon specific aspects of religion and other cultures to reconcile religious culture with their lived experiences, often modifying religious discourse and religious culture. Religion's effects in people's marriages fluctuated based on the utility of religious discourse and religious culture.

Eliciting religion in sacred marriages

Sacred marriages are not static, all-or-nothing forms that externally structure relationships. Rather, their importance in people's lives is based on social conditions and social contexts in which narratives are shared. Sacred marriages exist within a process in which people evaluate the utility of religious and nonreligious cultures in solving their problems, drawing from both disproportionately to solve their problems of action. Sacred marriages are social and as such are multistranded and intersectional. They are both sacred and secular at once, and the value of religion's effects in their telling is dependent on the social context in which they are shared.

For example, while George suggested that something supernatural drew him and Anne together, his rationale for their eventual marriage was a shared interest in the Portuguese language. Both Mary and Daisy held strong beliefs in gendered expectations for women of their generation to marry, have children, and be "housewives." While they described their fulfillment of these expectations as part of their religious experiences, they drew little on any supernatural explanations. Instead, they described the influence of the media and family in their decisions to marry and bear children. Kathleen and Wayne went so far as to suggest that the Church does not support marriage, but rather that marriage supports the Church. While their stories were filled with references to organized religion and divine intervention, they stressed no particular superhuman power in their decisions to marry and have large families in the stories they told. Instead, their decisions were based on their positive experiences of being raised in strong, large religious families. And, while Gary and Marie are devout Catholics, they are selective in which elements of religious discourse and religious culture they use in their sacred marriage.

Religion is not an outward source that produces effects in sacred marriages. Sacred marriages are overwhelmingly mundane. The stories people told me centered around everyday experiences of marriage and family life that could have happened to anyone, with or without religious context. Religion's influence on marriage does not exist in purely sacred spaces or religious contexts. Sacred marriages are secular marriages told in terms of religious discourse and religious culture. As a form of culture and discourse, religion writes on the subjectivities of actors and is rewritten by those actors. Sacred marriages are constructed through people's narratives of religion in which they highlight religion's influences to greater or lesser degrees based on social context. Sacred marriages are both sacred and secular at once, and the effects of religion in sacred marriage varies based on social context and who is listening to the stories people tell. Religion is most salient in people's lives when their religious identities are most valued by those with whom they are interacting at the time. Sacred marriages are produced in interaction, retold through religious discourse, and reworked into new sacred meanings and culture through subsequent interactions.

Religion provides people an ordered mechanism of interaction that is socially approved. Religious institutions and other organized settings provide people the opportunity to interact, to talk, to think, and to express feelings that are part of their mundane experiences of marriage but experienced through a lens of religion and the sacred. When people are more involved in these religious settings, they develop their religious acuity and learn to express themselves in religious ways, they also learn to listen to religious stories. They need not share in any specific doctrines for them to use religion to talk, think, feel, and act in ways that convey religious associations in their everyday experiences of marriage and family life. While religion's influence may not necessarily be consistently found in any one aspect of marriage or family, the dialectic associations within sacred marriages matter.

At the outset of this study, I intended to capture religion's influence on sacred marriages by using an extremely broad conceptualization of sacred as a construct. To that end, and in contrast to more psychological studies of sacred marriage premised on indexes and scales of people's perceptions of God's involvement in their lives, I included couples who agreed that marriage was sacred for religious reasons. What I discovered is that the selection criteria for inclusion in this study represented far less of an intellectual conviction that was well thought out and reasoned than an assent to a dominant culture of religion. Rather than expressing a considered, theological opinion, the couples who agreed to participate in this study were more likely attempting to align themselves with dominant cultural norms and position themselves within a religious community. Thus, when I encountered participants who were clearly atheists, who rarely referred to their religious beliefs or practices in the telling of their stories, and who openly argued that religion had little influence on the most salient elements of their enduring marriages, I ultimately realized that what I was originally perceiving as outliers were actually the presence of sociological forces at work. The power of religion cannot be measured in a linear fashion in which one more degree of religion results in one more degree of religious meaning or religious outcomes in sacred marriages. Instead, while religious meanings are important and the sacred is a powerful form of discourse that promulgates meanings, the true salience of the sacred is found in belonging.

Sacred marriages provide a social space in which people interact using their cultural repertoires and religious scripts with others who view marriage through a lens of religion and who share religious discourse, religious culture, and religious meanings. At the heart of that discourse is the acceptance of supernatural intervention. The devout are typically the most well-versed in the language of religion and are able to translate the mundane everyday experiences of marriage into shared religious meanings using a culture of religion, especially among others who are devout who listen for supernatural intervention in people's lives. Thus, the effects of religion on marriage lie not in a scale of objective absolutes, but rather in individual identities and the acceptance and mutual understandings of religious discourse based on social context and community.

The sacred is a means of interacting, of forming communities, of uniting disparate, fragmented cultural scripts and strategies of actions in ways that others will accept and embrace. Religion has the most effect in marriages and families when people are able to share their stories of their marriages and families with others who see marriage through the lens of the sacred. Thus, despite the many variations of religious practices, church teachings, and religious dogma, the sacred unifies people, brings competing religious doctrines together, and provides a social context in which people can bring strong emotions and ideologies together under a protective umbrella of acceptance. At the same time, this protective umbrella must be protected from intrusion if it is to remain powerful. It must sacralize the mundane in ways that order and structure strategies of action to exclude individual variation that might threaten the sacred.

Belonging to sacred marriages

The harm in sacralizing marriages lies in the perception of religious failure as a form of internal pathology rather than as a failure of discourse and culture. To explain this concept, I turn to the Christian marriage advice manuals. As a whole, these texts are self-help guides. They are intended to improve marriages and strengthen people's faith, commitment to marriage, and marital satisfaction and quality. But they are also defenders of the sacred. They actively suppress, minimize, and demonize that which threatens the sacred. In their construction of sacred marriages, they castigate and lambast changes in culture that challenge the sacred consciousness they attempt to create.

Divorce is the greatest threat to sacred marriages, and for Catholics it can mean spiritual separation from the Church (Dodaro 2014). In comparing Bartkowski's (1989) *Prayers for Married Couples* with Koenig-Bricker and Dziena's (2014) *Catholic Prayer Book for the Separated and Divorced*, the moralization of divorce is immediately apparent. Married couples are instructed to pray together for blessings on their marriages, loving each other, facing life together, getting along with each other, living with children, and for special occasions (e.g., vacations, birthdays, and the birth of babies). While married couple prayers include dealing with conflict, the tone of the prayers has a positively oriented outcome. The prayers seek God's intervention in controlling the couple's thoughts, feelings, and actions to allow God to bless the marriage through conformity with Church teachings. In contrast, Koenig-Bricker and Dziena (2014) introduce the prayers for the separated and divorced with the five stages of grief and loss. The prayers in this text address worries about children not being cared for properly by former spouses, not loving stepchildren, fighting with stepchildren, scandals with former spouses, conflict-filled interactions with former spouses, and separation from children when they depart for other parents' homes.

The tones of these two Catholic prayer books could not be more different. A comparison of these prayer books clearly indicates that marriage is filled with positive experiences, and even when conflicts arise, positive outcomes are intended for those conflicts. In contrast, people who have divorced should feel "anger," "isolation," and "depression." More than merely constructing a sacred consciousness of Christian marriage that favors marriage over other forms of relationships, the manuals condemn divorce and marginalize those who divorced through an attempt to normalize divorce as a form of death that permanently severs people's inclusion in the community of the sacred.

Just as the manuals use divorce as a device to separate people from the sacred, gender too is used to separate people from membership in the sacred. While at first it appears that the manuals provide guidance for men and women to assume their roles as husbands and wives in sacred marriages, their use of embodied gender represents a disenfranchisement from the community of the sacred. Consider Kimberly Hahn's (2007: 33) use of embodied gender practices as a rhetorical device to exclude gendered strategies of action that do not align with the dominant religious discourse of the sacred consciousness in Catholic marriages.

> Our culture characterizes the husband's position as primary provider for his family as a "cultural conditioning" for the purpose of denying women education, careers, prestige and meaningful work. (Besides, just think of what two incomes can mean). However, God commands men to provide for their families. First Timothy 5:8. . .
>
> [. . .]

Our culture belittles a wife's homemaker role as a cultural ploy to limit women to menial work – child care, cleaning, cooking – as the unpaid maid. However, Saint Paul addresses the value of this work . . .

[. . .]

A woman's care for her family ennobles her. Even her body reveals that caring for children is primarily her task: her body makes milk to feed her baby. . . . The woman receives the seed from the man.

[. . .]

Men tend to lead with rationality; women tend to lead with emotional sensitivity, and consequently they have a stronger integration of their bodies and emotions.

Hahn (2007: 36) then draws on the words of Pope John Paul II in upholding the Virgin Mary as "the model of the genius of womanhood in general and of motherhood" in the coexistence of virginity and motherhood in women that is not mutually exclusive or limiting.

While Hahn's (2007: ix) stated hopes for her Christian marriage advice manual – which she describes as a Bible study – are sharing lived wisdom among generations of women, providing context to better understand the principles of Christian marriage, and enabling engaged couples to explore their hopes and dreams for a fulfilling marriage, her actual use of embodied gender discourse separates, marginalizes, and disenfranchises women from belonging within the community of the sacred. Women who use contraceptives, have sex outside marriage, work due to economic circumstances, are single mothers, are divorced, and do not breast feed are discursively constituted as "impure," "unholy," and enjoined from inclusion in sacred marriages. Hahn (2007: 37) compares these women to prostitutes who have sex with anyone, dress seductively, lack dignity, and are ultimately frantic, ill-mannered, attention-getters who do not know the names of the men with whom they have sex (Hahn 2007: 39).

While sociologists of culture have argued that people can be content using culture to form strategies of action even when they lack understanding and meaning, there is little discussion of why people can be so blissfully ignorant and still function. The answer lies in belonging and the community of the sacred. People use culture to fit into social contexts. Strategies of action are only valuable if they can be perceived to be of value by others. I offer contraception as an example of religious belonging in sacred marriages.

It was no surprise that so many people I interviewed had almost no understanding of – and often stated with vehemence their desire not to understand – the mechanics of in vitro fertilization and a variety of forms of contraception. Even when wives had taken medications to promote fertility or had been surgically sterilized, they and their husbands offered explanations why they had not violated Catholic Church teachings. There were many participants who had used contraception that violated Church teachings, but when asked if the Church should change its stance on contraception, they almost always said no.

While O'Toole (2008) describes a tumultuous history in which Catholics became divided within the Church over teachings concerning the use of contraception, the divisions were largely based on pragmatics and not theology. O'Toole (2008) couches the division of Catholics over the use of contraception as part of a larger framework in which religion become more personalized, and it became easier to disregard specific Church teachings and still retain their Catholic identities. In attempts at reconciliation, a culture of religious ideology developed in which choices about the use of contraception remained a private matter without promoting changes in Church teachings, as most Catholics held, "a mixed collection of views on the issues that so enflamed the partisans on one side or the other," of the issue (O'Toole 2008: 244).

At first, respondents' personal rejection of Church teachings concerning contraception and their recommendation not to change those teachings seemed irreconcilable. But, their stories reflect their desire to remain connected to the religious community and those who value their sacred marriages. Changes in Church teaching concerning contraception, could negatively impact the sacralization of marriage because being willing to bear children as a result of sex is a fundamental component of the theology of sacred marriages (Pérez-Soba and Kampowski 2014).

Why would anyone violate Church teachings, provide sound reasons for their decisions to do so, and then overwhelmingly advocate for the Church to maintain its position on contraception? The answer is in part that they wanted to continue to unite with the community that believes in sacred marriages. Even when strategies of action sourced from the culture of religion failed to solve their problems of action, couples rarely faulted religion, but instead blamed themselves for not having enough resolve or being weak Christians. Just as the Christian marriage advice manuals protect the sacred, the couples I interviewed retained belonging with the sacred by protecting the sacred through marginalizing and disenfranchising discourse that could threaten it, not because of deeply shared religious meanings, but to maintain membership with the community with whom they could share in the ways they act, talk, think, and feel about sacred marriages. In the community of sacred marriages, people with widely diverse religious backgrounds can unite and form bonds, often outside of religious discourse and religious culture.

The couples in this study used religion to talk, think, feel, and act in ways that bound them with the community of the religious. Their almost universal denunciation of abortion when questioned about their sex lives – although I never asked any questions about abortion – gives a glimpse into the ways they actively sought connections to the sacred in marriage through religion, and the ways they separated themselves in their stories from that which they perceived would distance them from their religious communities. Through an extension of Verter (2003), I suggest that people use religious discourse and religious culture to connect with other people who belong to broader communities of sacred marriages.

The search for the communities of sacred marriages begins in the blending of religion and leisure in childhood. Marks (1996: 5) suggests that religion and leisure promulgate a range of implicit and explicit values and beliefs. The couples in this study described wiener bakes (i.e., eating hotdogs in the church basement), roller skating parties, dances, sporting events that began with prayer, and family-friendly movies projected on the side of a downtown hardware in a small, rural community. While the couples in this study maintained their own individual agencies, and hypothetically could have attended any leisure activities they wished as children and during courtship, the hegemony of their religious and generational cultures limited their choices. Many other activities simply did not exist, and others were unthinkable. While they were likely not cognizant of the cultural forces at play as children and young adults, their parents, church leaders, and schools organized their leisure activities within religious frameworks supportive of sacred marriages. The couples overwhelmingly framed their leisure experiences in value-laden discourse using a blended sacred-secular language when describing their leisure activities as children and during their courtships. Examples of this language include "wholesome," "family-oriented," "protected," "dignified," "respectable," and "good, clean fun." Church-related leisure activities were often one of the few social activities available to the couples in this study in their early years, especially for those living in small communities. It is not surprising that they sought out mates and other couples after their marriages who were supportive of their shared value for sacred marriage, often without reflecting significant religious commitment.

There is no question that religious institutions and their institutional power over marriage has changed through time (Coontz 2005; O'Toole 2008; Witte 1997). And the religious cultures and identities of congregations have changed accordingly (Ammerman et al 1998). But community is an essential aspect of sacred marriages because religion is not one-sided. Religious discourse and religious culture is valuable only in as much as it is shared. In contrast to the manuals, which produce religious culture through religious discourse to establish the boundaries of sacred marriages, often through a juxtaposition of the secular with the religious to limit, restrict, and regulate behavior, the couples in this study shared stories of their lived experiences of marriage through a sacred lens. They shared stories that connected them to a community of sacred marriages by framing their experiences in sacred language to promote unity with their communities.

When religious discourse or religious culture did not solve problems of action in their lived experiences of marriage, they almost never overtly rejected religious discourse or religious culture to remain within accepted boundaries of the sacred and the religious community in which it is located. Instead, they united with their religious communities through explanations like, "God won't give you more than you can take," "Our ways aren't his ways," "God always answers prayer, but sometimes the answer is no," and, "It just wasn't in God's plan." Openly rejecting religious discourse and religious culture, even when religious scripts fail to solve problems of action, can impact belonging in communities of sacred marriages. Sacred marriages also promote unity. Even when people disagree about Church teachings, belong to different denominations, or even if they are atheists, they can still belong to a community of people who believe that marriage is sacred.

Belonging to communities of sacred marriages is not dependent on direct relationships with the supernatural, nor does it require specific sacred experiences. Sacred marriages are part of religious tradition and invoke religious narratives and experiences, whether people understand or deeply internalize those traditions or not. Rather than promulgating specific religious truths about marriage, most of the people in this study simply shared stories about the ways they think people ought – and ought not – talk, think, feel, and act in sacred marriages as part of the larger relationships – both human and divine – to which they belong.

8 Reproducing sacred marriages

This chapter comes full circle from the use of religion to sacralize marriage and sacred aspects of marriage like love, sex, and childbearing to the reproduction of religious culture that frames sacred marriages when religious culture fails to solve people's problems of action. Given the plasticity of religion, couples are able to draw on sacred meanings and understandings of marriage to transform their sacred marriages.

Religion and the sacred are different (Burr et al 2012). Not all aspects of religion are sacred. Religion is organized and institutionalized. Religion is ordered and systematic. Religion is observable and therefore has been a practical means of studying marriage and family. But sacred is abstract and broad in scope. Reframing segments of religious culture through religious discourse of sacred marriages requires no logical connections between strategies of action and sacred meanings people ascribe marriages. The discourse of sacred marriages is filled with everyday emotions and experiences that anyone can experience but that are transformed and that morph from the mundane to a realm of existence that is transcendental. Whether sacred marriages are objective realities or imagined, the phenomenological aspects of the ways people talk, think, feel, and act about and towards their sacred marriages solve their problems of action. Sacred marriages represent the nexus between religious culture and the sensate emotional experiences that comprise the most fundamentally important, meaningful, and salient relationships in most people's lives.

Sacred marriages include both theistic and the nontheistic landscapes (Burr et al 2012). While theists may cite numerous sacred aspects of religion, many people describe emotional, inspiring, or transcendental experiences as sacred. For example, some of the couples in this study and some of the Christian marriage advice manuals refer to sacrifice, parenthood, commitment to a spouse, commitment to the institution of marriage, and forgiveness as sacred aspects of marriage that inspire a sense of reverence and respect. Even for those couples who did not reference the sacred in their narratives, they live in a social world in which they routinely interact with others who think, talk, feel, and act in reference to ideas, events, or objects associated with marriage that they find sacred, awe inspiring, or holy.

There is power in the way people use their sacred marriages. While some people may be highly religious and act in ways that are detrimental to their marriages and families, others may not be particularly religious but act in ways that benefit their marriages and families. The sacred can cross the divide between religious meanings and inconsistent actions. While people's cultural repertoires are filled with inconsistent, competing, segmented, incomplete fragments of culture that they draw upon to frame their experiences, culture is not without limitation in organizing people's experiences. As I have suggested before, there is no reason to assume that everyone has an equal capacity to use their cultural toolkits to solve their problems of action. There is no evidence that people are equally capable of investing in, negotiating, or effectively doing cultural work necessary to solve their problems of action. There are times that culture is not sufficient to tell their stories in meaningful ways that order their experiences and solve their problems of action. Additionally, people's stories may not be equally valued among all audiences, in which case people may not be able to capitalize on shared cultural meanings and therefore experience marginalization. The couples in this story serve as examples of situations in which their use of religion ultimately resulted in marginalization within their communities and required bending of religion to produce new sacred marriages.

The people I interviewed say that marriage takes work. They often used religion to do the work they believe sustains their marriages and improves the quality of their relationship with their spouses, their children, their extended families, and others with whom they form social bonds. While some of the couples I interviewed used specific Christian marriage advice manuals I analyzed for this study to work towards changing themselves and their marriages, others used religious culture and religious discourse in more broad terms to work on their marriages. Sometimes couples used religion to work on their relationships in ways that really did not require much change in their religious identities (e.g., attending religious services together or praying for their marriages). At other times, people described significant changes in their own religious identities (e.g., converting to the same denomination as a spouse to strengthen their marriages). Changing one's identities to strengthen marriage is a common theme among the couples I interviewed. And, the Christian marriage advice manuals I analyzed offered instruction in the specifics of how to use religion to work on the self to strengthen Christian marriages, based on a comingling of religious and nonreligious discourses.

Rather than examine the advice proffered in the marriage manuals I analyzed as a product of an objective, external reality of religion that prescribes specific actions to sustain marriage, here I examine the discursive power of these texts as reflective of a structuring of possible strategies of actions. From this perspective, the significance of the bases of the advice offered in the texts, or lack thereof, pales in comparison to the role such advice plays in structuring religious culture and promoting particular power systems. This addresses one potential criticism that could be levied against this study. That criticism is that the content of any one, or all for that matter, of the Christian marriage advice manuals may not be known to one or more of the participants in this study. It is highly unlikely that any of the participants in this study has read all of these manuals, especially given the denominational differences in the theological bases of some of these texts and the local origins of these books within the homes and lending libraries of specific churches to which all participants did not share access. However, the participants need not know the specific content of all these texts for the manuals to reflect the manner in which the culture of religion structures the strategies of actions associated with sacred marriages.

A consistent theme within Christian marriage advice manuals is that marriage is divined by God. The secular nature of marriage as a legal contract sanctioned by the State is given little, if any, significance in these texts. Instead, many focus on the supra-human origins of marriage, the supra-human purposes of marriage, and the belief that, with only a limited number of exceptions (e.g., physical abuse), marriages should and can last. At the same time, there is a clear recognition in these texts that Christian marriages may not last and Christian marriages do frequently end.

Consistent with Swidler's (2001) findings, the couples in this study do active cultural work to bridge the gap between expectations that marriage is indissoluble and the fragility of marriage. There is a recognition that marriage is a choice and that even the Church has no ultimate power to prevent the dissolution of a marriage. The existence of so many Christian marriage advice manuals in itself – and I certainly did not analyze them all – attests to the salience of religious discourse in reconstructing religious culture.

Swidler (2001: 136) suggests that culture structures strategies of action that influence social bonds like marriage. At the heart of her reasoning is the assertion that "social bonds are products of voluntary individual choice." And, "people must choose whom and whether to marry and whether or not to stay married." Thus, "individuals create social ties by their free choices." Culture structures strategies of action people can use to sustain relationships based on their subjectivities and the ability to make individual choices within conditions necessary to make authentic and valid choices. It is not a unity of belief that creates a culture of voluntarism in social bonds but rather the deinstitutionalization of structures that promotes the shared elements of a culture. Most important to this study, "beliefs about personal traits and predispositions and theories of what changes or stabilizes the self are critical . . . to theories of relationships."

These observations explain how people's divergent expectations, unique sociocultural histories, disparate religious beliefs, and theological differences in the construction of consistent themes about the nature of sacred marriages can coexist. While each person or author of a manual may approach marriage from a different angle, and while each person may hold unique religious meanings associated with marriage and family relationships, there is a consistency to the themes of the work required to change oneself for the greater good of the marriage, to be more disciplined, and to seek genuine relationships that satisfy the needs of both parties. Religious culture is one of many cultural logics that can provide coherent, although culturally commingled, strategies of action. But do people use the culture of religion and religious discourse the same way they do other cultures and discourses? Or, are religious cultural tools non-unique resources?

Rather than examining how people use religious culture to sustain relationships in their sacred marriages, here I turn the analysis on its head. By examining the failure of religious discourse and religious culture to sustain family relationships, we can better understand how the sacred functions within the commingled cultural resources in people's cultural toolkits and religion's contribution to cultural repertoires. Religion is one of many pieces in the cultural landscape that structure strategies of action, and it sometimes fails to solve problems of action. When nonreligious culture also fails to produce solutions to people's problems of action as well, they turn to the sensate in their sacred marriages.

Sometimes there are disconnections between people's acceptance of religious culture and religious scripts that result in fractured family relationships. The challenges of maintaining family bonds can result in imbalances in interactions that can weaken relationships, block reconciliation, and result in unpredictable and unstable emotions. While religion can regulate and control family relationships, cultural repertoires and religious discourse may conflict with the individual agencies of family members. Riis and Woodhead (2010) offer a framework for their study of religious emotion that I borrow from here because they focus on the interaction of individual agency, community, and religious symbols. Religious culture is most powerful when people identify with shared symbolic meanings of sacred marriages found in religious discourse. When individual choices violate religious meanings or when religious meanings are not shared, people can face insurmountable problems of action that result in the loss of relationships.

Estrangement

Frank and Frieda are Evangelical Baptists who have been married 51 years. They are retired teachers. Born during the Great Depression, they both embrace a culture of hard work and frugality consistent with their generation. And, although they never directly referred to the term stewardship, their narratives are at times consistent with elite religious discourse associated with stewardship and predestination. In analyzing their narratives, I felt at times as though I were observing a model type of Weber's theory of the Protestant ethic. Although all of the couples in this study were sharing stories based on retrospective accounts of their lives, more so than most others, Frank and Frieda seemed to be living in their pasts. They offered no descriptions of happy moments as a family. Instead, their transcripts read more like a defense of the choices they made in their marriage, the processes and failures of the decisions they made as spouses and parents, and their rationales for why they took the actions they did.

Their interviews were different than the other couples in this study. While they were both polite, they were distant and cautious. I was met by Frank at the front door and led immediately to their home office. He shut the door and shared that his wife was reluctant to participate. They had been told about the interview process I had planned by another couple whom I had previously interviewed and who asked Frank and Frieda to participate in the study on my behalf. Before my arrival, Frank and Frieda had agreed not to be interviewed together prior to or after their individual interviews. Frank was to be interviewed first. He explained that the door was to remain closed in the room during each individual interview, and I had to promise that I would not mention any of the answers Frank gave to my questions during Frieda's interview that would follow. At the conclusion of Frieda's interview, she led me out of the house. I never saw Frank and Frieda at the same time while I was in their home. And, although their interviews are inconsistent with the specific interview methodology for this study, the study is much richer due to their involvement.

Before I asked any questions, Frank said the following:

> Our son has had a lot of drug problems, and we haven't communicated with our daughter in 15 years. I know where she is, and I can find her on the computer. She's only an hour's drive away. She married a Jew. He worked for an oil company and is doing very, very well. She is doing some writing, and I can see her website and kind of keep track of her. But, I've never talked with her in 15 years. You lose track of time but it's been 15 years. She's got three kids. We know that. We were still talking when her son was born. But we haven't seen the daughter or the second daughter.
>
> She was involved in church and was president of the youth group for the whole state at one time. She really zeroed in on religion. When she left to go to college, she went to the Midwest Baptist University, which is where we sent her. She got off on the wrong track. She got off on the wrong track. I don't know if she's Christian anymore or not with the influence of a Jew.
>
> But through that time – and it was tougher for my wife than it was for me – we stayed together. Even now, when I pull something up on the computer about our daughter, she won't look at it. So I don't even do things like that now.
>
> [. . .]
>
> She never expressed why, but she blew up with my wife. I kind of avoided it. She went into the thick battle with our daughter, and she got hurt pretty badly. But through those times with our son and daughter we got closer by supporting each other. Today we're okay. We're doing fine. My wife won't tell you about any of this. It's just not in her anymore. Now you can ask your questions.

Both Frank and Frieda shared early in their interviews that Frieda could not have children. They adopted a boy and later a girl as infants. When I asked Frieda about the influence of religion on their decision to adopt, she shared the following.

> We're Baptists. The church really didn't support us because when we were trying to start a family, we were spending as much time with his parents or my parents and being at their places on the weekends and going to home churches. So, we didn't really establish a church. We started going to one here in town, but we live too far away from it. So, finally we moved to the northeast side of town, and we said we're going to find a church that's close.

Frank and Frieda were both raised in devout families in small, rural communities. They described childhoods of poverty and working their way through college. They dated for several years as they completed graduate school before marrying. There is an inconsistency between their strong, conservative, Evangelical beliefs, and their sparse references to organized religion in their narratives.

When I asked Frank if religion had influenced his marriage, his response shifted to themes of choice and accountability with only tangent reference to religion. Throughout his interview, he made references to "God's plan" and "God's choice." But at one point, Frank began to question his adoptive children's backgrounds and "God's choice" of children for him. Then, he suddenly stopped himself when he realized his story was headed in that direction.

> My wife and I got through with our kids because we worked hard, and we knew how to work hard. That's been God's saving grace. We had an education, and we worked hard. Problems can be turned around for the good – all challenges can. We have two kids who were adopted, so we don't know about their backgrounds.
>
> [Frank raised his hands in front of his body motioning to stop, as he stuttered and stumbled over these next words.]
>
> But, but we don't want to make that as an excuse. I don't think that had anything to do with it. I'm not so sure that we handled everything right. We made many, many, many mistakes and ignored some things that we should have picked up on. Good gracious, we should have picked up on some of the stuff. Our encouraging to go on to college was a given, but that in itself led to problems. I think in both of their minds they thought it was just going to happen, and they wouldn't have to do very much to get there, because that was just the way it was going to be. What kind of foundation did they have to get there? They didn't work hard to go to college. They didn't have the work ethic to succeed in college and beyond.

Frieda also repeatedly stressed choices in her interview. She was critical of her own choices concerning conflict resolution in her relationship with Frank.

> I don't deal with conflict very well. I can tell you that. There were times that I hate to admit that I turned over with my back to Frank. That's not what you're supposed to do. But those are the kind of things you have to work through.

Although she never made specific reference to the conflict she has with her son or her daughter, towards the end of the interview she attempted to collect her thoughts into a larger narrative of religion's influence on her marriage.

> I think that we're both involved – not as much as when we were younger. We were involved with church, and we did things as a family at church, and we knew that this was God's plan. Once you make a decision, that's it. Love is

wonderful when you first start out but it becomes a choice later. If you fall in love with someone – mind over matter – you've made a decision. You have to make a decision to continue to love them. I don't think that you can say, "Hey I'm not in love with this person anymore because they've changed a little bit, and I changed a little bit." You've made a conscious decision to love whether it's towards your kids, your spouse, relatives, or whoever. You made that decision to love them, and therefore, that's what God wanted you to do. So, that's what we are going to do the best we can.

I don't know that we ever argued enough to say, "This is it. We're getting divorced." Not out loud. Maybe in our mind. That just wasn't a choice to get divorced. You were going to work it out. We have been to Christian counseling over the years during the growing up of the kids age. We have done bible studies in church on family relations. We did a retreat one time in Wisconsin for a marriage encounter. We make conscious choices to do things to enrich our lives to get along. Because you've made a decision already, and you stick to your decision. When you made the decision to marry the person, you made a decision to love and to follow God's choices. It just didn't seem like an option to do anything else. I may have been mad enough one time to think about it, but not seriously. It just wasn't a choice.

Throughout their interviews, when asked specific questions about religion's influence on multiple aspects of their marriage, Frank and Frieda rarely referred to organized religion, sacred texts, religious books, or elite religious discourse specifically. They do not lack the knowledge. Nor do they lack the ability to express themselves, which is evident given their level of education and as retired educators.

At first it may appear that religious culture was unable to provide solutions to the problems they faced in their marriage. However, they both retain their individual agency and collective agency as a couple, notwithstanding the hegemony of culture or the power of discourse in their lives. There is no reason to assume everyone is equally capable of using culture to solve their problems, or that their chosen strategies of action to solve their problems were choices that would lead to solutions. Culture does not guarantee outcomes, but couples may not share in the cultural means of aligning their practices with their perceived goals. While by all appearances they had cultural repertoires of religion available to them, that they could have used to form strategies of action to solve their problems – as other couples in this study were able to do – Frank and Frieda both repeatedly mentioned their work ethic in their narratives and their reliance on therapeutic culture. Their stories about why they became estranged from their children focused on their children's lack of work ethic as the central reason for them not being prepared for adulthood (e.g., college, the paid labor force, marriage, parenthood, and managing a household). Frank and Frieda also both mentioned the negative influence of their own work ethic as parents (e.g., "working too many hours," "attending too many school functions," "bringing work home"). Even their social lives centered around their work. While they placed high value on their identities as Baptists, in their lived experiences, they placed more value in a culture that valued work over other cultures and discourses.

By pointing out the role of agency in religion's influence on sacred marriages, I imply no normative value on people's choice of discourse and culture to attempt to solve their problems. I am also not moralizing people's decisions. I am instead suggesting, as I have throughout this book, that people are not passive recipients of discourse or culture. They are active agents and bricoleurs who reproduce discourse and culture. If, as Swidler (2001) argues, people do cultural work because relationships are fragile and dependent on individual choice, then the role of individual agency and the collective agency of the couple cannot be overlooked. People's cultural toolkits and their cultural repertoires are not just the resources available from which people form strategies of action, they are, in part, the result of their own agency. They choose strategies of action within power discourses and hegemonic cultures, but they do choose. This leaves us with a question similar to that posed by Durkheim in his search for the basis of solidarity, why do people stay married in sacred marriages, especially when religious culture seems not to solve their problems of action?

Despite their limited use of religious discourse to explain their lived experiences, Frank and Frieda turned to the sacred meanings they ascribe all marriage, and theirs in particular, in their narratives. As a couple and as individuals, Frank and Frieda have worked to change their subjectivities, their marriage, and their relationships. Despite their fractured relationships with their children, they argue that these experiences have brought them closer together as a couple and strengthened their marriage.

Consistent with the sacred consciousness of marriage I have described throughout this book, Frank and Frieda did not seriously consider ending their marriage because marriage is sacred to them. Many of the people I interviewed said they did not consider the choice to end their marriages as valid, authentic, or legitimate. More importantly they suggested that their belief that they did not truly have a choice to end their marriage was not their own decision but rather the result of "God's will." They obviously knew they had the choice to end their marriages, but they did not consider it a legitimate choice because their choices were guided by the symbolic and sacred meanings found in sacred marriages that are tied to social emotions within the strategies of action that order their individual agency and their collective agency as a couple.

For many of the couples I interviewed, the sacred meanings they ascribed marriage are more important than their agency. Religious emotional regimes in sacred marriages order discourse, culture, and agency, influencing how people talk, think, feel, and act in sacred marriages. Frieda articulated the sense of an inability to exert her free will because marriage is sacred. However, her relationship with her daughter was not sacred. She actively worked to maintain their estrangement. Regardless of the reasons why, this clearly indicates that sacred marriages embody a unique relationship between husband and wife. While the sacralization of marriage includes the sacralization of love, the sacralization of sex, and the sacralization of childbearing, it does not sacralize other relationships. In fact, the sacralization of marriage orders the relationship between husband and wife above all other relationships. According to the manuals, the relationship between husband and wife is further sacralized in the belief that Christ is a third member of the sacred union between husband and wife in the sacrament of marriage (Burke 2015; Sheen 1996; Shivanandan 1999). Religion represents a unique contribution in the structuring of the relationship between husband and wife and the ordering of all other relationships as subordinate to that relationship. The manuals describe no relationship in sacred marriages, other than that between husband and wife, as sacred. This is not to suggest that other nonreligious discourses and cultures do not also frame the relationship between husband and wife as supraordinate to other relationships, but nonreligious discourses and cultures cannot base supraordination on religious discourse and religious culture because they are by definition nonreligious.

Marriage matters. It is not like any other relationship. I am not asserting a normative value to marriage. My assertion is simply that marriage is a unique form of relationship that influences how people talk, think, feel, and act in all of their relationships. Those who believe that marriage is sacred are able to talk, think, feel, and act in ways that are meaningful to them and others. The sacred allows people to pick up the pieces of commingled cultural resources and order them within their marriage to create religious meanings based on the endurance of their marriages, even when individual strategies of action fail to solve problems of action.

While the capacity of people to act is affected by a range of factors, a wide range of emotions have a place, and religious emotions constitutive of religious culture and religious discourse in sacred marriages hold unique power. Rather than thinking of the sacred as a way of creating functional, coherent meanings, I suggest the presence of power systems in sacred marriages influences the ways people talk, think, feel, and act about the unique social bond they believe exists between spouses. Sacred marriages give people unique religious motivations – constructed from a blending of religious and nonreligious spheres – to form and end relationships. While severing a relationship with one's adult child may be culturally frowned upon, ending the relationship due to religious dissonance may be cause for sorrow and regret but still be supported within a religious community. Sacred marriages can be used to justify people's choices of strategies of action and the ways they talk, feel, think, and act as agents. In the case of Frank and Frieda, the sacred supports their decisions to remain married while severing their relationship with their son and daughter.

According to Riis and Woodhead (2010: 152),

> emotions can themselves be a stimulus to action – that is to see emotions as sources of power rather than just reactions to power. We present emotions as active, relational 'stances' within the world; as means by which individuals and groups actively negotiate their relational standing, as well as monitoring and reacting to their social and material-symbolic positioning.

The power of emotions in sacred marriages is directly related to the way people feel. Sacred marriages are concentrated forms of strategies of action constitutive of religious culture and religious discourse. Swidler (2001: 149) argues that, "Only the self's free choices make action legitimate." However, this account does not consider the power of emotions in individual agency. Religious culture and religious discourse give sacred meaning to Frieda's emotions and decision not to interact with her daughter. Her sacred marriage not only legitimizes Frieda's decision to sever ties with her daughter, it allows her to deny her own agency in the telling of her stories. In her narrative, she is no longer the actor. It is "God's will" that directs her actions and structures her emotions. Her sacred marriage acknowledges the dysfunction in her relationship with her daughter while promoting the longevity of her marriage and her bond with her husband. Frank and Frieda weave a tale of emotional struggles that ends ultimately in an ordering of events in which their emotions and decisions outweigh the emotions and decisions of their daughter because they are in the religious "right" and their daughter is in the religious "wrong." While they recognize that specific religious strategies of action failed, promoting dysfunction in their relationships with their children, they shared in sacred meanings that subordinated other cultural resources and the emotions of others in the ways they talked, thought, felt, and acted as a couple in a sacred marriage within their stories, despite their choice of a culture of work over other cultural resources available to them in their narratives.

Sacred marriages hold power to order discourses and cultures because sacred aspects of marriage are venerated. The sacred exists above the mundane, although it incorporates the mundane. It is nebulous by design. It informs how people talk, think, feel, and act because it is an intangible construct that evokes powerful agency and emotions. While speaking religion is a form of discourse that offers people cultural means of feeling, thinking, talking, and acting in religious ways, speaking the sacred personifies the ultimate, supreme, and purest aspects of marriage as an emotionally-bound touchstone to which people can turn when they choose cultures that fails to solve their problems of action.

Marriage endurance

As evidence of the power of the sacralization of marriage in people's lives, I offer a common response participants had to my questions about the endurance of their marriages. Several couples explained the endurance of their marriages through an ontological tautology by referring to the persistence of their marriage (e.g., he's/she's still here, we're still married, he/she still puts up with me, he/she hasn't left yet) as though continued participation in the marriage was self-evidence of the reasons why their marriages had endured. While I initially dismissed these responses as people's attempts at humor, it was when I asked probing questions of respondents about why they and their spouses continued to remain married that it became apparent that the endurance of their marriages was a constitutive component of what they believed to be sacred about their marriages. All the couples I interviewed described challenges to their marriages to different degrees, and many couples I interviewed described problems of action and the inability of the cultural strategies they chose to resolve their problems. It was when they were describing their decisions and their spouses' decisions to remain in their marriages that they were most likely to make reference to sacred aspects of their marriages.

Sacred marriages are more than religion. Just as religious discourse and religious culture blend religious and nonreligious spheres, couples held both religious and nonreligious reasons for their beliefs that marriage is sacred. In a similar fashion to the rhetorical devices employed by the authors of some of the Christian marriage advice manuals, some participants framed their sacred marriages through a juxtaposition of their marriages with secular culture. Some participants even shared stories in which they argued that their marriages were sacred by identifying what they believed to be failures of both religious culture and secular culture to solve their problems of action. In so doing, they selected discourse and cultural strands that framed their marriages within the realm of the sacred, somehow above both the secular and religious spheres.

New sacred meanings

Corrine and Ray's marriage was stressed by Ray's ongoing infidelity. Corrine believes she neglected Ray in different ways because she put her role as a mother over her role as a wife. When she learned of Ray's infidelity she turned to religious texts, secular counseling, and rejected divorce. She claimed she did not reject divorce due to sacred meanings in her marriage, but due to her divorced neighbor's experiences.

Ray struggled to verbalize a consistent narrative in response to my questions about religion and his infidelity.

> We need to get better sermons. How much time have you got, and I'll tell you everything the church needs to do? I like going to gentlemen's clubs on Sunday night, but what does that have to do with what you do when you go to church? And when do they really give you a sermon, the last 20 minutes? Even after that 20 minutes, can you remember anything? It used to be that father Rick would give a sermon, and you could not leave without taking something away. I think people would've followed him. They'd follow him still now. He's got a big family in town that does a lot for the Catholic Church. Why don't they give better sermons? Why is it when I go to the Cathedral I don't understand a word they say? We have a priest that does nobody any good because I don't know what he's saying, and nobody else knows what he's saying. We're all trying, but all I hear is words. Sometimes I hear a word like sacrifice, and I'd like to tell you the rest but I can't. How come the monsignor isn't in the back of the church listening to him, giving him a scorecard. He doesn't even read his scorecard. I look around. Is anybody getting this? Nobody's getting this.
>
> The thing that hurts the most in a marriage and a family is all the stuff on TV and at gentlemen's clubs. It's the outside coming in that messes up

everything. It truly is. I mean, I go to clubs, and those things are just filthy dirty. You can't open yourself up to that. You can't do that on one hand, and say you are a shining example on the other hand. You can hardly watch TV, or any sitcoms anymore, without them pushing the envelope as far as they can push it. How can you do that? I don't know. I don't know. I don't know the answer to that. All that outside stuff is killing us.

"If the clubs are hurting your marriage, why do you frequent them?" I asked.

"Because there aren't any sermons anymore and that stuff is everywhere. Listen, it works for Corrine. We've talked about it a lot. But, I can't figure out how to make sense of it anymore because there isn't a sermon anymore. I don't know." Ray concluded.

Ray's response is rich with contradictions, yet there is a consistent voice. He cannot justify his behaviors with religious discourse other than to point to the harms of secular culture and deficiencies he sees in the Church. Thus, he blames the Church for what he perceives as a failure to provide homilies that are understandable and applicable in his everyday life. At the same time, he draws upon his father's infidelity and 60-year marriage as an example of the way couples can "make it work, if they want to" as a rationale for the survival of his marriage despite his infidelity and attendance at strip clubs on Sunday nights. Ray stated several times that "marriage is sacred" but quickly diverted the discussion to immorality in society and the Church's failures when questioned about the influence of religion in his marriage. He has reframed his infidelity in discourse in which the Church needs to strengthen its teachings. Clearly, Ray and Corrine do not share in this reframing and Ray's actions continue to reduce their overall marriage quality and satisfaction.

The rejection of lines of action and religious meanings is an essential component of sacred marriages. Couples in this study often used an overt religious framing of their lived experiences of marriage and family because they were being asked about the influence of religion on their marriages. Connie stayed married to her "unfaithful" husband Ray because she did not want the life of her divorced neighbor. She never wanted to be what she described as a "lonely, single mother." While she "detests" Ray's infidelity, Connie continues to believe that "God can change him," and that she will be "rewarded in heaven" for her decision to remain married, consistent with the manual she asked me to include in this study, *Unfaithful: Hope and Healing after Infidelity* (Shriver and Shriver 2009). Ray draws heavily on religious culture to describe marriage making frequent reference to elite religious discourse, but then abandons religion completely when it fails to coincide with his infidelity. Then he reframes religion as lacking meaning and as incomprehensible because of what he describes as failures of the church.

Connie is hardly an oppressed woman who suffers in silence at her husband's indiscretions. Instead, she has produced a new sacred meaning in their marriage and a new subjectivity as a wife, consistent with Allen and her colleague's (2005) findings concerning people's responses to infidelity in relationships.

"I don't stay with Ray because I love him like I did when we first met. I love Ray because he's not going to make me a liar to God. My vow is sacred to me," Connie explained. Connie's love for Ray is based on a sacred "love for God," part of which includes loving Ray and remaining married to him because Ray is a "gift from God, that I'd like to return." Both Connie and Ray described their marriage in terms of a need for one another.

"What would either of us be without the other?" Ray asked.

By abandoning traditional sacred meanings in marriage and specific religious scripts found in Catholicism, Connie and Ray have formed a new sacred marriage by bending religious discourse and religious ways that produce new sacred meanings in their marriage.

Sacred marriages as ongoing negotiation and positioning

At first, Ray's explanation of his infidelity in terms of weak sermons seems a contradiction, but that is because marriage is not sacred by degrees. Sacred marriage is sacred by cultural context and discursive positioning. People draw on a culture of religion and religious discourse as pieces from the whole, and different strands of religious culture and segments of religious discourse can influence different aspects of infidelity in marriage (Atkins et al 2001; Atkins and Kessel 2008). They use religious discourse and religious culture to explain their marriage longevity, as long as a religious framing of their lived experiences of marriage and families works to solve their problems of action in their stories with their audience. Although they clearly shift easily between various cultural frames that are at times religious and at times nonreligious, they also reframe religious meanings as they address problems of action rejecting those cultural strands of religion that do not meet their needs and adapting religious discourse in ways that satisfy their understandings of sacred marriages.

The couples in this chapter exemplify the segmented application of religious discourse and religious culture to construct their sacred marriages. And while it may seem illogical that Ray suggests bad sermons are one of the causes of his infidelity, both he and Connie hold fast to their belief that marriage is sacred, divined by God, and that they are expected to remain married.

When religious culture fails to solve problems of action, people reframe their sacred marriages using segments of religious discourse and segments of religious culture that solve their problems of action to give new religious meanings to their sacred marriages. Sacred marriages are not objective realities, but rather they are a process of ongoing negotiation of changes in religious meanings articulated through religious discourse that solve problems of action when elite religious discourse fails to solve problems of action in everyday lived experiences of marriage. Just as people can switch among various cultural frames to address problems of action, they can reframe cultural frames they value highly producing new cultural forms and meanings.

The couples I interviewed who were unable to solve their problems of action with religious culture drew from their experiences and the sacralization of their marriages to order and bend religious culture and reproduce and reconstruct new sacred marriages. They were able to validate their individual choices regarding marriage by committing to their marriages and spouses by turning to the sacred nature of their relationships as husbands and wives. Through a reframing of sacralized loved they were able to find personal rewards for their reinvestment in the endurance of their marriages. They ordered their religious emotional tools and competing cultures of love by balancing cultural contradictions in their marriages through a reframing of their sacred marriages in ways that brought them "closer to God." They exhibited new religious strategies as they sought out new sacred meanings and sacred understandings from the margins of their stressed sacred marriages. They normalized, legitimized, moralized, and sacralized their emotions and relationships through narratives they told themselves and others. These narratives were attempts to explain and persuade listeners that their marriages were still sacred. They reconstructed their sacred marriages by doing and using segmented religious discourse and religious culture to redefine their problems of action and bend religious discourse and religious culture in the production of their new sacred marriages.

Through the bending of religious culture, these couples were able to incorporate contradictory emotions in their relationships that ranged from disgust, to hatred, to sorrow, to guilt, to joy, to happiness, by anchoring these feelings within new religious meanings and subjectivities. These were sacred marriages of difference. They drew upon competing religious discourses to elide those discourses that were inconsistent with their solutions to the problems they faced. They sought out segments of religious culture that supported their emotions, even when their emotions clashed with other morals and mores. These sacred marriages often exhibited a one-sided tilt towards the subjective emotions of one or both spouses over the socially imposed emotions and strategies of action in religious culture. These couples found a niche within the complexities of religious culture that much of the community of sacred marriages may not accept as fully religious or fully sacred. However, even when they are unable to reconcile their lived experiences with other religious communities, they embraced their sacred marriages despite their detachment from traditional religious contexts – placing them at the margin of their communities – but still producing new emotional and cultural standards when they found other social domains emotionally meaningless or too constraining.

9 Conclusion

Throughout this book, I have suggested an extension and redirection of the scholarship examining sacred marriages with a strong focus on the social. I have argued against objectivist and reductionist paradigms in favor of a more fluid understanding of the blending of religious and nonreligious spheres in the sacralization of marriages. I have also suggested that a wide range of emotions (e.g., sensate emotions, social emotions, and religious emotional regimes) serve as powerful movers in people's sacred marriages. Marriages are sacralized by sacralizing various domains of people's lives (e.g., sacralized love, sacralized sex, and sacralized childbearing). And, while the importance of culture cannot be overlooked in the sacralization of marriage, neither can powerful gendered, embodied discourses in the reproduction of cultural strategies of action that people use to solve their problems. People in sacred marriages often find and seek supernatural interventions in their lives to mask their individual agency and collective agency as a couple. Ultimately, religion acts *in* sacred marriages and not *on* sacred marriages by connecting people's stories of their sacred marriages with others who share their stories of sacred marriages. By bending religious discourse, people can construct sacred marriages of difference located at the margins of their communities that endure. But, much like gender difference, sacred marriages are socially constructed as different, requiring people to navigate private and public boundaries in religion (Coltrane 1996).

While my intention has not been to normalize or promote marriage, this book is about sacred marriages. It describes a sample of mostly white, U.S. Midwestern, middle-class, educated grandparents and great-grandparents who are heterosexuals. They have also all been married at least 40 years. The Christian marriage advice manuals are drawn from the sample's homes, churches, and publishing companies they believe represent their religious denominations. But, all the interviews were conducted in English, and the manuals were written in English. All the data is representative of a particular religious culture of Christianity that exists within a strongly divided political culture in the early 21st century. The couples and the manuals exist within a social and political history that has experienced tremendous changes in gender, love, religion, and marriage (Browning 2003; Burns 2005; Griffith 2017; Haag 2011; Nock et al 2008). Taking these factors and others into consideration, there are clearly limitations to this study. I have no reason to assume that my findings concerning the influences of gendered discourse and culture on sacred marriages are generalizable to any broader population, but I also have no reason to assume they are not. However, the impacts of religion in how people live in sacred marriages, assuming sacred marriages even exist in every culture, could vary widely from the findings in this study. Nonetheless, my findings are significant and add to the scholarship of religion and sacred marriages.

Sacred marriages are private and public

There is power in the ways people act, think, feel, and talk in and about their sacred marriages and the sacred marriages of others. The ways people act, think, feel, and talk in and about their sacred marriages and the sacred marriages of others are not static, but are embedded in and reflect changes in culture. Sacred marriages exist at the nexus of the individual and the collective. When people have exhausted their cultural toolkits to solve problems of action in which their marriages are threatened, they sometimes bend religion and reinvest in sacred aspects of their lives to give new and altered meanings to the ways they talk, think, feel, and act. They share stories in which they position themselves in places, times, groups, and contexts in which others not only share but seek supernatural interventions in their sacred marriages.

Most of the time the couples I interviewed expressed ideas about religion's influences in their marriages in terms of the nature of God, organized religion, spirituality, faith, and the social world in which their marriages exist. It is in these stories of the sacred, whether religious or nonreligious, that people found and sought ideas, causes, and solutions to their problems of action. As Ammerman (2014) suggests, stories exist at the nexus of public and private, and stories about the sacred allow people to position themselves within broader narrative frames accounting for their thoughts, feelings, and actions. People's stories identified where they belonged within culture, what they did with culture, and why they did it. People's stories intertwined their individual narratives with public, shared stories. They not only described how they talked, felt, thought, and acted individually, but also how others like them talked, felt, thought, and acted. Their sacred stories elevated the importance of mundane experiences in their sacred marriages, giving them power and salience through a wide range of emotions (e.g., sensate emotions, social emotions, and religious emotional regimes). The power and feelings people shared often did not represent order, coherency, or logic individually, but they gave powerful meanings to their use of culture. Their stories of their sacred marriages described aspects of their pasts, expectations of their futures, and positioned their interactions and relationships within strategies of action.

Segmented sacralization

While a minority of the couples I interviewed and a handful of the manuals I analyzed described a general sacralization of marriage in terms of a divine plan for the salvation of humanity, the primary mechanism through which marriages were sacralized occurred through a segmented sacralization of various domains of marriage. First, marriage itself was sacralized through a discursive positioning of contrasted cultures. This occurred through a juxtaposed framing of marriage in religious and secular cultures, as though religious and nonreligious spheres are dichotomous and ordered with the religious sphere superordinate to the nonreligious sphere. The sacralization of marriage is dependent on separation from and delegitimization of all relationships that are not sacred marriages. If love, sex, and childbearing are sacred only within marriage, then all other forms of relationship structures, love, sex, and childbearing must be perceived as threats to sacred marriages.

Second, emotions – especially sensate emotions – were sacralized by linking them to love, sex, and childbearing, again through positioning emotions within contrasted cultures. Sacred marriages are produced through discourse within a power system in which religious culture is framed as authentic, natural, legitimate, and moral, while nonreligious culture is framed as corrupt, unnatural, illegitimate, and immoral. Embodied religious practices in sacred spaces are sacralized, while the nonreligious body is considered disgusting, sinful, unworthy, and not to be trusted. Sacralized sex is framed as only legitimate within marriage, and any sex other than heterosexual sex within marriage serves as a threat to sacred marriages. Love is described as an inherent attribute of sex, and sex between husbands and wives mirrors sacred love for humanity. Childbearing is linked with divine love which empowers sex between husbands and wives with the potential to share in the creative power of the divine, allowing human thoughts, feelings, and actions to temporarily enter the realm of the sacred, giving love, sex, and childbearing the power of the sacred.

Bending religion

While the couples I interviewed shared stories about their marriages using elements of the segmented sacralization of marriage I have described, religion was far more malleable, plastic, and fluid in the production of their sacred marriages. They also altered religion to form new sacred marriages. Many couples told stories about religious rituals they believed held sacred importance in their marriages. But, they almost always referred to the uniqueness of these rituals in their own experiences as contrasted with the experiences of others who participated in the same rituals as a means to further sacralize and privatize their own experiences of the rituals common to the broader community. Whether it was being intoxicated and vomiting on the minister, changing a Church marriage document, standing off the alter, spilling wine on a wedding dress before the ceremony, or refusing to attend a wedding, the couples in this study were constrained and limited by religion but were also liberated by creatively bending it to their needs to find solutions to their problems of action. Consistent with Gerson (2010) the couples in this study were able to cross gendered religious boundaries and blur sacred meanings in search of more effective ways to solve their problems of action.

When the cultural tools found in traditional religious practices no longer held their utility or sacred meanings, they forged new cultural repertoires incorporating new and altered cultural tools from both religious and nonreligious spheres. Whether it was deceiving the Church and not acquiring a state-issued marriage license, embracing a therapeutic culture to deal with children's addictions, or disregarding Church teachings about contraception, or remaining married to a husband who engages in extramarital sex, the couples in these sacred marriages were able to bend religion to fit their needs and create new and altered sacred marriages. Through dialectic relations and altering religious emotional regimes associated with comprising, couples were able to engage in transformative processes in their marriages that promoted self-regulation of their relationships.

Sacred marriages operate within other cultures

Sacred marriages do not exist in a cultural vacuum or exclusively within religious culture. Instead, the couples I interviewed produced sacred marriages within broader cultural and social contexts. They sought out communities of believers within cultures of diversity, caregiving, family support, social justice, and politics to tell their stories of sacred marriages, to listen to others' stories of sacred marriages, and to belong to the broader narratives of sacred marriages. While elite religious discourse was important to many of the people I interviewed, there was almost no couple who agreed completely with all Church teachings. There were also no two couples who experienced religious involvement the same, although there were similarities and patterns that emerged among the couples. Consistent with Ammerman (2005), that which was most important for the majority of couples in this study, when searching for a community with whom to experience and practice religion, was the culture of that community. Specific religious scripts were far less salient in their choices of physical and social spaces to live their sacred marriages than were nonreligious cultures that framed those spaces.

Effects of religion in sacred marriages

Sacred marriages are messy. Neither religion nor the sacralization of marriage are panaceas for people's problems. In this book, I have included only a few of the many challenges couples in this study faced. Believing marriage is sacred does not absolve people from their choices and their use of cultural tools to structure the ways they think, talk, feel, and act in their lived experiences of religion, marriage, and family. Almost everyone in this study had one or more siblings or children who divorced. Many couples described unresolved conflicts they had with spouses, with children, with siblings, with coworkers, with religious leaders, and with members of their religious communities. The challenges people faced often served as the source of remedies in their marriages that they argued further sacralized their marriages through privatization and a sense of ownership of their problems. Others, rejected completely their own agency in the solutions they chose to address their problems of action, turning instead to supernatural intervention as a means of masking their failures and attributing their successes to a power greater than themselves.

Changes to religion and sacred marriages

Mostly, religious discourse and religious culture provide sacred marriages with stable strategies of action and cultural tools that people generally know how to manipulate to solve their problems. Certainly the manuals, and almost all of the people I interviewed, had no desire for changes in religious discourse or religious culture concerning sacred marriages.

Clarence is a retired school administrator who is Methodist. He grew up helping his family operate a small general store in a rural community. He was demonstrative in his response to my questions about changing the Church and its teachings, raising his voice and gesturing emphatically with his hands he said the following:

> The Church has definitely changed. The Church is catering to numbers. [. . .] They're trying to get people into the Church, so they have lost the ability to teach what really is in the Bible. [. . .] Because if they do they're going to offend somebody, and that's the way I see it. If you don't want to offend somebody because you're afraid you'll lose numbers, then you don't teach things. . . . The Church was designed to teach you how to worship God. . . . It was there to teach you what to do. And now we just teach what people want to hear.

Phil reflected on many changes in the Catholic church throughout his interview without being prompted. He shared several concerns about what he believed were falling numbers of Christians globally, Catholic parishes closing due to low membership, and a general decline of the Church as a social institution.

> I read an article in the paper the other day about the liberal and the conservative Catholic bishops. [. . .] I think there is some kind of a split coming someday. Back in the 60s, when Pope John wrote his encyclical that allowed nuns not to wear habits, during that time – I think they called it Vatican II – they kind of said, "Okay, go ahead and do your own thing." [. . .] Once you change things and let people try to do things their own way the old way kind of becomes gone. If you're going to do that think about it in 40, 50, or 60 years from now. Things are going to be a lot different. They're not going to be the way they are now. [. . .] You know there's a lot of people . . . and churches saying it's okay to have gay marriage, or live together, or yada, yada, yada. It's like with your kids . . . there has to be certain rules, and whether they like it or not, they have to follow them. Otherwise go do your own thing, but don't

tell me you're Catholic. Otherwise, marriage isn't a sacrament. What does it mean if you change it?

Like many participants in this study, Marvin was concerned that the church is not doing enough to prevent changes in Church teaching.

> The Church should continue the same thing that they have had for 2,000 years. [. . .] The strength of the Church is that they are consistent with the teachings of the apostles. [. . .] The first thing is that the Church is not from the pulpit giving a consistent message of this is right and this is wrong. [. . .] I'm tired of hearing that it's too hard to understand it all too. You don't have to understand the Catechism, let's say, to follow it. Where else are these kids going to turn to learn about God's plan for marriage?

Richard was conflicted about existing changes in the Catholic Church. After describing his dissatisfaction with Vatican II, changes he witnessed like the service no longer being conducted in Latin, the removal of the communion rail, and no longer having a four-page Latin card that he "used and didn't even know what [he was] saying," he shared the following:

> We go to church every day and I wonder why [did they change that]? Why are they changing again? What is the purpose of sticking that in there? What does this mean? What does that mean? I think people nowadays aren't the way they were a few years ago. I was born and raised Catholic and that's my faith. I think nowadays people go if it's convenient, and they don't if it's not. I think if you're Catholic you've at least got to go to church on Sunday. [. . .] I wouldn't even call them Catholic. I don't care what you believe, and everyone can dissent if they don't want to follow what the church teaches, but if you're Catholic, you're Catholic.

Some wives were direct and forceful in their answers to my questions about changing Church teachings. Josephine actually reached across the table and grabbed my forearm, pulling me closer to her as she said, "Hell yes, the Church has to change. I had six pregnancies, and I was a nervous wreck. The Church needs to stay out of people's sex lives and stop putting pressure on people to have families that meet the Church's definition of what a family is."

But, the majority of wives were contemplative in their responses. Mary Jo's and Patsy's narratives exemplify the reflective tone of most of the wives.

Mary Jo said, "There are a lot of things that probably should change in the Church, but I'm not sure they should. There are a lot of things we could change, but I think God's word is powerful because it is unchanging."

Patsy was particularly reserved, "I have no opinion on the Church's positions. That doesn't change my behavior any. I just kind of stay out of that in a way. I don't have any real opinion on it. You have to answer to your maker at the end and explain to him what you've done. But I will say, it's between you and your maker, not you and the Church."

Cynthia shared,

> You know, let them change whatever they want. I am very trusting. If they say there needs to be change, I just try to be obedient because it doesn't change how I feel about God. These men can say whatever they want, and it won't change what God means to me, whether I decide to do what they say or not. God's love isn't in the words of men. It won't change my relationship with God one whit.

As Marcia formed her answer to my questions about changes in the Church, she paused several times to carefully consider her next words.

> I am a cradle Catholic. [Long pause] My views on things have changed over the years. [Long pause] I see more of the perspective of what the Church is teaching from a more holistic perspective. [Long pause] They are trying to put us in the frame of mind where we are truly serving God and not serving ourselves. If we are serving ourselves we're putting God off to the side. We are creating our own gods, [long pause] whatever they might be. If it's your obsession with money or some hobby – and it can be a lot of things – but if you become obsessed about things, then you're pushing God aside. [Long pause] It's still something I struggle with. Every time I think I'm in alignment with the Church on these issues, I see some situation that comes up, and I think, "Well, wait a minute." [Long pause] The struggle for me is how do I put aside my logical nature at times and trust that the position the Church takes is the right one. It's not that I want to follow blindly but I want to follow with faith. [Long pause] I don't begrudge others for the actions they take, in that's their decision to make. [Long pause] If asked, I would give someone my opinion, but I wouldn't try to force anyone to accept it.

The negotiation of religious discourse and religious culture in the production of sacred marriages is an ongoing process. Sacred marriages are built and rebuilt within the quotidian realities of married life. The people I interviewed were just trying to live their lives. They went to school, had careers, ran households, raised children, enjoyed vacations, and tried to be good people. They experience religion in different ways. While a few mentioned miracles in their lives, even they shared these sacred stories sparingly. The people in this study believed marriage was sacred for religious reasons, but they did not let religion control their lives. Consistent with Ammerman's (2014) findings, religious meanings are less salient in people's lives when their everyday experiences impinge on their religious lives. Although almost everyone I interviewed attended church with regularly frequency, there were only a few exceptions in which people did not miss because of school, work, household responsibilities, childrearing, or travel. Every event was not sacred in their lives. Most of the time, they lived their lives through routine employment of cultural repertoires they used to resolve their problems. In fact, people were often leery of those whom they found to be too religious. They were cautious of those who too frequently proffered sacred attributes to daily life. Instead, their perception of the sacred was premised on individual agency, personal decision-making, and personal effort as motives for evaluating marriage and family outcomes.

Gender

Sacred marriages are gendered. Gender affects emotion work in sacred marriages, as well as how people act, think, talk, and feel about their love relationships with their spouses and others. Love itself is gendered, and husbands and wives negotiate religion in their sacred marriages in tandem to reflexively produce gendered sacred meanings. Marriages are sacralized through the sacralization of sex and childbearing using discourses of gendered embodiment. The sacred takes on an embodied transcendence that is both father and mother, sexualized, and gendered as masculine but with feminine qualities. Marriage is sacralized by constraining sex and empowering both men and women as co-creators with the divine. Marriages are sacralized by discursively positioning sacred gendered roles of husbands and wives against secular culture's eschewance of traditional gender roles. The sacralization of marriages is reproduced through rituals that forge embodied memories of social emotions in sacralized everyday spaces. Ultimately, rituals and religious practices are performed in gendered spaces within gendered communities designed to promote and support gendered expectations in sacred marriages.

Implications

Sacred marriages are largely unconscious in people's lives. They do not have to question whether others believe that sex is a sacred aspect of their marriage, or that the birth of a child was a sacred moment between them, or that experiencing the death of a child was a sacred time that they shared together outside the gaze of others. They recognize that people generally attend weddings, first communions, baptisms, confirmations, and funerals because elements of each of these rituals are sacred in life, but they are mostly a time to gather family and friends together in celebration and recognition of achievement and the passing of time. Most of the lived experiences of sacred marriages goes unquestioned and unexplained in the routine of life.

   My findings suggest that there is tremendous value in the study of sacred marriages. Given that the sacred is rarely consciously employed in couples lived experiences of religion in their marriages, the reasons it is employed prove salient in the study of religion's influences in marriage and family processes. The times that people in this study told stories in which they acknowledge their use of sacred meanings in their marriages were typically situations when they refused to compromise (e.g., not attending a wedding, severing a relationship with a daughter, severing relationships with extended family, and remaining married in the midst of infidelity). It appears that sacred marriages are most important in people's lives at the extremes of marriage and family processes at the points where their relationships are most fragile and risk dissolution. At those times, people forge new sacred marriages with new ways of talking, feeling, thinking, and acting. Future research may benefit from less focus on individual beliefs about the sacred and more on what people do and how they do it during these extreme circumstances.

Appendix
Methodology

For this study of religion and sacred marriages, participants were interviewed over a three-year period beginning in 2011. Interviews were conducted in Indiana, Ohio, and Michigan. There were two criteria for inclusion in the study. First, participants had to be married to the same person for at least 40 years. Second, both spouses had to be self-reported Christians who held religious beliefs that marriage is sacred. The initial two couples were approached for inclusion because they are each highly visible, prominent members of a large Catholic and Methodist church, respectively. They then helped recruit additional participants for the study.

Given that many couples in the sample are Catholic, and given this study's theoretical frame, I wanted to include couples married prior to or near the time of the Second Vatican Council (informally known as Vatican II) which closed in 1965 and represented a significant shift in the lived experience of Catholicism for many Catholics. A shared sociocultural history is an important aspect of this study. Being married 40 years or more also means that the majority of couples I interviewed were born by about 1950 and were married by about 1975. Thus, the participants share a common culture of the 1960s, were witnesses to the space race, Neil Armstrong's stepping on the moon, the gender movements, the Cold War, and the war in Vietnam. Most importantly their marriages endured during a period in time that arguably experienced the sharpest rise in divorce rates in U.S. history; yet, their marriages endured.

Interview methodology

For the interview portion of the study, I used intensive interviewing. Interviews were conducted in couples' homes. I interviewed couples for approximately two hours separately followed by an interview of about one hour together. Spouses were interviewed separately because it allowed a more detailed examination of the ways in which each spouse constructed the links between religion and their sacred marriages. It also allowed them to openly and honestly discuss sensitive issues like infidelity and marital conflict. After separate interviews, the couples were interviewed together. Given the heavy reliance of most studies conducted over the past decade on self-reports of religiosity and family relationships (Mahoney 2010), I also interviewed couples both separately and together to increase the accuracy of responses. This provided the opportunity for couples to fill in gaps in each other's recollections, share different kinds of knowledge held by each individual, and to remind and correct each other of shared experiences. I was also able to observe some of their nonverbal communications. Examples of these portrayals included holding hands, head nods, discerning looks, and the presentation of symbolic and sacred objects (e.g., wedding photos, small gifts between spouses, a wedding dress, jewelry, and various religious objects such as palm fronds, and a family bible including significant wedding and birthdates in their family). One couple actually encouraged each other by kissing when they perceived they had given "good" answers to my questions and discouraged each other by playfully nudging each other when either spouse felt the other's response gave a negative connotation to their marriage, family, or faith.

Sample

The sample consisted of 43 heterosexual couples married over 40 years who were self-proclaimed Christians who hold religious beliefs that marriage is sacred. The average length of marriage was 50.91 years (range = 41 to 71). The sample included 22 Catholic couples and 21 Protestant couples: 10 Methodist, two Lutheran, three Evangelical Baptist, two Presbyterian, and two couples belonging to the Church of Christ. The remaining two Protestant couples claimed no religious denomination reporting only that they were "Christians," and that they attended a nondenominational, Protestant church. Although several individual respondents indicated they had converted between denominations prior to their marriage, all respondents indicated they attended the same church as their spouse throughout their entire marriage.

Couple-based demographic data

Although what follows is not traditionally presented in methodology portions of studies, I want to stress the importance of viewing the demographic data through a married, couple-focused lens. Sacred marriages are conceptualized and operationalized through couple-based processes in this study taking seriously individual agency as well as each couples' collective agency. And while individual-level data contribute to the unique sociocultural historical experiences of each spouse, there is equally a unique sociocultural historical experience for each married couple. Although I have separated the data and codified the data as distinct ontological constructs, they do not take on the same meanings for the couples in this study as they do for researchers. These data represent an extreme reductionist view of the complex subjectivities of the couples I interviewed and should be viewed only as a small part of a greater whole.

Educational attainment is a commonly measured sociological construct used to describe a sample for a study. The couples in this study shared stories about significant periods in their lives as a married couple using education not as an individual attainment but rather as an aspect of married life. For example, Phyllis holds a bachelor's degree in education and taught high school math and science her entire life except for the time she stopped teaching to have children. Her husband Arnold holds a master's degree and worked as a senior executive in the defense industry. "Once I finished my bachelor's degree, *we* decided to have *our* first child, while *we* were getting *our* master's degree." (Italics has been added for emphasis). Notice that Phyllis said "our" master's degree, although she does not have a master's degree. Arnold has a master's degree. Likewise, Arnold incorporated Phyllis' experience of childbearing into his educational attainment. "*We* were *blessed* with our daughter Betsy when *we* were finishing college. *We* had Robby when *we* started at StarDefense Industries." Both Phyllis and Arnold describe their educational attainment, childbearing, and employment using plural pronouns with a focus on a lifetime as a married couple, and not as individual attainments. Based on the couple-focused presentation of demographic data within the narratives of the couples interviewed for this study, and the poststructuralist theoretical orientation of this study, I have attempted to present demographic data that describes the sample in terms of married couples, while still providing sufficient data to construct pertinent individual-level measures to describe the sample.

I intentionally did not use a separate respondent survey to gather demographic information from each participant individually. Again, I felt it important to gather demographic data within the narratives provided by the respondents as individuals and as couples. Questions about frequency of attendance, prayer, age at marriage, number of children, extended family, and education are filled with powerful meanings embedded in religious discourse. For example, a few couples had advanced degrees and had either dated or married during graduate school. This allowed me to question where they attended church during their courtship, how pursuing their degrees influenced frequency of church attendance, and the role of their faith in decisions to marry, have additional children, and manage financial conflicts.

The following demographic data are provided as a reflection of the social context in which study participants lived their lives. Additionally, given the retrospective nature of the accounts of the participants throughout the interviews, the demographic data were generated in an attempt to better understand the significance they had to the participants within their own narratives. These demographic data changed through the participants' life courses as well. For example, men almost always began their narratives about their families of origin by describing their fathers' employment, while women were far more likely to begin their narratives by describing the structures of their families of origin (e.g., number of aunts, uncles, and siblings). I sought out demographic information to determine where participants positioned that data within the narratives of their marriage.

The education categories I used included some graduate school or completion of graduate school, some college or completion of an undergraduate degree, high school graduate, and no high school graduation. Seven husbands had graduate degrees as did all their wives except one who had some college and another who graduated high school. Of the 12 husbands who had attended or completed college, all of their wives also had some college except for one wife with a graduate degree, two wives with high school degrees, and one wife who did not graduate high school. Of the 20 husbands with high school educations, all of their wives had high school educations as well with the exception of one wife with a college education and four wives with no high school education. Only one husband did not graduate high school, and his wife did graduate high school. Thus, 23 percent (n = 10) of the sample couples have graduate degrees, 28 percent (n = 12) of the couples had some college education, 47 percent (n = 20) of the couples had high school educations, and one couple consisted of a wife with a high school education and a husband who did not graduate high school.

All of the couples were white, although five couples included a spouse who was non-white. Everyone in the sample had children and grandchildren with the exception of one couple who had no children. Although I did not specifically ask about great-grandchildren, several couples reported being great-grandparents. Four couples had adopted children, and all but one of them had at least one non-white child. The participants' ages ranged from 62 years old to 92 years old. I did not gather specific birth year data on each participant given the relative homogeneity of their ages, however I did gather specific data on year of marriage and age at marriage. Sixteen percent (n = 7) of the sample is in their 60s, 72 percent (n = 31) of the sample is in their 70s, and 12 percent (n = 5) of the sample is over 80 years old. Two participants were divorced before marrying their current spouse. Almost the entire sample married by the age of 22 (n = 42), with the vast majority marrying within one year of high school graduation (n = 35). The oldest person to marry for the first time was a 27-year-old-woman. Twenty-two couples married while the husband was in military service.

It is difficult to describe the couples in terms of income across their life course because many started poor but built wealth through time. Given that I interviewed all of them near or after retirement age, their current incomes do not accurately represent their lived experiences of religion, marriage, and family. It is also not possible to reflect income in terms of constant dollars in a given year for comparative purposes based on the narrative methodology I chose. However, almost all 43 husbands had consistent outside employment with only minor interruptions due to job transitions throughout their lifetimes. In contrast, most wives took time off from the paid labor force for childrearing.

I ultimately decided to code income based first on husband's employment and then on spouse's employment. The categories included high income (e.g., large business owners, senior attorneys, senior accountants, school or university administrators, nursing supervisors, and senior executives), medium income (e.g., skilled factory workers, middle managers, small business owners, professors, and school teachers), and low income (e.g., entry-level minimum wage jobs). The additional category of none represents wives who were lifetime "homemakers" or "stay-at-home moms," as they described themselves, but had no consistent, paid employment outside the home. Despite their full-time homemaker status, they sometimes took jobs to supplement family income. However, this income offers little probative value to this study. Only three of the wives of high income husbands had low or no income. The wives of the medium income husbands ranged from no income to medium income. Of the five low income husbands all of their wives are low income or had no income. In sum, of the married couples in this study 37 percent (n = 16) are high income, 49 percent are medium income (n = 21), and 14 percent (n = 6) are low income.

Many of the couples I interviewed included at least one spouse who experienced some form of family trauma or parental absence during their childhood. Of the 86 individual spouses I interviewed, 29 experienced an event during childhood that has been associated with marriage instability in the literature. Some spouses had fathers who were frequently absent (n = 7), experienced the death of a parent during their childhood (n = 12), experienced the death of a sibling during childhood (n = 4), experienced childhood physical or sexual abuse (n = 9), were abandoned by biological parents and raised by grandparents (n = 3), had parents who were alcoholics (n = 17), had a parent with mental illness (n = 13), or whose parents were unwed, teenagers (n = 4). Although these estimates represent unduplicated counts, several spouses experienced more than one of these traumatic events in their childhoods. Some spouses also married other spouses who experienced these traumatic events as children, resulting in 54 percent (n = 23 couples) of the couples in this study having experienced familial traumas as children that have been attributed to marital instability.

One criticism that could be levied against this study is that the sample is largely homogenous and lacks diversity. The sample consists primarily of predominantly white, Midwestern, grandparents, in their 70s, who married young, are middle income, and are college educated. However, that is by design and an artifact of the intentionality of the sampling method I used. Snowball sampling was chosen for this study because it was important to capture similar religious discourses and lived experiences within their shared religious cultures across the participants' lifetimes. Subjectivity and social imaginaries are dependent on construed futures based on lived experiences; therefore, the more common the lived experiences and social contexts within the sample, the better I was able to isolate the processes in the sacralization of marriage and observe when and how religious and nonreligious discourse and culture was used to sacralize marriages.

The lack of variation based on race within the sample is also intentional. The "effects of race" in sociological studies is not based on skin color or behavior. According to Zuberi and Bonilla-Silva (2008: 7), "Race is about an individual's relationship to other people within the society." Race is a social construction dependent on "the merging of self-imposed choice within an externally imposed context." Additionally, religious discourse and the interpretation of religious discourse is highly dependent on race. Given the importance of lived experiences in social contexts associated with race specifically (Marks et al 2008), and the role of context in the social construction of race as part of subjectivity and social imaginaries, it was important to seek a homogenous sample. Given the influence of race on the formation of social networks, it is not surprising that this sample is predominantly white, given the sampling methodology.

While I did not intentionally seek participants who were related or members of the same congregations, the overlap of social networks among the participants strengthened the sample's exposure to shared culture and religious discourse. The people I interviewed all draw from a common pool of religious discourses and religious cultures. Often they shared sacred spaces, friendships, and kinship ties. I interviewed cousins and their spouses, siblings and their spouses, people who had attended the same churches as other couples I interviewed, and two couples who were in-laws because the son of one couple married the daughter of another couple.

Ultimately, the representativeness of the sample is inconsequential in certain respects. I do not generalize the findings of my research to the population at-large. I also do not use the data in this study as evidence of any influence of religion on sacred marriages among other religions or racial or ethnic groups beyond that of the sample. Most importantly, the theoretical perspective guiding my analysis is not dependent on correctly characterizing a particular religious discourse or particular person in a particular moment. However, I see no reason to assume that the theoretical processes I suggest in this study work differently for others than the study sample. Although it is beyond the scope of this study, the theoretical processes I describe are likely universal for all sacred marriages, but further research is required.

Transcript analysis

With the participants' permission, I audio-taped the in-depth interviews and personally transcribed them. I used open coding to identify major themes in the data. During open coding, labels were given to recurring concepts to create related groups. Axial coding was then employed to collapse themes into fewer, broader themes. In a second phase of axial coding, links were constructed and deconstructed between groups. I concluded this triadic coding process with selective coding to identify overarching themes. The resulting major themes were reduced by combining themes and removing less salient themes. A final formal review of the transcripts occurred to identify instances that did not support the resulting themes and concepts. Concurrently, I attempted to find additional evidence supporting, broadening, and refining the final themes and concepts identified in the analysis stage to bring greater validity to the study.

While I used the same interview questionnaire for each interview, I let the person being interviewed take the lead in sharing the story of their marriage and family. I let participants share what they felt were the most salient aspects and least significant elements of religion in their marriages, and in the order they chose within their narratives. Although I ensured that all of the essential elements of the study were addressed in the narratives, I let participants take the lead in sharing what they knew about religion, how they learned what they knew, when they learned it, and how they used it.

By pushing participants to explain what they meant by phrases like "God's plan," "the power of prayer," "we're blessed," "God's will," and "sacred," I sought out the manner in which people put religion to use in their marriages. I wanted to know the origins of their religious knowledge as well as its benefit in dealing with the challenges they faced in their marriages. I was interested in knowing how religion shaped the way they talked, thought, felt, and acted in their marriages. More than that, I wanted to know how they thought and felt about the ways they used, rejected, or modified religious discourse and culture. While Swidler (2001) examined how people use culture, I also examined how people felt and thought about how they used religious culture in their marriages. Most importantly, I sought out examples of how, when, and where people believed that religion acted of its own accord in their lives exhibiting supra-human agency that often conflicted with the agency of individual participants in this study.

In-depth interview questionnaire

Based on selective elements of the work of Gallagher (2003), Bartkowski (2001), and Swidler (2001), the interview instrument included questions covering five areas: sociocultural context, meaning of marriage and commitment, religiosity, love, and family life.

In-depth individual spouse interview questionnaire (investigator-administered)

[Read at the beginning of each interview]

This is a study of the things married couples do that bring their relationship closer together and make it last. I'm asking couples who have been married for a long time to tell me a little about what seems important in their personal relationships, what some of their greatest problems are, what seems to work well, and what some sources of difficulty have been. It isn't a study where there are right answers or wrong answers. I'm just interested in trying to better understand the influence of religion on marriages that have lasted a long time. I will not share anything you tell me with your spouse, and I won't share anything your spouse tells me with you.

1   First, can you tell me a little about yourself? Where are you from? Where you worked, or used to work, if you're retired?

   Probing Questions if Needed:
   Age? Occupation? Education? Residential history? How long were parents married?
   Do you have siblings and how long have they been married? Children and are they married and for how long? When is your anniversary? How old were you when you got married?

2   Can you tell me about some of the major things you are doing now, at this point in your life? Is there anything especially important or unusual happening in your life now? What? Is there anything special you are trying to do? What? Or is it just a normal time? Normal in what way?

3 What has your relationship been with the Church? To which local church do you belong, and how has it played a role in your family?

Autobiographical – cultural history

4 Can you tell me something about your background?

Probing Questions if Needed:
Where you grew up? What your family was like? Can you tell me about your religious upbringing? Where you lived? What your childhood was like? (Happy, secure, less happy?) What activities did you participate in that you do or did with your family as an adult? (birthdays, movies, holidays, weddings, religious activities, games, tv, family meals?)

5 Tell me about married life. Have you ever been divorced or cohabitated with someone other than your current spouse? Tell me more about that relationship.

Probing Questions if Needed:
How long did it last? Were you happy in that relationship? Did you love that person? Why did the relationship end? How did that relationship influence your current marriage?

6 And now I'm particularly interested in what ideas about love, marriage, or personal relationships you might have had when you were young.

What ideas about love do you think you might have gotten from the Church? Were your parents religious? Did they have any influence? Other relatives? Friends?

7 Thinking back now, say to when you were younger, maybe a teenager, do you remember what you thought love was, or what you expected it to be? What role did the Church and your faith play in shaping your thoughts about love?

Probing Questions if Needed:
Do you know where you got those ideas? Family? Friends? Popular songs, books, TV, movies? And did you ever think you were in love? How did you know? What did it feel like?

8 Tell me about a time when you would say you were really in love with your husband/wife?

Probing Questions if Needed:
What made you think it was love? Is that an idea of love you still hold? How has your understanding of love in marriage changed through time? What things did you first do to show your spouse you loved them? Are those still things you do to show your love? How have those things changed through time? What role did your church, faith, and God have in shaping your understanding of love?

Sacred meanings in marriage

9   What can you tell me about marriage and your church, your faith, and God?

Probing Questions if Needed:
How did you meet? Did God have a role in you meeting your spouse? How long did you date? What did you do on dates? Were others present on dates? Do you think your beliefs influenced what you did or where you went on dates? How did you decide that this was the person you wanted to marry? What role did God, your church, or your beliefs play in your decision? Did you think or know that you were in love? Was love an important consideration? How did you recognize it as love? Were you sure or unsure? What questions did you ask yourself? What did it feel like? Did your beliefs or God influence what you experienced as love? Did you love them right away, or was it something that grew gradually? Did God have a hand in you growing to love your spouse? Were you sure that this was the right person to marry? Unsure? Why? Did your faith or God influence your decision? Was deciding who to marry hard or easy? What did you do to show them you loved them? Did the kinds of activities you did together change through time? What role did the church, God, and your beliefs have in preparing you for marriage?

10   During your marriage, have your ideas about love and your faith changed? How? Why do you think they haven't changed?

Probing Questions if Needed:
What have you done differently in your marriage than you did at first to strengthen it? Has the Church shaped your understanding of what you should do to demonstrate love? Has God had a role in shaping your marriage?

11   What have been the most important things you've learned about relationships from the Church and your beliefs? What have been the hardest issues to deal with? Have there been unexpected things? Good? Bad? What role did God or your faith have in these events?

12   On the whole would you say it is a good marriage, a good relationship? In what ways is it good, bad, and could it be better? How do you think your faith influences your answer?

General ideas about love and marriage

13   Tell me about your beliefs, love, and marriage.

Probing Questions if Needed:
Does love and marriage require some sort of intense, ecstatic experience?
If so, what do you do to keep that experience from dying out? If not, do you worry about missing that? What role does your church, God, and your faith play? Does loving imply obligation to certain activities? How does

your church, faith, and God influence your answer? What responsibilities do families and couples have to each other? How does your church, faith, and God influence your answer? What about sacrifice? Should people make sacrifices for those they love? How does your church, faith, and God influence your answer? Does love have to be permanent in a marriage? If not, what should people do to keep their marriage going, if they don't feel love? Has the Church, your faith, or God ever helped you as an individual or as a couple to get more emotional energy from your marriage and family?

Conflict and Marriage

14 Tell me about your beliefs and conflict in marriage.

Probing Questions if Needed:

When there is conflict, should you do what's best for yourself or best for the other person in the relationship? What things have you done or do you do now that you do to prevent conflict? How does your church, faith, and God influence your answer? What are some activities you've participated in with your spouse or apart from your spouse that have been sources of conflict? Has the Church, God, or your faith ever been a source of conflict?

Why were they sources of conflict and how did you manage to stay married during these conflicts?

Rituals

15 What are some things you do without your spouse that you think strengthen your marriage and have allowed you to stay married for so long? Do they involve the church, your faith, or God? How?

16 What are some things your spouse does without you that you think strengthen your marriage and have allowed you to stay married for so long? Do they involve the church, God, or your faith? How?

17 What are some things you do with your spouse that you think strengthen your marriage and have allowed you to stay married for so long? Do they involve the church, your faith, or God? How?

18 I want to know about your day-to-day activities. What things do you do with your spouse? Just describe a normal day from the time you get up until the time you go to bed, and tell me where your spouse is in relationship to these activities.

19 Has this routine changed through time? How has it changed through time? What makes it different? Why did it change? Has the role of the church, God, and your faith changed in your family and marriage through time?

20 Tell me about the influence of your church, your faith, and God on lasting marriages.

Couple Interview

[These questions were asked with both spouses present]

[Begin by clarifying any inconsistencies from the individual interviews and ask probing questions about important issues from those interviews].

1   Tell me about the presence of the church, your faith, and God in your home.
2   What is the most important thing about the church, your faith, and God that have directly impacted your marriage?
3   What would you change about your church or faith related to your marriage?
4   To be included in this interview, you stated that you felt marriage was sacred. What does it mean for a marriage to be sacred? After talking with me, do you think your marriage is still sacred?
5   Does your church or God have a plan for marriage and your marriage specifically?
6   Do you think God is part of your marriage?
7   Describe your religious life together as a married couple please.

Textual analysis methodology of Christian marriage advice manuals

Given the importance of discourse and culture to the theoretical framework of this book, and the centrality of Christian marriage advice manuals as a form of discourse to my analysis of religion in sacred marriages, the method I used to analyze these primary source documents demands a more detailed description. This study includes 58 Christian advice manuals, all of which are referenced directly in this book.

The reason these manuals bear significance in this study is that these texts serve as exemplars of the dominant, elite religious discourses pertinent to the lived experiences and meanings couples shared during their interviews. They represent the predominate religious discourses to which the couples in this study have been exposed specifically, as well as being indicative of the dominant religious discourses the larger body of married Christians negotiate in their marriages. They purport themselves to link conflicting secular and spiritual discourses in coherent schemata as model types worthy of emulation, even to the extent of creating ties between atheist discourse and Christian discourse (McGowan 2014).

The centrality of the discourses in these manuals in the production and maintenance of subjectivity are clearly present in the stories couples shared about their churches, their religion, themselves, and their marriages. Couples I interviewed frequently made use of concepts found in the marriage advice manuals in their responses. For example, one local Methodist minister had recently offered a five-week-long Bible study based on Gary Chapman's (2010), *The Five Love Languages: The Secret to Love that Lasts*, for married couples in his church. Some of the couples I interviewed had attended the Bible study, and one couple in particular had just finished their daily scripture readings before I arrived at their home.

Eleanor and Tom shared that they try to pray together and read something their pastor recommends every day. They had been praying to better understand each other's "love languages" to strengthen their marriage. Their stories were peppered with the term "love language," and they repeatedly described each other's communication styles within a sacred and "love language" framework.

These texts are not simply a means of conveying information and opinions, but rather they are representative of the power of discourse and culture as ontologically formative and as a salient component of the process by which couples sacralize their marriages and use religion in their lived experiences. The texts offer specific cultural scripts and explain to Christians how they are supposed to use religion to talk, think, feel, and act in their marriages. Several of the manuals were sanctioned specifically by the Church, especially in Catholic publications by the *Nihil Obstat*, which is a certification from a Church censor indicating the text is not objectionable on doctrinal or moral grounds, and the *Imprimatur*, which is a declaration by a Church official to print a religious text. In most cases, these texts represent a Church-approved blueprint for how Christians should talk, think, feel, and act in their marriages. This allowed me to examine how married couples *were supposed to use* religion in their marriages by juxtaposing these texts against *how people actually did use* religion in their marriages.

The Christian marriage advice manuals blend gendered discourse seamlessly into a religious culture. For many of the Catholic manuals, this gendered discourse is sanctioned as elite religious discourse. For example, Fisher (2014a: 13) explicitly states in her bulleted list of what her "book is not about," that, "It's not going to spell out the theological argument against contraception." But, in the very next bullet point she grants herself authority as a Catholic author when she writes, "It's not going to make a secular case for NFP [Natural Family Planning]. I'm Catholic, and I write like a Catholic, so there." While some of the authors claim their gendered rhetoric is not theological and merely a reflection of their own experiences, the fact that they are published by a religious press grants them authority and legitimacy. The front matter of these manuals often make reference to sacred texts like *The Revised Standard Version of the Bible: Catholic Edition*, the *Holy Bible, New International Version*, the *Catechism of the Catholic Church* for the United States of America, the *Catechism of the Catholic Church: Modifications from the Editio Typica*, and *The Roman Missal*. This suggests that the gendered discourse used in the manuals to sacralize marriage is supported by the Church.

Selection of Christian advice manuals

There were three criteria for inclusion of each manual in this analysis. First, I asked each participant the following question: "Do you know of any good Christian marriage advice manuals?" Participants frequently directed me to their bookshelves where I wrote down the titles and authors of the books they indicated. Several couples attended churches with lending libraries containing marriage advice manuals. Many participants eagerly shared these titles with me, almost as a badge of honor that their church offered couple's marriage advice manuals. One husband from a large congregation chaired a marriage committee and said, "You've got to teach these young couples how to have godly marriages and our church does that." No one appeared to hesitate to share what they were reading with me. This may be attributable to the fact that I was in the first year of my own marriage when I began the interviews, and almost every couple I interviewed asked me about my own marital status at some point during the interviews.

Second, I specifically asked participants if they knew of any publishing companies that sold Christian marriage advice manuals. Often these publishers were well known to participants because some publishers have denominational affiliations. For example, it was not surprising that Catholic couples recommended Our Sunday Visitor, Ignatius Press, and Ave Maria Press, all of which market to the Catholic community. Similarly, Methodist participants recommended publishing companies like Abington Press and Cokesbury. I mention these examples of publishing companies to highlight the denominational nature of the publishing companies and the denominational connection they have to the churches participants attended.

This threefold sampling methodology (e.g., manuals couples owned, manuals in church lending libraries, and recommendations of Christian publishers) for inclusion of Christian marriage advice manuals ensures that the texts that are included in my analysis have meaning in the lives of the study participants. They are directly tied to the participants' denominations as well as the participants' churches. They are readily available within the participants' religious communities. More importantly, on multiple occasions, participant narratives made reference to the themes in these texts, evincing the influence of religious discourse and religious culture in sacred marriages.

Given this study's reliance on religious culture and religious discourse specifically, the voice of the Christian marriage advice manuals is particularly of interest. While qualitative sociologists make reference to the voices of underrepresented groups (e.g., women, ethnic minorities, the LGBTQ community, and the disabled), rarely do they refer to the voice of texts. But texts carry the voice of groups as well, except that voice is in the form of written words rather than symbols or spoken language. In my examination of Christian marriage advice manuals, I inadvertently engaged in a dialog with participants in which I questioned the authority of the texts they recommended. I informally asked about what made one book better or worse than another. I discovered during these exchanges, that Christian marriage advice manuals that couples shared with me had four sources of authority. Not all of the books include all three sources of authority, but some do. Others contain only one source of authority.

The four sources of authority in the Christian marriage advice manuals analyzed in this study are sacred texts, the professional expertise of the author, scholarly studies, and marital status and life experiences of the author. Many of these texts make reference to sacred texts like the Bible, encyclicals, other papal writings, and catechisms. Often authors described their professional expertise as a source of authority. Examples of such professional authority included, but were not limited to, a licensed marriage and family counselor who claims to be a Christian, a minister who counsels couples, a Bishop who authored a practical guide to marriage, a couple who hosts a talk show about marriage for a local Christian radio station, and a Christian attorney who serves on a Catholic annulment tribunal for his diocese. Christian marriage advice manuals sometimes made reference to scholarly articles about marriage and family to lend credibility and a sense of authority to the books. Finally, the marital status and life experiences of the authors as Christians were frequently included as a source of authority. Some authors were divorced and remarried, others reported surviving turbulent times in their marriages, others simply stated that they had been married for many years and had several children and grandchildren as evidence of their authority to write a Christian marriage advice manual.

I mentioned the voices in the Christian marriage advice manuals because the sources of authority of the texts were often linked to and augmented by louder and quieter voices within the manuals. As an example, when scholarly research was introduced in texts, it was often used to demonstrate the decline and deinstitutionalization of marriage. Often, authors made reference to "university studies" demonstrating some outcome in marriage, without providing a reference to the study, effectively silencing the voice of the scholarship surrounding the study. At other times, authors provided quotations from the Bible, but then extended the explicit words in the quote by describing the Hebrew origins of specific words and then offering alternative translations of the words to make specific points, again changing the voice of the original quote from the Bible by extolling other sources of authority in justifying and legitimizing the authors' argument.

Any reading of these texts results in one consistent finding. There is no objective "elite religious discourse" that defines sacred marriages. Instead, sacred marriages are constructed through religious and nonreligious discourse in ways that are oft competing, conflicting, and inconsistent. Just like the people I interviewed, these texts provide cultural skills and abilities that people can use as part of their cultural toolkits and repertoires to form strategies of action that are often illogical but that are still meaningful to people. Despite these inconsistencies, there were overarching themes present in the texts, which I report throughout this book. Additionally, and more importantly, couples were overwhelmingly content with these inconsistencies and contradictions. They served as yet another source of multiple sacred meanings they could use to cope with adversities and to pursue their social imaginaries of a shared future together.

Analysis of Christian marriage advice manuals

The analysis began by dividing the manuals into three groups: Catholic (n = 22), Secular (n = 15), and Protestant (n = 21). Each manual was then analyzed within each group for 1) sacred meaning of terms (e.g., marriage, longevity, love, and identity), 2) the rationales for the advice (e.g., scripture, religious documents and teaching, anecdotes from marriage and family counselors, personal experience, ancient marriage contracts, other marriage advice manuals, and cultural artifacts in the form of movies, books, and poetry), and 3) the source of the authority of the author (e.g., Church leader, licensed counselor, leader of Christian marriage foundation, and Christian couple serving as a role model to others). During the analysis, I gave special attention to the author's rationale explaining why the advice was religious, spiritual, or sacred in nature.

During the initial reading of the manuals I created a list of recurrent themes. I then refined the coding scheme by rereading the manuals to ensure all manuals were read through the same thematic lens and interpretive frame. I then read the manuals a third time to identify contradictory evidence for specific themes. This reading of the manuals as a whole was designed to find inconsistencies and conflicting discourses within the manuals. The fourth and final reading of the manuals occurred after reading the interview transcripts. This allowed me to identify the presence, and absence, of dominant themes in the manuals within the narratives of the couples I interviewed.

This systematic process of analyzing Christian marriage advice manuals, benefited the study in three specific ways. First, the literature extant does not adequately capture the importance of the sacralization of love, sex, and childbearing in sacred marriages. Repeatedly, the manuals described love between husband and wife in comparison to Christ as savior loving and being married to the church. Thus, religious culture includes a sacred dimensionality and meaning of love in sacred marriages that links religious emotional regimes with the way people think, talk, feel, and act. Second, almost all of the manuals are predicated on the conceptualization of marriage as indissoluble. Although the risk of divorce is mentioned in many of these manuals, it is not offered as a legitimate option to married Christians. Third, categorizing the manuals as either Catholic, secular, or Protestant yielded no significant variations in the discourse they contained, although the theological basis of the discourse varied by denomination. This is consistent with the theoretical perspectives used in this study, suggesting that religion is constituted through a blending of religious and secular spheres. These findings have significantly shaped this study. They support the decision to use culture theory and discourse theory in this study. This analysis shifted the study away from the influence of doctrine and variations in Church teachings based on participants' denominations towards a more nuanced and complex analysis and understanding of discourse and culture in religion's influences in sacred marriages.

References

Abdhalla, Stéphanie Latte. 2009. "Fragile Intimacies: Marriage and Love in the Palestinian Camps of Jordan (1948–2001)." *Journal of Palestine Studies* 38:47–62.

Alexander, Jeffrey C., and Steven J. Sherwood. 2002. "Mythic Gestures: Robert N. Bellah and Cultural Sociology." Pp. 1–14 in *Meaning and Modernity: Religion, Polity, and Self.* Berkley: University of California Press.

Allen, Elizabeth S., David C. Atkins, Donald H. Baucom, Douglas K. Snyder, Kristina Coop Gordon, and Shirley P. Glass. 2005. "Intrapersonal, Interpersonal, and Contextual Factors in Engaging in and Responding to Infidelity." *Clinical Psychology: Science and Practice* 12:101–130.

Allison, Steven, Kathleen Stacey, Vicki Dadds, Leigh Roeger, Andrew Wood, and Graham Martin. 2003. "What the Family Brings: Gathering Evidence for Strengths-based Work." *Journal of Family Therapy* 25:263–284.

Amato, Paul R. 2007. "Transformative Processes in Marriage: Some Thoughts from a Sociologist." *Journal of Marriage and Family* 69:305–309.

Amato, Paul R., and Shelley Irving. 2006. "Historical Trends in Divorce in The United States." Pp. 41–58 in *Handbook of Divorce and Relationship Dissolution*, edited by Mark A. Fine and John H. Harvey. Mahwah, NJ: Erlbaum.

Ammerman, Nancy T. 2014. *Sacred Stories, Spiritual Tribes: Finding Religion in Everyday Life*. Oxford: Oxford University Press.

Ammerman, Nancy T. 2005. *Pillars of Faith: American Congregations and Their Partners*. Berkley: University of California Press.

Ammerman, Nancy T., Jackson W. Carroll, Carl S. Dudley, and William McKinney. 1998. *Studying Congregations: A New Handbook*. Nashville: Abingdon Press.

Arbuckle, Gerald. 2013. *Catholic Identity or Identities: Refounding Ministries in Chaotic Times*. Collegeville, MN: Liturgical Press.

Archdiocese of Philadelphia and the Pontifical Council for the Family. 2014. *Love Is Our Mission: The Family Fully Alive. A Preparatory Catechesis for the World Meeting of Families*. Huntington, IN: Our Sunday Visitor.

Atkins, David C., Donald H. Baucom, and Neil S. Jacobson. 2001. "Understanding Infidelity: Correlates in a National Random Sample." *Journal of Family Psychology* 15:735–749.

Atkins, David C., and Deborah E. Kessel. 2008. "Religiousness and Infidelity: Attendance, but Not Faith and Prayer, Predict Marital Fidelity." *Journal of Marriage and Family* 70:407–418.

Bachand, Leslie L., and Sandra L. Caron. 2001. "Ties That Bind: A Qualitative Study of Happy Long-term Marriages." *Contemporary Family Therapy* 23:105–121.

Baggett, Jerome P. 2009. *Sense of the Faithful: How American Catholics Live Their Faith.* Oxford: Oxford University Press.

Bartkowski, John P. 1996. "Beyond Biblical Literalism and Inerrancy: Conservative Protestants and the Hermeneutic Interpretation of Scripture." *Sociology of Religion* 57:259–272.

Bartkowski, John P. 1997. "Debating Patriarchy: Discursive Disputes Over Spousal Authority Among Evangelical Family Commenters." *Journal for the Scientific Study of Religion* 36:393–410.

Bartkowski, John P. 2001. *Remaking the Godly Marriage: Gender Negotiation in Evangelical Families.* New Brunswick, NJ: Rutgers University Press.

Bartkowski, John P. 2004. *The Promise Keepers: Servants, Soldiers, and Godly Men.* New Brunswick, NJ: Rutgers University Press.

Bartkowski, Renee. 1989. *Prayers for Married Couples.* Liguori, MO: Liguori.

Beck, Ulrich, and Elisabeth Beck-Gernsheim. 1995. *The Normal Chaos of Love.* Cambridge, UK: Polity Press.

Beck, Ulrich, and Elisabeth Beck-Gernsheim. 2014. *Distant Love: Personal Live in the Global Age.* Cambridge, UK: Polity Press.

Bell, Robert R. 1974. "Religious Involvement and Marital Sex in Australia and the United States." *Journal of Comparative Family Studies* 5:109–116.

Bellah, Robert N., Richard Madsen, William M. Sullivan, Ann Swidler, and Steven M. Tipton. 1985. *Habits of the Heart: Individualism and Commitment in American Life.* Berkley: University of California Press.

Bennett, Art, and Laraine Bennett, eds. 2014. *Catholic and Married: Leaning into Love.* Huntington, IN: Our Sunday Visitor.

Berger, Peter, and Thomas Luckmann. 1966. *The Social Construction of Reality.* Garden City, NY: Doubleday.

Berscheid, Ellen. 2010. "Love in the Fourth Dimension." *Annual Review of Psychology* 61:1–25.

Biddle, Perry H., Jr., 1974. *A Marriage Manual.* Grand Rapids, MI: William B. Eerdmans Publishing Company.

Black, Keri, and Marie Lobo. 2008. "A Conceptual Review of Family Resilience Factors." *Journal of Family Nursing* 14:33–55.

Blackburn, Jim. 2011. *101 Quick Questions with Catholic Answers: Marriage, Divorce, and Annulment.* San Diego, CA: Catholic Answers.

Blyth, Catherine. 2011. *The Art of Marriage: A Guide for Living Life as Two.* New York: Penguin Books.

Bosio, John. 2008. *Happy Together: The Catholic Blueprint for a Loving Marriage.* New London, CT: Twenty-third Publications.

Bosio, John. 2012. *Blessed is Marriage: A Guide to the Beatitudes for Catholic Couples.* New London, CT: Twenty-third Publications.

Bourdieu, Pierre. 1977. *Outline of a Theory of Practice.* London: Cambridge Unviersity Press.

Brasher, Brenda E. 1998. *Godly Women: Fundamentalism and Female Power.* New Brunswick, NJ: Rutgers University Press.

Brown, Teri, Yaxin Lu, Loren Marks, and David C. Dollahite. 2011. "Meaning Making Across Three Dimensions of Religious Experience: A Qualitative Exploration." *Counselling and Spirituality* 30:11–36.

Browning, Don S. 2003. *Marriage and Modernization: How Globalization Threatens Marriage and What to Do About It.* Grand Rapids, MI: William B. Eerdmans Publishing Company.

Broyles, Anne. 1993. *Growing Together in Love: God Known Through Family Life*. Nashville, TN: Upper Room Books.

Burke, Cormac. 2015. *The Theology of Marriage: Personalism, Doctrine, and Canon Law*. Washington, DC: The Catholic University of America Press.

Burns, Gene. 1992. *The Frontiers of Catholicism: The Politics of Ideology in a Liberal World*. Berkley: University of California Press.

Burns, Gene. 2005. *The Moral Veto: Framing Contraception, Abortion, and Cultural Pluralism in the United States*. Cambridge: Cambridge University Press.

Burr, Wesley R., Loren D. Marks, and Randal D. Day. 2012. *Sacred Matters: Religion and Spirituality in Families*. New York: Routledge.

Burris, Jessica, Gregory T. Smith, and Charles R. Carlson. 2009. "Relations Among Religiousness, Spirituality, and Sexual Practices." *Journal of Sex Research* 46:282–289.

Call, Vaughn R. A., and Tim B. Heaton. 1997. "Religious Influence on Marital Stability." *Journal for the Scientific Study of Religion* 36:382–392.

Canary, Daniel J., Laura Stafford, and Beth Semic. 2002. "A Panel Study of the Association Between Maintenance Strategies and Relational Characteristics." *Journal of Marriage and Family* 64:395–406.

Cancian, Francesca M. 1986. "The Feminization of Love." *Journal of Women in Culture and Society* 11:692–709.

Caughlin John P., and Ted L. Huston. 2006. The Affective Structure of Marriage. Pp. 131–155 in *The Cambridge Handbook of Personal Relationships*, edited by Anita L. Vangelisti and Daniel Perlman. New York: Cambridge University Press.

Champlin, Joseph M. [1970] 2012. *Together for Life: Celebrating and Living the Sacrament*. Notre Dame, IN: Ave Maria Press.

Chapman, Gary. 2010. *The 5 Love Languages: The Secret to Love That Lasts*. Chicago: Northfield.

Cherlin, Andrew. 2009. *The Marriage-Go-Round: The State of Marriage and the Family in America Today*. New York: Vintage Books.

Chodorow, Nancy J. 1999. *The Power of Feelings: Personal Meanings in Psychoanalysis, Gender, and Culture*. New Haven, CT: Yale University Press.

Christopher, F. Scott, and Tiffani S. Kisler. 2004. "Exploring Marital Sexuality: Peeking Inside the Bedroom and Discovering What We Don't Know – But Should!" Pp. 371–384 in *The Handbook of Sexuality in Close Relationships*, edited by John H. Harvey, Amy Wenzel, and Susan Sprecher. Mahwah, NJ: Erlbaum.

Clack, Beverly. 1996. "God and Language: A Feminist Perspective on the Meaning of God." Pp. 148–158 in *The Nature of Religious Language: A Colloquium*, edited by Stanley Porter. London: Bloomsbury T&T Clark.

Clinton, Tim, and John Trent. 2009. *The Quick-reference Guide to Marriage and Family Counseling*. Grand Rapids, MI: Baker Books.

Cloud, Henry, and John Townsend. 1999. *Boundaries in Marriage: Understanding the Choices that Make or Break Loving Relationships*. Grand Rapids, MI: Zondervan.

Coleman, Paul. 2006. *The 30 Secrets of Happily Married Couples*. Avon, MA: Adams Media.

Collins, Nancy L., Heidi S. Kane, Molly A. Metz, Christena Cleveland, Cynthia Kahn, Lauren Winczewski, Jeffrey Bowen, and Thery Prok. 2014. "Psychological, Physiological, and Behavioral Responses, to a Partner in Need: The Role of Compassionate Love." *Journal of Social and Personal Relationships* 31:601–629.

Coltrane, Scott. 1996. *Family Man: Fatherhood, Housework, and Gender Equity*. New York: Oxford University Press.

Coontz, Stephanie. 2005. *Marriage, a History: How Love Conquered Marriage*. New York: Penguin Books.

Curtis, Kristen Taylor, and Christopher G. Ellison. 2002. "Religious Heterogamy and Marital Conflict." *Journal of Family Issues* 23:551–576.

D'Antonio, William V., James D. Davidson, Dean R. Hoge, and Mary L. Gautier. 2007. *American Catholics Today: New Realities of Their Fath and Their Church*. Walnut Creek, CA: Rowman and Littlefield Publishers.

D'Antonio, William V., James D. Davidson, Dean R. Hoge, and Katherine Meyer. 2001. *American Catholics: Gender, Generation, and Commitment*. Walnut Creek, CA: Rowman and Littlefield Publishers.

Davis, Kathy. 1997. *Embodied Practices: Feminist Perspectives on the Body*. London: Sage.

Davidson, James D. 2005. *Catholicsm in Motion: The Church in American Society*. Liguori MO: Liguori/Triumph.

Davidson, James D., Andrea S. Williams, Richard A. Lamanna, Jan Stenftenagel, Katheleen Maas Weigert, William J. Whalen, and Patricia Wittberg. 1997. *The Search for Common Ground: What Unites and Divides Catholic Americans*. Huntington, IN: Our Sunday Visitor.

DeMaris, Alfred, Annette Mahoney, and Kenneth I. Pargament. 2010. "Sanctification of Marriage and General Religiousness as Buffers of the Effects of Marital Inequity." *Journal of Family Issues* 31:1255–1278.

Damasio, Antonio R. 1994. *Descartes' Error: Emotion, Reason, and the Human Brain*. New York: G.P. Putnam.

Denzin, Norman K. 1983. "A Note on Emotionality, Self, and Interaction." *American Journal of Sociology* 89:402–409.

Dewey, John. [1910] 1997. *How We Think*. Mineola, New York: Dover Publications.

Dillon, Michele. 1999. *Catholic Identity: Balancing Reason, Faith, and Power*. New York: Cambridge University Press.

Dollahite, David C., Alan J. Hawkins, and Melissa R. Parr. 2012. " 'Something More': The Meaning of Marriage for Religious Couples in America." *Marriage and Family Review* 48:339–362.

Dollahite, David C., and Loren D. Marks. 2009. "A Conceptual Model of Family and Religious Processes in Highly Religious Families." *Review of Religious Research* 50:373–391.

Dodaro, Robert, editor. 2014. *Remaining in the Truth of Christ: Marriage and Communion in the Catholic Church*. San Francisco, CA: Ignatius Press.

Dunbar, Robin. 2012. *The Science of Love*. Hoboken, NJ: John Wiley and Sons.

Durbin, Karen. 1998. "On Sexual Jealousy." Pp. 36–45 in *Jealousy*, edited by Gordon Clayton and Lynn G. Smith. Lanham, MD: University Press of America.

Edmisten, Tom, and Karen Edmisten. 2014. "Forward." Pp. 7–14 in *Catholic and Married: Leaning into Love*, edited by Art Bennett and Laraine Bennett. Huntington, IN: Our Sunday Visitor.

Eggerichs, Emerson. 2005. *Love and Respect Workbook: For Couples, Individuals, or Groups. The Love She Most Desires: The Respect He Desperately Needs*. Nashville, TN: Thomas Nelson.

Elder, Glen H., Jr., 1999. *Children of the Great Depression: Social Change in Life Experience*. Boulder, CO: Westview.

Fairclough, Norman. 2003. *Analyzing Discourse: Textual Analysis for Social Research*. New York: Routledge.

Fincham, Frank D., Scott M. Stanley, and Steven R. Beach. 2007. "Transformative Processes in Marriage: An Analysis of Emerging Trends." *Journal of Marriage and Family* 69:275–292.

Fisher, Simcha. 2014a. *The Sinner's Guide to Natural Family Planning.* Huntington, IN: Our Sunday Visitor.

Fisher, Simcha. 2014b. "Mirrors around a Flame." Pp. 15–28 in *Catholic and Married: Leaning into Love,* edited by Art Bennett and Laraine Bennett. Huntington, IN: Our Sunday Visitor.

Flam, Helena. 2009. "Extreme Feelings and Feelings at the Extreme." Pp. 73–93 in *Theorizing Emotions: Sociological Explorations and Applications,* edited by Debra Hopkins, Jochen Kleres, Helena Flam, and Helmut Kuzmics. Frankfurt, Germany: Campus Verlag.

Foley, Gerald. 1992. *Courage to Love . . . When Your Marriage Hurts.* Notre Dame, IN: Ave Maria Press.

Ford, Judy. 2010. *Every Day Love: The Delicate Art of Caring for Each Other.* Berkley, CA: Viva Editions.

Foster, Michael. 1990. *Annulment: The Wedding That Was. How the Church Can Declare a Marriage Null.* New York: Paulist Press.

Gallagher, Sally K. 2003. *Evangelical Identity and Gendered Family Life.* New Brunswick, NJ: Rutgers University Press.

Garascia, Anthony. 2007. *Before "I do": Preparing for the Sacrament of Marriage.* Notre Dame, IN: Ave Maria Press.

Gerson, Kathleen, editor. 2010. *The Unfinished Revolution: Coming of Age in a New Era of Gender, Work, and Family.* Oxford: Oxford University Press.

Giddens, Anthony. 1992. *The Transformation of Intimacy: Sexuality, Love and Eroticism.* Cambridge: Polity Press.

Goodman, Michael A., and David C. Dollahite. 2006. "How Religious Couples Perceive the Influence of God in their Marriage." *Review of Religious Research* 48:141–155.

Goodman, Michael A., David C. Dollahite, Loren D. Marks, and Emily Layton. 2013. "Religious Faith and Transformational Processes in Marriage." *Family Relations* 68:808–823.

Grandos, Carlos, editor. 2014. *The Hope of the Family: Dialogue with Gerhard Cardinal Müller.* San Francisco: Ignatius.

Greeley, Andrew M. 1991. *Faithful Attraction: Discovering Intimacy, Love, and Fidelity in American Marriage.* New York: Tom Doherty Associates.

Green, Nile, and Mary Searle-Chatterjee, editors. 2008. *Religion, Language and Power.* New York: Routledge.

Griffith, R. Marie. 1997. *God's Daughters: Evangelical Women and the Power of Submission.* Berkley: University of California Press.

Griffith, R. Marie. 2004. *Born Again Bodies: Flesh and Spirit in American Christianity.* Berkley: University of California Press.

Griffith, R. Marie. 2017. *Moral Combat: How Sex Divided American Christians and Fractured American Politics.* New York: Basic Books.

Griffith, R. Marie and Barbara Dianne Savage. 2006. *Women and Religion in the African Diaspora.* Baltimore: John's Hopkins University Press.

Guarendi, Ray. 2011. *Marriage: Small Steps, Big Rewards.* Cincinnati, OH: Servant Books.

Haag, Pamela. 2011. *Marriage Confidential: The Post-romantic Age of Workhorse Wives, Royal Children, Undersexed Spouses and Rebel Couples Who are Rewriting the Rules.* New York: HarperCollins.

Hahn, Kimberly. 2007. *Chosen and Cherished: Biblical Wisdom for Your Marriage*. Cincinnati, OH: Servant Books.

Hahn, Kimberly. 2001. *Life-giving Love: Embracing God's Beautiful Design for Marriage*. Cincinnati, OH: St. Anthony Messenger Press.

Hall, David D., editor. 1997. *Lived Religion in America: Towards a History of Practice*. Princeton: Princeton University Press.

Hatfield, Elaine, and Richard L. Rapson. 1993. *Love, Sex, and Intimacy: Their Psychology, Biology, and History*. New York: HarperCollins.

Hawkins, Daniel N., and Alan Booth. 2005. "Unhappily Ever After: Effects of Long-term, Low-quality Marriages on Well-being." *Social Forces* 84:451–471.

Heaton, Tim B. 1984. "Religious Homogamy and Marital Satisfaction Reconsidered." *Journal of Marriage and Family* 46:729–733.

Heaton, Tim B., and Stan L. Albrecht. 1991. "Stable Unhappy Marriages." *Journal of Marriage and Family* 53:747–758.

Heaton, Tim B., Stan L. Albrecht, and Thomas K. Martin. 1985. "The Timing of Divorce." *Journal of Marriage and Family* 47:631–639.

Heaton, Tim B., and Edith L. Pratt. 1990. "The Effects of Religious Homogamy on Marital Satisfaction and Stability." *Journal of Family Issues* 11:191–207.

Hegi, Kevin E., and Raymond M. Bergner. 2010. "What is Love? An Empirically-based Essentialist Account." *Journal of Social and Personal Responsibilities* 27:620–636.

Hernandez, Krystal M., Annette Mahoney, and Kenneth I. Pargament. 2011. "Sanctification of Sexuality: Implications for Newlyweds' Marital and Sexual Quality." *Journal of Family Psychology* 25:775–780.

von Hildebrand, Dietrich. 1991. *Marriage: The Mystery of Faithful Love*. Manchester, NH: Sophia Institute Press.

Hochschild, Arlie R. 1979. "Emotion Work, Feeling Rules and Social Structure." *The American Journal of Sociology* 85:551–575.

Hochschild, Arlie R. [1983] 2012. *The Managed Heart*. Berkley: University of California Press.

Hochschild, Arlie R. [1989] 2003. *The Second Shift*. New York: Penguin Books.

Hochschild, Arlie R. 2013. *So How's the Family? And Other Essays*. Berkeley: University of California Press.

Hook, Derek. 2001. "Discourse, Knowledge, Materiality, History: Foucault and Discourse Analysis." *Theory and Psychology* 11:521–547.

Hopkins, Debra, Jochen Kleres, Helena Flam, and Helmut Kuzmics, editors. 2009. *Theorizing Emotions: Sociological Explorations and Applications*. Frankfurt, Germany: Campus Verlag.

Iida, Masumi, Gwendolyn Seidman, Patrick E. Shrout, and Kentaro Fujita. 2008. Modeling Support Provision in Intimate Relationships. *Journal of Personality and Social Psychology* 94:460–478.

Illouz, Eva. 2012. *Why Love Hurts: A Sociological Explanation*. Cambridge: Polity Press.

Jenkins, Kathleen E., 2005. *Awesome Families: The Promise of Healing Relationships in the International Churches of Christ*. New Brunswick, NJ: Rutgers University Press.

Jenkins, Kathleen E., 2014. *Sacred Divorce: Religion, Therapeutic Culture, and Ending Life Partnerships*. New Brunswick, NJ: Rutgers University Press.

Jones, Stanton L., and Heather R. Hostler. 2005. "The Role of Sexuality Inpersonhood: An Integrative Exploration." Pp. 115–132 in *Judeo-Christian Perspectives on Psychology: Human Nature, Motivation, and Change*, edited by William R. Miller and Harold D. Delaney. Washington, DC: American Psychological Association.

Kalmijn, Matthijs. 2004. "Marriage Rituals as Reinforcers of Role Transitions: An Analysis of Weddings in the Netherlands." *Journal of Marriage and Family* 66:582–594.

Kaslow, Florence W., and Helga Hammerschmidt. 1992. "Long-term "Good" Marriages: The Seemingly Essential Ingredients." *Journal of Couples Therapy* 3:15–38.

Kaslow, Florence W., and James A. Robison. 1996. "Long-term Satisfying Marriages: Perceptions of Contributing Factors." *American Journal of Family Therapy* 24:153–170.

Keller, Timothy, and Kathy Keller. 2011. *The Meaning of Marriage: Facing the Complexities of Commitment with the Wisdom of God*. New York: Riverhead Books.

Kephart, William M. 1967. "Some Correlates of Romantic Love." *Journal of Marriage and Family* 29:470–474.

Koenig, Harold G. 2001. "Religion and Medicine II: Religion, Mental Health, and Related Behaviors." *International Journal of Psychiatry in Medicine* 31:97–109.

Koenig-Bricker, Woodeene, and David Dziena. 2014. *Catholic Prayer Book for the Separated and Divorced*. Huntington, IN: Our Sunday Visitor.

Konieczny, Mary Ellen. 2013. *The Spirit's Tether: Family, Work, and Religion Among American Catholics*. Oxford: Oxford University Press.

Krumrei, Elizabeth J., Annette Mahoney, and Kenneth I. Pargament. 2009. "Divorce and the Divine. The Role of Spirituality in Adjustment to Divorce." *Journal of Marriage and Family* 71:373–383.

Lasnoski, Kent J. 2014. *Vocation to Virtue: Christian Marriage as a Consecrated Life*. Washington, DC: The Catholic University of America Press.

Laumann, Edward O., John H. Gagnon, Robert T. Michael, and Stuart Michaels. 1994. *The Social Organization of Sexuality: Sexual Practices in the United States*. Chicago: University of Chicago Press.

Lawler, Michael G. 2002. *Marriage and the Catholic Church: Disputed Questions*. Collegeville, MN: The Liturgical Press.

Lawrence, Anna M. 2011. *One Family Under God: Love, Belonging, and Authority in Early Transatlantic Methodism*. Philadelphia, PA: University of Pennsylvania Press.

Lehrer, Evelyn L., and Carmel U. Chiswick. 1993. "Religion as a Determinant of Marital Stability." *Demography* 30:385–404.

Levine, Robert, Suguru Sato, Tsukasa Hashimoto, and Jyoti Verna. 1995. Love and Marriage in Eleven Cultures. *Journal of Cross Cultural Psychology* 26:554–571.

Lindsey, Jacquelyn, editor. 2003. *Catholic Prayer Book*. Huntington, IN: Our Sunday Visitor.

Lupton, Deborah, and Leslie Barclay. 1997. *Constructing Fatherhood: Discourses and Experiences*. Los Angeles: Sage.

Mahoney, Annette. 2010. "Religion in Families, 1999–2009: A Relational Spirituality Framework." *Journal of Marriage and Family* 72:805–827.

Mahoney, Annette, Kenneth I. Pargament, and Krystal M. Hernandez. 2013. "Heaven on Earth: Beneficial Effects of Sanctification for Individual and Interpersonal Well-being." Pp. 397–410 in *Oxford Book of Happiness*, edited by Susan A. David, Ilona Boniwell, and Amanda Conley Ayers. Oxford: Oxford University Press.

Mahoney, Annette, Kenneth I. Pargament, Aaron Murray-Swank, and Nicole Murray-Swank. 2003. "Religion and the Sanctification of Family Relationships." *Review of Religious Research* 44:220–236.

Mahoney, Annette, Kenneth I. Pargament, Nalini Tarakeshwar, and Aaron B. Swank. 2001. "Religion in the Home in the 1980s and 1990s: A Meta-Analytic Review and Conceptual Analysis of Links Between Religion, Marriage, and Parenting." *Journal of Family Psychology* 15:559–596.

Marks, Frederick W. 2001. *A Catholic Handbook for Engaged and Newly Married Couples*. Steubenville, OH: Emmaus Road.

Marks, Loren D. 2004. "Sacred Practices in Highly Religious Families: Christian, Jewish, Mormon, and Muslim Perspectives." *Family Processes* 43:217–231.

Marks, Loren D., Katrina Hopkins, Cassandra Chaney, Pamela A. Monroe, Olena Nesteruk, and Diane D. Sasser. 2008. "Together, we are Strong: A Qualitative Study of Happy, Enduring African American Marriages." *Family Relations* 57:172–185.

Marks, Lynne. 1996. *Revivals and Roller Rinks: Religion, Leisure, and Identity in Late-Nineteenth-Century Small-Town Ontario*. Toronto: University of Toronto Press.

McCubbin, Hamilton I., Anne I. Thompson, and Marilyn A. McCubbin. 1996. *Family Assessment: Resiliency, Coping and Adaptation: Inventories for Research and Practice*. Madison: University of Wisconsin Publishers.

McGuire, Meredith. 2007. "Embodied Practices: Negotiation and Resistance." Pp. 187–200 in *Everyday Religion: Observing Modern Religious Lives*, edited by Nancy T. Ammerman. New York: Oxford University Press.

McGowan, Dale. 2014. *In Faith and In Doubt: How Religious Believers and Nonbelievers Can Create Strong Marriages and Loving Families*. New York: AMACOM.

McGuire, Meredith. 2008. *Lived Religion: Faith and Practice in Everyday Life*. Oxford: Oxford University Press.

McSwite, O. C. 2001. "Reflections on the Role of Embodiment in Discourse." *Administrative Theory and Praxis* 23:243–250.

Morse, Jennifer Roback, and Betsy Kerekes. 2013. *101 Tips for a Happier Marriage: Simple Ways for Couples to Grow Closer to God and Each Other*. Notre Dame, IN: Ave Maria Press.

Mullins, David F. 2016. "Effects of Religion on Enduring Marriages." *Social Sciences* 5:24. DOI: 10.3390/socsci5020024. www.mdpi.com/2076-0760/5/2/24/html

Mullins, Larry C., Kimberly P. Brackett, Donald W. Bogie, and Daniel Pruett. 2004. "The Impact of Religious Homogeneity on Divorce in the United States." *Sociological Inquiry* 74:338–354.

Munson, Ziad. 2007. "When a Funeral Isn't Just a Funeral: The Layered Meaning of Everyday Action." Pp. 121–136 in *Everyday Religion: Observing Modern Religious Lives*, edited by Nancy T. Ammerman. New York: Oxford University Press.

Murray-Swank, Nichole A., Kenneth I. Pargament, and Annette Mahoney. 2005. "At the Crossroads of Sexuality and Spirituality: The Sanctification of Sex by College Students." *The International Journal for the Psychology of Religion* 75:199–219.

Nock, Steven L. 2001. "The Marriages of Equally Dependent Spouses." *Journal of Family Issues* 22:755–775.

Nock, Steven L., Laura A. Sanchez, and James D. Wright. 2008. *Covenant Marriage: The Movement to Reclaim Tradition in America*. New Brunswick, NJ: Rutgers University Press.

Northrup, Chrisanna, Pepper Schwartz, and James Witte. 2012. *The Normal Bar: The Surprising Secrets of Happy Couples and What They Reveal About Creating a New Normal in Your Relationship*. New York: Harmony.

O'Boyle, Donna-Marie Cooper. 2013. *Catholic Mom's Café: 5-Minute Retreats for Every Day of the Year*. Huntington, IN: Our Sunday Visitor.

O'Toole, James M. 2008. *The Faithful: A History of Catholics in America*. Cambridge, MA: The Belknap Press of Harvard University.

Pargament, Kenneth I., and Annette Mahoney. 2005. "Sacred Matter: Sanctification as a Vital Topic for the Psychology of Religion." *The International Journal for the Psychology of Religion* 15:179–198.

Pargament, Kenneth I., and Annette Mahoney. 2009. "Spirituality: The Search for the Sacred." Pp. 611–620 in *Oxford Handbook of Positive Psychology*, edited by Shane J. Lopez and C. R. Snyder. New York: Oxford University Press.

Pargament, Kenneth I., Gina M. Magyar, Ethan Benore, and Annette Mahoney. 2005. "Sacrilege: A Study of Sacred Loss and Desecration and their Implications for Health and Well-being in a Community Sample." *Journal for the Scientific Study of Religion* 44:59–78.

Peräkylä, Annssi, and Marja-Leena Sorjonen, editors. 2012. *Emotion in Interaction*. Oxford: Oxford University Press.

Pérez-Soba, Juan José, and Stephan Kampowski. 2014. *The Gospel of the Family: Going Beyond Cardinal Kasper's Proposal in the Debate on Marriage, Civil Re-Marriage, and Communion in the Church*. San Francisco: Ignatius Press.

Pew Research Center. 2010. "Religion Among the Millennials." Retrieved January 8, 2018 (www.pewforum.org/Age/Religion-Among-the-Millennials.aspx).

Pew Research Center. 2012. "2012 Values Survey: Section 6. Religion and Social Values." Retrieved January 8, 2018(www.people-press.org/2012/06/04/section-6-religion-and-social-values/).

Pinto, Henrique. 2003. *Foucault, Christianity, and Interfaith Dialogue*. London: Routledge.

Popcak, Greg. 2008. *For Better . . . Forever: A Catholic Guide to Lifelong Marriage*. Huntington, IN: Our Sunday Visitor.

Popcak, Greg, and Lisa Popcak. 2013. *Just Married: The Catholic Guide to Surviving and Thriving in the First Five Years of Marriage*. Notre Dame, IN: Ave Maria Press.

Post, Steven G., Lynn G. Underwood, Jeffrey P. Schloss, and William B. Hurlbut. 2000. *Altruism and Altruistic Love: Science, Philosophy, and Religion in Dialogue*. New York: Oxford University Press.

Rew, Lynn, Y. Joel Wong, and R. Weylin Sternglanz. 2004. "The Relationship Between Prayer, Health Behaviors, and Protective Resources in School-age Children." *Issues in Comprehensive Pediatric Nursing* 27:245–255.

Richardson, Ronald W. 2010. *Couples in Conflict: A Family Systems Approach to Marriage Counseling*. Minneapolis, MN: Fortress Press.

Riessman, Catherine Kohler. 1990. *Divorce Talk: Women and Men Make Sense of Personal Relationships*. New Brunswick, NJ: Rutgers University Press.

Rietti, Sophie. 2009. "Emotion-work and the Philosophy of Emotion." *Journal of social Philosophy* 40:55–74.

Riis, Ole, and Linda Woodhead. 2010. *A Sociology of Religious Emotion*. Oxford: Oxford University Press.

Roberts, Thomas W. 1992. "Sexual Attraction and Romantic Love: Forgotten Variables in Marital Therapy." *Journal of Marital and Family Therapy* 18:357–364.

Rosenau, Douglas E., and Michael R. Sytsma. 2004. "A Theology of Sexual Intimacy: Insights into the Creator." *Journal of Psychology and Christianity* 23:261–270.

Rostosky, Sharon Scales, Ellen D. B. Riggles, Crolyn Brodniki, and Amber Olson. 2008. "An Exploration of Lived Religion in Same-sex Couples from Judeo-Christian Traditions." *Family Process* 47:389–403.

Rubin, Zick. 1970. "Measurement of Romantic Love." *Journal of Personality and Social Psychology* 16:265–273.

Salzman, Todd A., Thomas M. Kelly, and John J. O'Keefe, editors. 2004. *Marriage in the Catholic Tradition: Scripture, Tradition, and Experience*. New York: The Crossroad Publishing Company.

Sayer, Liana C, and Suzanne M. Bianchi. 2000. "Women's Economic Independence and the Probability of Divorce." *Journal of Family Issues* 21:906–943.

Schultz, Valerie. 2008. *Closer: Musings on Intimacy, Marriage, and God.* Notre Dame, IN: Ave Maria Press.

Sheen, Fulton J. [1951] 1996. *Three to Get Married.* New York: Scepter.

Shelly, Rubel. 2011. *Divorce and Remarriage: A Redemptive Theology.* Abilene, TX: Leaf-wood Publishers.

Shimoff, Marci. 2010. *Love for No Reason: 7 Steps to Creating a Life of Unconditional Love.* New York: Free Press.

Shiota, Michelle N., and Robert W. Levenson. 2007. "Birds of a Feather Don't Always Fly Farthest: Similarity in Big Five Personality Predicts More Negative Marital Satisfaction Trajectories in Long-term Marriages." *Psychology and Aging* 22:666–675.

Shivanandan, Mary. 1999. *Crossing the Threshold of Love: A New Vision of Marriage in the Light of John Paul II's Anthropology.* Edinburgh: T&T Clark.

Shotter, John, and Kenneth J. Gergen, editors. 1989. *Texts of Identity.* London: Sage.

Shriver, Gary, and Mona Shriver. 2009. *Unfaithful: Hope and Healing After Infidelity.* Colorado Springs, CO: David C. Cook.

Slider, John W. 2011. *Free Methodist Handbook: Marriage and Weddings. Virtual Church Resources.* Self-Published, Create Space Independent Publishing Platform.

Sprecher, Susan, and Beverly Fehr. 2011. "Dispositional Attachment and Relationship-specific Attachment as Predictors of Compassionate Love for a Partner." *Journal of Social and Personal Relationships* 28:558–574.

Swidler, Ann. 1986. "Culture in Action: Symbols and Strategies." *American Sociological Review* 51:273–286.

Swidler, Ann. 2001. *Talk of Love: How Culture Matters.* Chicago: University of Chicago Press.

Thaagard, Tove. 1997. "Gender, Power, and Love: A Study of Interaction Between Spouses." *ACTA Sociologica* 40:357–376.

Thomas, Gary. 2000. *Sacred Marriage: What if God Designed Marriage to Make Us Holy More than to Make Us Happy?* Grand Rapids, MI: Zondervan.

Thorton, Arland, and Donald Camburn. 1989. Religious Participation and Adolescent Sexual Behavior. *Journal of Marriage and Family* 51:641–652.

Turner, Johathan H., and Jan E. Stets. 2005. *The Sociology of Emotion.* New York: Cambridge University Press.

Uebbing, Jenny. 2014. "Catholic Marriage and Contraception." Pp. 79–92 in *Catholic and Married: Leaning into Love*, edited by Art Bennett and Laraine Bennett. Huntington, IN: Our Sunday Visitor.

Underwood, Lynn G. 2005. "Interviews with Trappist Monks as a Contribution to Research Methodology in the Investigation of Compassionate Love." *Journal for the Theory of Social Behaviour* 35:285–302.

United States Conference of Catholic Bishops. (n/d). "Liturgy of the Eucharist." Retrieved January 8, 2018 (www.usccb.org/prayer-and-worship/the-mass/order-of-mass/liturgy-of-the-eucharist/).

Vaaler, Margaret L., Christopher G. Ellison, and Daniel A. Powers. 2009. "Religious Influences on the Risk of Marital Dissolution." *Journal of Marriage and Family* 71:917–934.

Vanderwell, Howard, and Norma de Waal Malefyt. 2010. "The Service of the Lord's supper (Bible Study)." Calvin Institute of Christian Worship for the Study and Renewal of Worship. Retrieved January 8, 2018 (https://worship.calvin.edu/resources/resource-library/the-service-of-the-lord-s-supper-bible-study-/).

Verter, Bradford. 2003. "Spiritual Capital: Theorizing Religion with Bourdieu against Bourdieu." *Sociological Theory* 21:150–174.

Wallin, Paul. 1957. "Religiosity, Sexual Gratification, and Marital Satisfaction." *American Sociological Review* 22:300–305.

Wallin, Paul, and Alexander L. Clark. 1964. "Religiosity, Sexual Gratification, and Marital Satisfaction in the Middle Years of Marriage." *Social Forces* 42:303–309.

Walsh, F. 1998. *Strengthening Family Resilience*. New York: Guilford.

Weedon, Chris. 1992. Feminist Practice and Poststructuralist Theory. Oxford: Blackwell.

Weigel, Daniel J., and Deborah S. Ballard-Reisch. 1999. "How Couples Maintain Marriages: A Closer Look at Self and Spouse Influences Upon the Use of Maintenance Behaviors in Marriages." *Family Relations* 48:263–269.

West, Christopher. 2007. *Good News about Sex and Marriage: Answers to Your Honest Questions about Catholic Teaching*. Cincinnati, OH: Servant Books.

White, Nancy, Judith Richter, Jane Koeckeritz, Kristy Munch, and Patty Walter. 2004. "Going Forward": Family Resiliency in Patients on Hemodialysis." *Journal of Family Nursing* 10:357–378.

Wilcox, W. Bradford. 2004. Soft Patriarchs, New Men: How Christianity Shapes Fathers and Husbands. Chicago: University of Chicago Press.

Wilcox, W. Bradford, and Kathleen Kovner Kline, editors. 2013. *Gender and Parenthood: Biological and Social Scientific Perspectives*. New York: Columbia University Press.

Wilcox, W. Bradford, and Steven L. Nock. 2006. "What's Love Got to do with It? Equality, Equity, Commitment and Women's Marital Quality." *Social Forces* 84:1321–1345.

Wilcox, W. Bradford, and Nicholas H. Wolfinger. 2016. *Soul Mates*. Oxford: Oxford University Press.

Wilkins, Amy C. 2008. "Happier than Non-Christians: Collective Emotions and Symbolic Boundaries Among Evangelical Christians." *Social Psychology Quarterly* 71:281–301.

Williams, Alan. 2008. "The Continuum of 'Sacred Language' from High to Low Speech in the Middle Iranian (Pahlavi) Zoroastrian Tradition." Pp. 123–142 in *Religion, Language and Power*, edited by Nile Green and Mary Searle-Chatterjee. New York: Routledge.

Witte, John Jr., 1997. *From Sacrament to Contract: Marriage, Religion, and Law in the Western Tradition*. Louisville, KY: Westminster John Knox Press.

Worthington, Everett L., Jr. 2005. *Hope-focused Marriage Counseling: A Guide to Brief Therapy*. Downers Grove, IL: InterVarsity Press.

Wrona, Patricia A. 2004. *The Exclamation: The Wise Choice of a Souse for Catholic Marriage*. Bloomington, IN: Xlibris Self-Publishing Company.

Xu, Xiaohe, and Martin King Whyte. 1990. "Love Matches and Arranged Marriages: A Chinese Replication." *Journal of Marriage and Family* 52:709–722.

Young, Michael, Raffey Luquis, George Denny, and Tamera Young. 1998. "Correlates of Sexual Satisfaction in Marriage." *The Canadian Journal of Human Sexuality* 7:115–127.

Zuberi, Tukufu, and Eduardo Bonilla-Silva, editors. 2008. *White Logic, White Methods: Racism and Methodology*. Lanhan, MD: Rowan and Littlefield Publishers.

Index